AF469258

MAJORCA

ISLAND PANORAMAS 360°

Photographs
Werner Weiler

Authors
Helga Neubauer
Wolfgang Vorbeck

360° Panoramic Photos

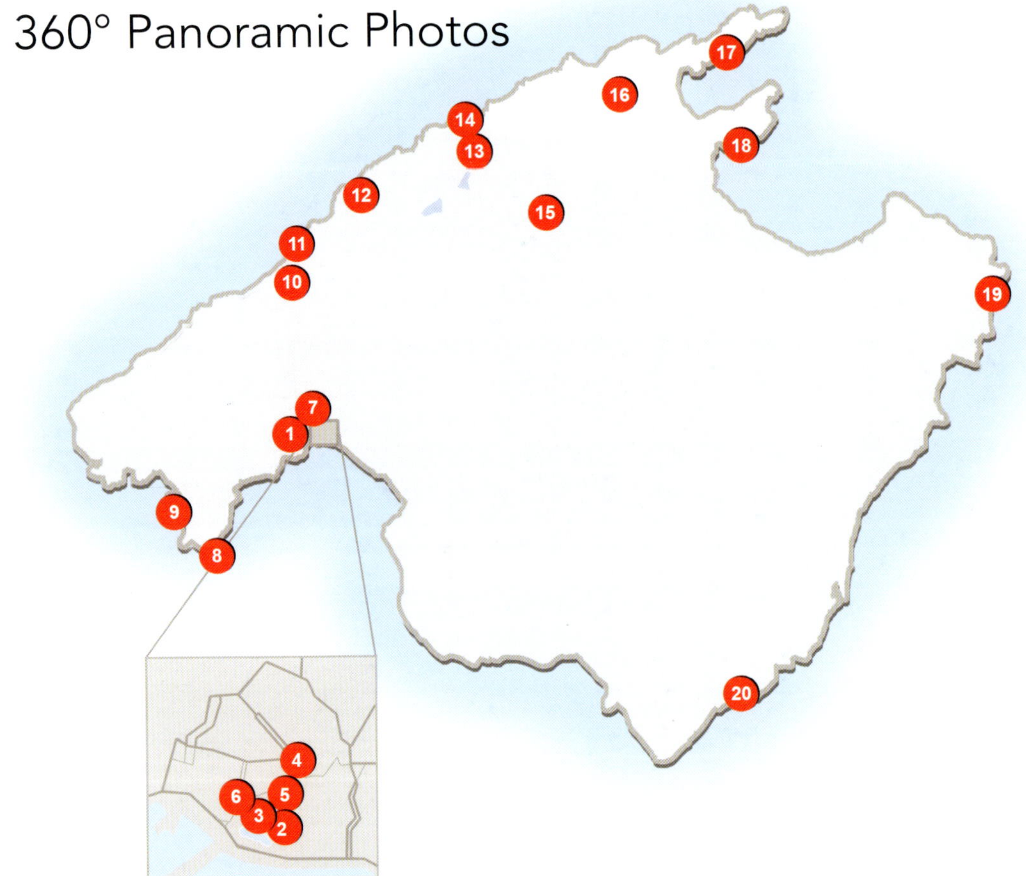

1. Palma – *Castell de Bellver*
2. Palma – *Cathedral La Seu*
3. Palma – *Cathedral La Seu*
4. Palma – *Plaça Major*
5. Palma – *Plaça Cort*
6. Palma – *S'Hort del Rei*
7. Palma – *Pueblo Español*
8. Portals Vells – *Cala Portals Vells*
9. Santa Ponsa – *Cala de Santa Ponsa*
10. Valldemosa – *Plaça de la Cartoixa*
11. Son Marroig – *Son Moragues*
12. Sóller – *Port de Sóller*
13. Sa Calobra – *Mirador, Nus de sa Corbata*
14. Sa Calobra – *Torrent de Pareis*
15. Caimari – *Almond Bloom*
16. Pollença – *Plaça Major*
17. Cap Formentor – *Cala Pi de la Posada*
18. Alcúdia – *Port d'Alcúdia*
19. Cala Rajada – *Port de Cala Rajada*
20. Cala Figuera – *Torrent dels Oms*

The Spanish Mediterranean island of Majorca is the biggest of the Balearic Islands with 3,640 km^2. It has about 880,000 inhabitants, almost 400,000 of which live in Palma, the island's capital. Majorca is divided into six "Comarques" (regions): Palma, Serra de Tramuntana, Llevant, Pla de Mallorca, Raiguer and Migjorn. The bigger towns include Calvià, Manacor, Llucmajor, Marratxi, Inca, Felanitx, Pollença, Alcúdia and Sóller.
The island's mild climate brings forth a rich flora with more than 1,500 species, turning the meadows and field paths into a riot of colour. Wild, fragrant herbs line the roads, and a variety of shrubs and creepers cover property walls built from natural stone. The island's fauna includes many species of birds and only a few mammals. The national park Archipiélago de Cabrera, 6 nature parks, 5 nature reserves and the natural monument Ses Fonts Ufanes offer fantastic opportunities for hikes and day trips. The mountain ranges of Serra de Llevant with peaks of over 500 m and Serra de Tramuntana frame the island. The highest mountains are located in the Serra de Tramuntana area (including Puig Major at 1,443 m) and the well-known canyon Torrente de Pareis. Majorca's coast line of 554 km with more than 170 bays is very varied, offering steep cliffs, jagged rocks, small shingle beaches and long stretches of sandy coves.
The plain of Es Pla, broken by only a few low ranges of hills, covers the centre of the island, bounded by the big bays of Pollença and Alcúdia to the north-east and Palma to the south-west.
The first traces of human settlements date back to the pretalayotic times (2000 to 1400 BC). Around 1400 BC, new tribes reached the island from the eastern Mediterranean. The culture of the Talayots was followed by a Roman invasion in 123 BC. Majorca was subsequently conquered by the Vandals in 450 AD, by Byzantine troops in 534 AD and by Moors in 902 AD. During the "Reconquista", Aragon troops regained control over the island in 1229 Majorca, and in 1276, Jaime II. proclaimed the kingdom of Majorca. In 1349, Jaime III was ousted by Pedro IV of Aragon, and the island became a province of Aragón. During the Spanish Civil War of 1936, Majorca fell under the control of the Falange. Spain became a parliamentary monarchy in 1978, and in 1983, the Balearics were declared an autonomous region.
Majorca's oldest structures date back to the Talayots, followed by architectural remnants from Roman times. Palma in particular bears witness to Moorish rule. Important sacred and secular buildings were erected under Jaume I. Many magnificent country mansions and city palaces were built in the 18th and 19th century. The Gran Hotel in Palma is a great example of Catalan Art Nouveau. Many contemporary artists have been inspired by the magic of the island. The famous painter and sculptor Joan Miró made his home on the island in 1945. One belonging to the younger generations of resident artists is the painter Miquel Barceló, born in 1956.
Majorca's economy is characterized by tourism, which began to boom in 1960. Other important industries include farming, mining (mostly marble) and light industry (leather, pottery, pearls, glass). In the fertile valleys, peach trees prosper, apricots and medlar, which the Arabs brought along with carob. The oranges harvested here are particularly aromatic, and the area of Sóller is famous for its citrus fruit. On the terraces on the northwest coast, olive trees grow in great numbers, and about 7 million almond trees are an attraction for thousands of visitors when they begin to bloom in January.
Palma de Mallorca is the capital and political, economical and cultural centre of the island. The old part of the city is one of Europe's largest and best preserved. As a UNESCO World Heritage Site, it contains a number of protected monuments.
For more than 600 years, people on the island have been playing the Majorcan bagpipes "Sa Xeremia". The folk songs reflect Majorca's many different reigns, going back to Moorish times. The earthenware pots made from brown clay, "Olles" and "Greixoneres", normally used for cooking stews, are popular souvenirs, just as the Phoenician-Carthaginian clay pipes called "Siurells".
Many fragrant bakeries produce the sweet buns called "Ensaïmades", the pizza-like vegetable pies "Coques" and many other delicacies. Bite-sized "Tapas", the toasted bread "Pa Amb Oli", the sausage "Sobrassada" and many tasty soups make for great snacks. These days, only a few restaurants still serve the hearty traditional Majorcan dishes, usually accompanied by island wine served in earthenware jugs.

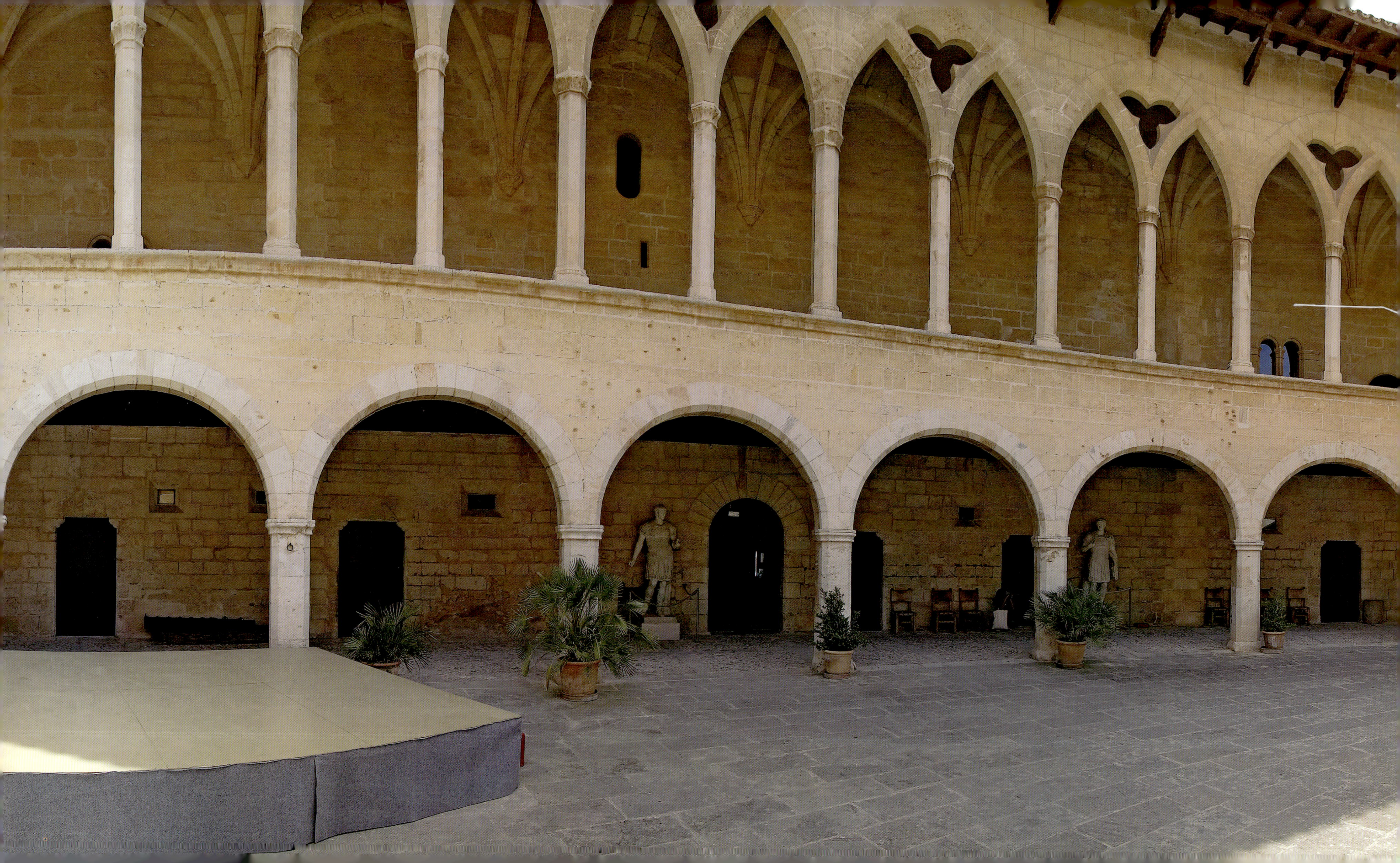

Castell de Bellver

Following the conquest of Palma in 1229, Jaime I. decided to build a monument for himself and his troops. But it took until 1300, until architect Pere Salvá was ordered to build Spain's only round two-storey fortress, 112 m above Palma, which was completed in 1309. The lower level is dominated by impressive Romanesque arcades, while the colonnade above was built in the Gothic style. Three round towers stand not much taller than the structure that is surrounded by a moat with a width of 4 m. "Torre de l'Homenatge", the fourth and tallest tower stands outside the fortress, connected by a drawbridge. The terrace was built as a strategic lookout. It also served as an access to the dungeon, a part of the cave system "Coves d'Avall", which was created during construction. "Castell de Bellver" was only briefly used as a royal seat, because the building became a prison in the late 14th century, first for the Jews of Palma, later on for a number of famous prisoners, including justice and tax minister Gaspar Melchor de Jovellanos between 1802 and 1809. Prisoners were thrown from the "Torre de l'Homenatge" for a 5 m drop into the dungeon. Today, a part of the building houses a museum, illustrating the history of Palma.

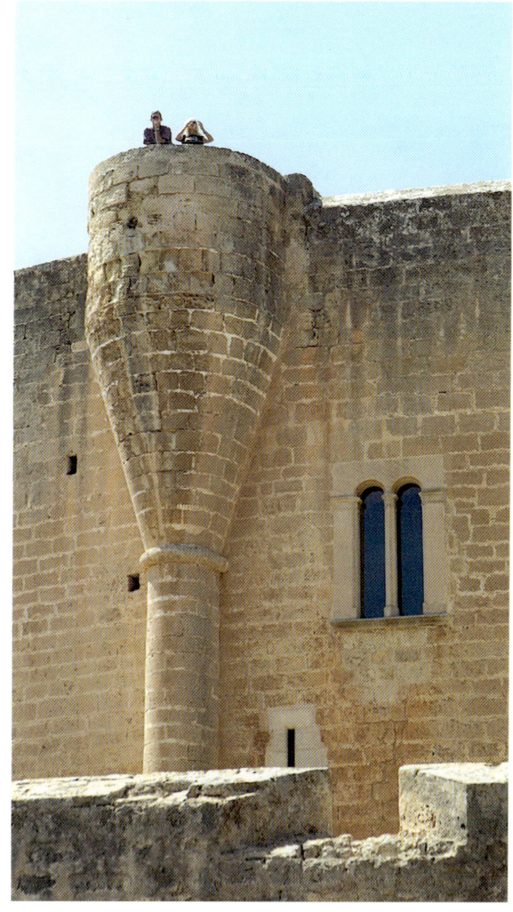

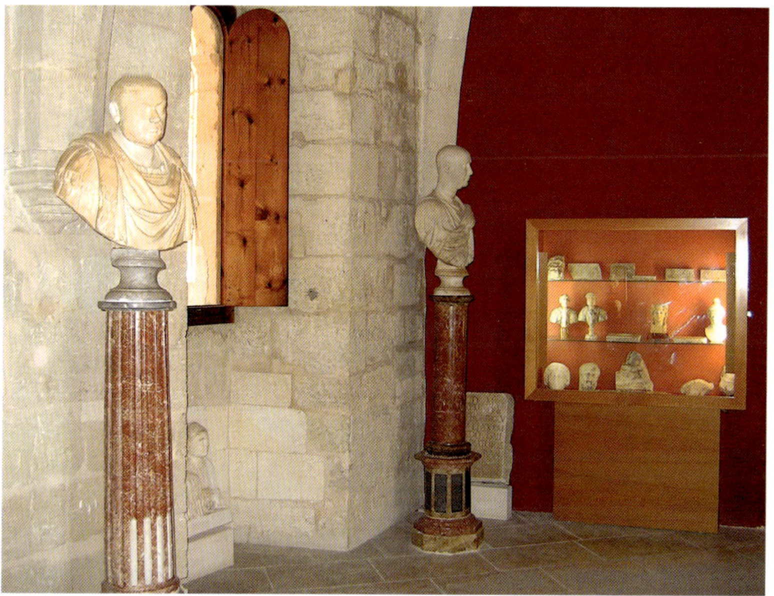

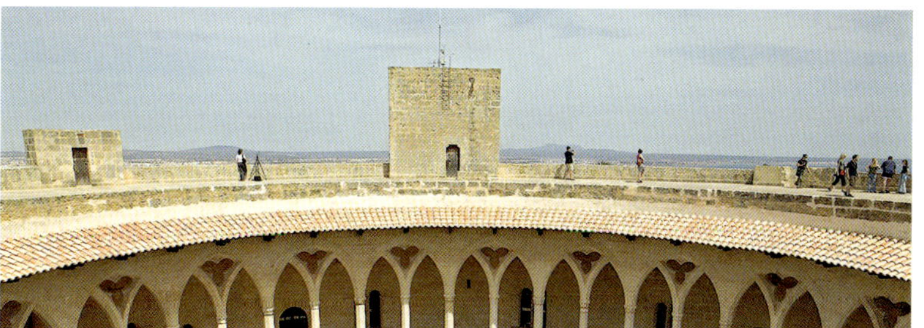

Castell de Bellver

360° panoramic photo: The inner courtyard of Castell de Bellver 1

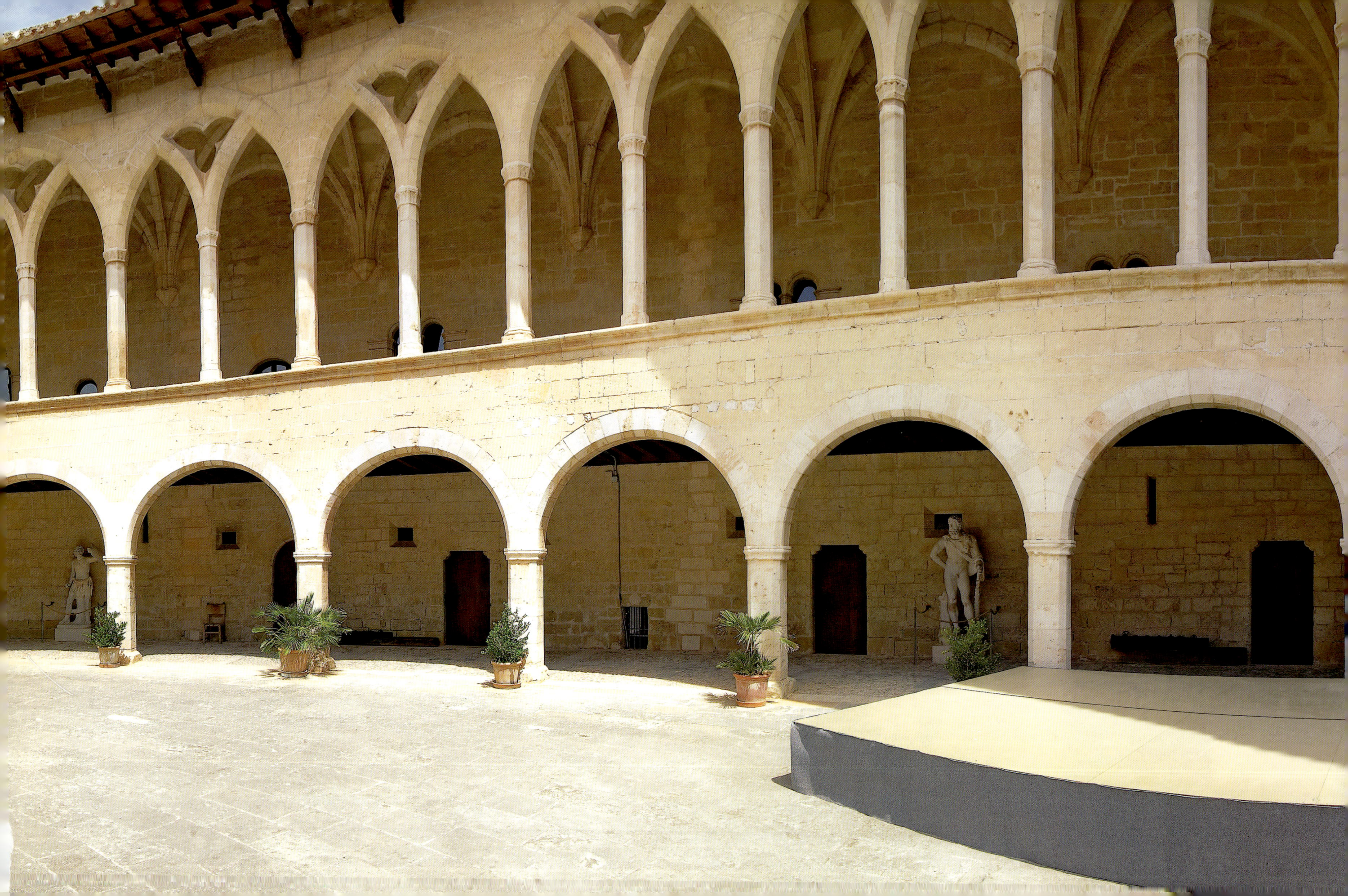

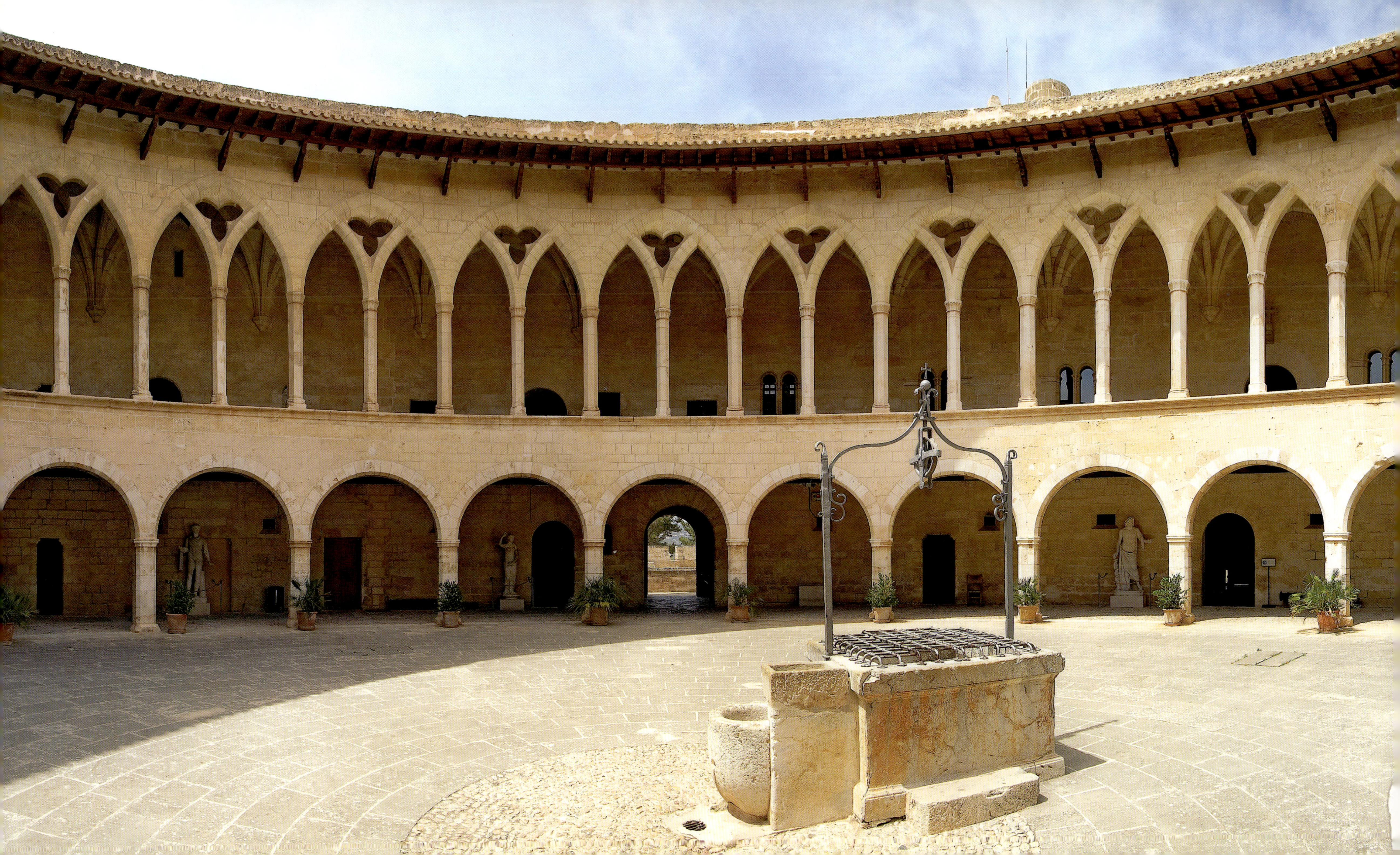

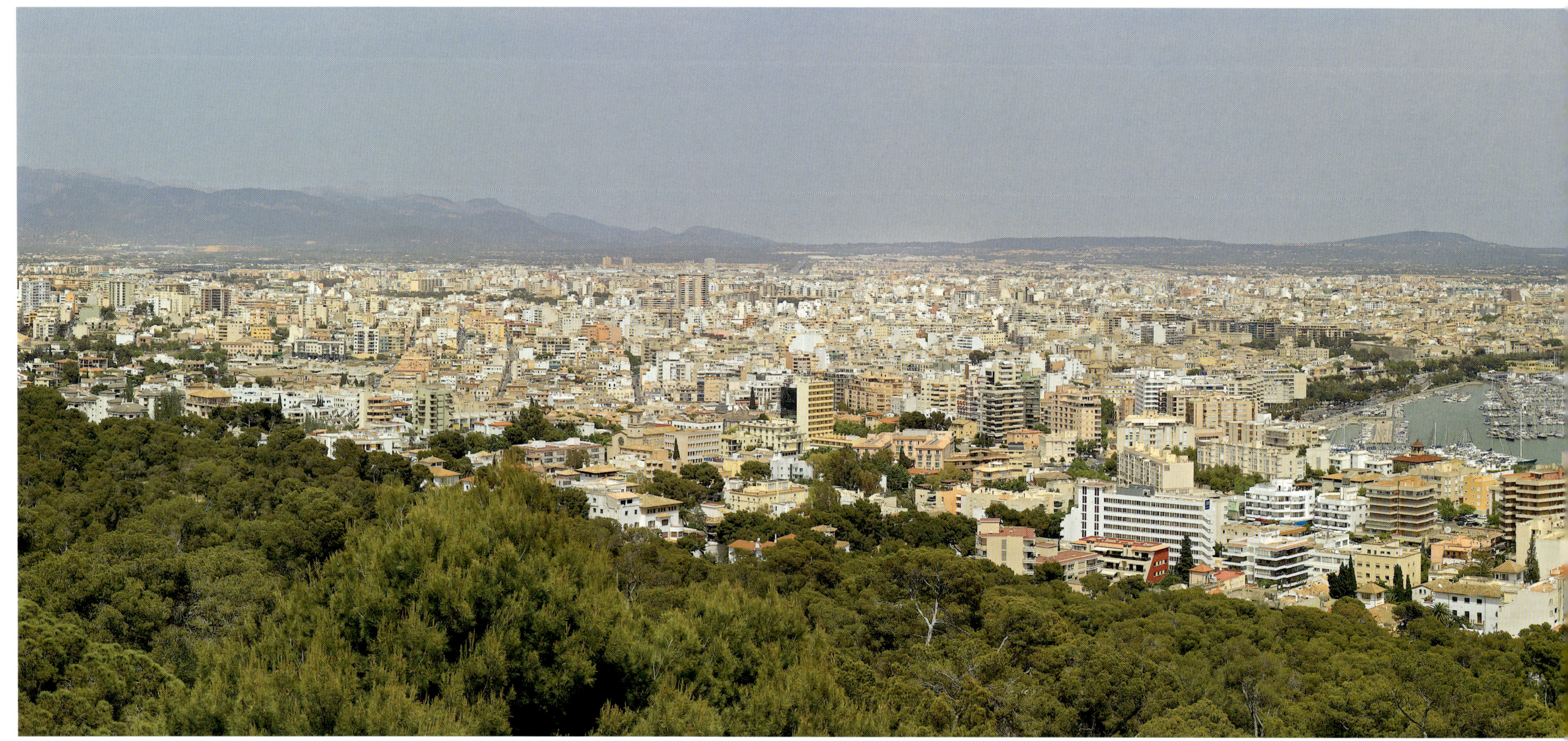

Palma de Majorca

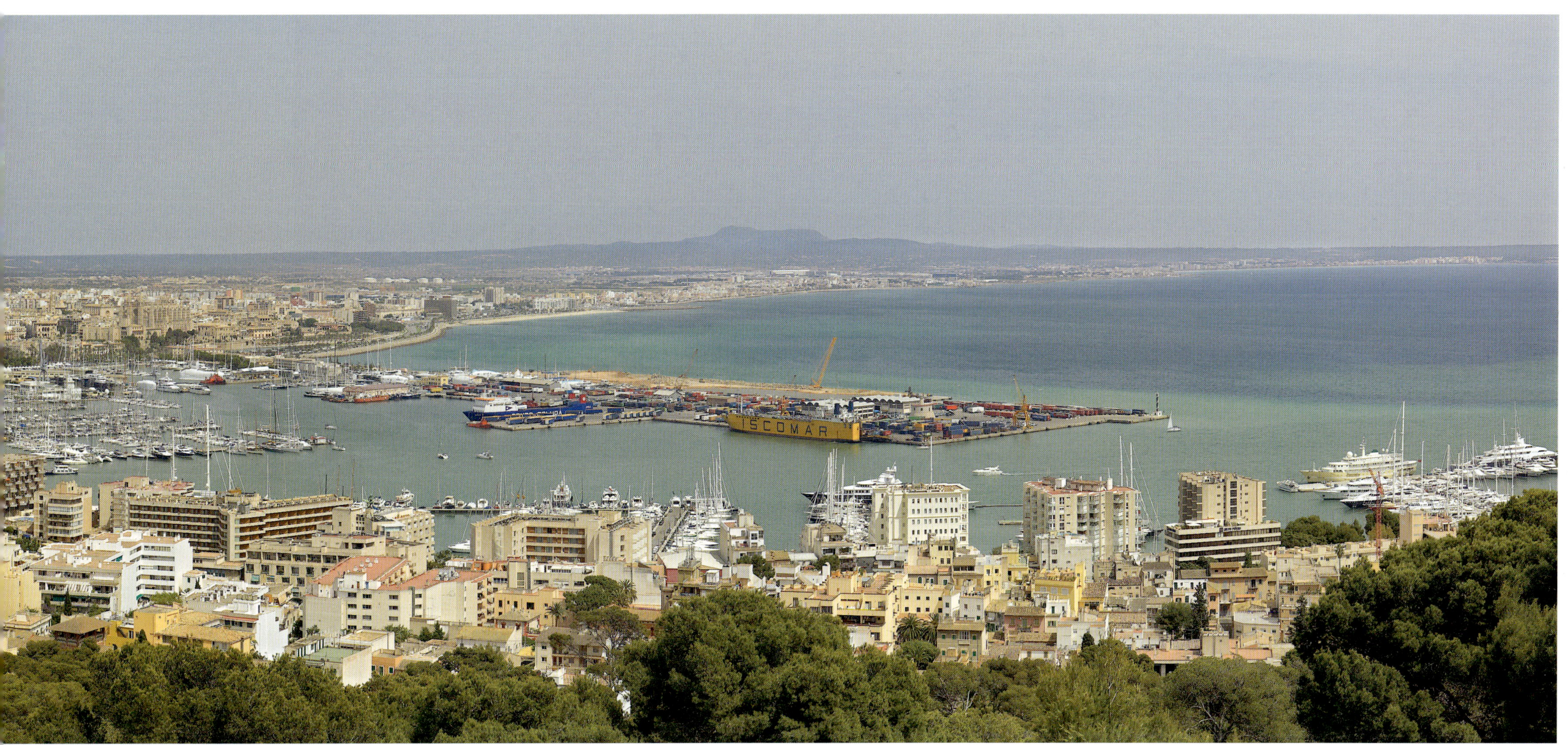
ISCOMAR

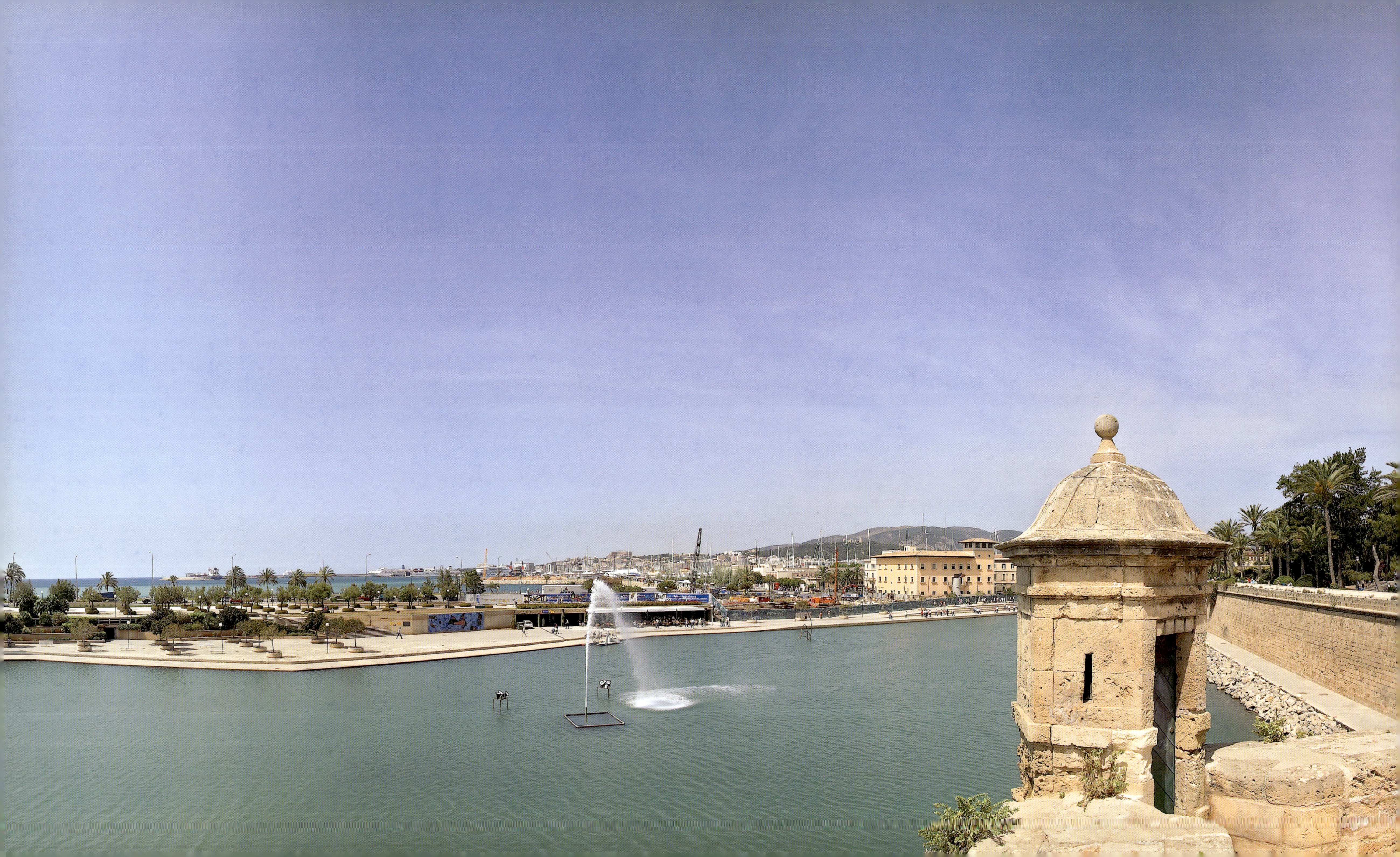

Cathedral La Seu

The port of Palma is towered by the 44 m high Gothic cathedral on the Plaça de l'Almoina, which was begun under the reign of Jaime I. in 1230. A monument of gratitude for the victory over the Moors, the cathedral was built on the ruins of the main Moorish mosque. In 1360, under Jaime II., construction of the nave began, which was finished in 1587. In 1601, the main portal was opened, but the facade was not completed until the 20th century. In 1851, the cathedral sustained heavy damage in an earthquake, and in 1902, Antoni Gaudi was contracted to renovate the building in a neo-Gothic style. For almost ten generations, thousands of people transported the rectangular ashlars on mule-drawn carts. Wooden scaffolding and blocks and tackles were used to put the huge stones together and bind them with plaster. The 15 m tall portal "El Mirador" is one of the most beautiful examples of Spanish lancet architecture.

The cathedral, built on 6,600 m² and one of the world's four most beautiful Gothic cathedrals, features columns with a height of 22 m but a diameter of only 2m, which carry the lancet arches of the roof construction.

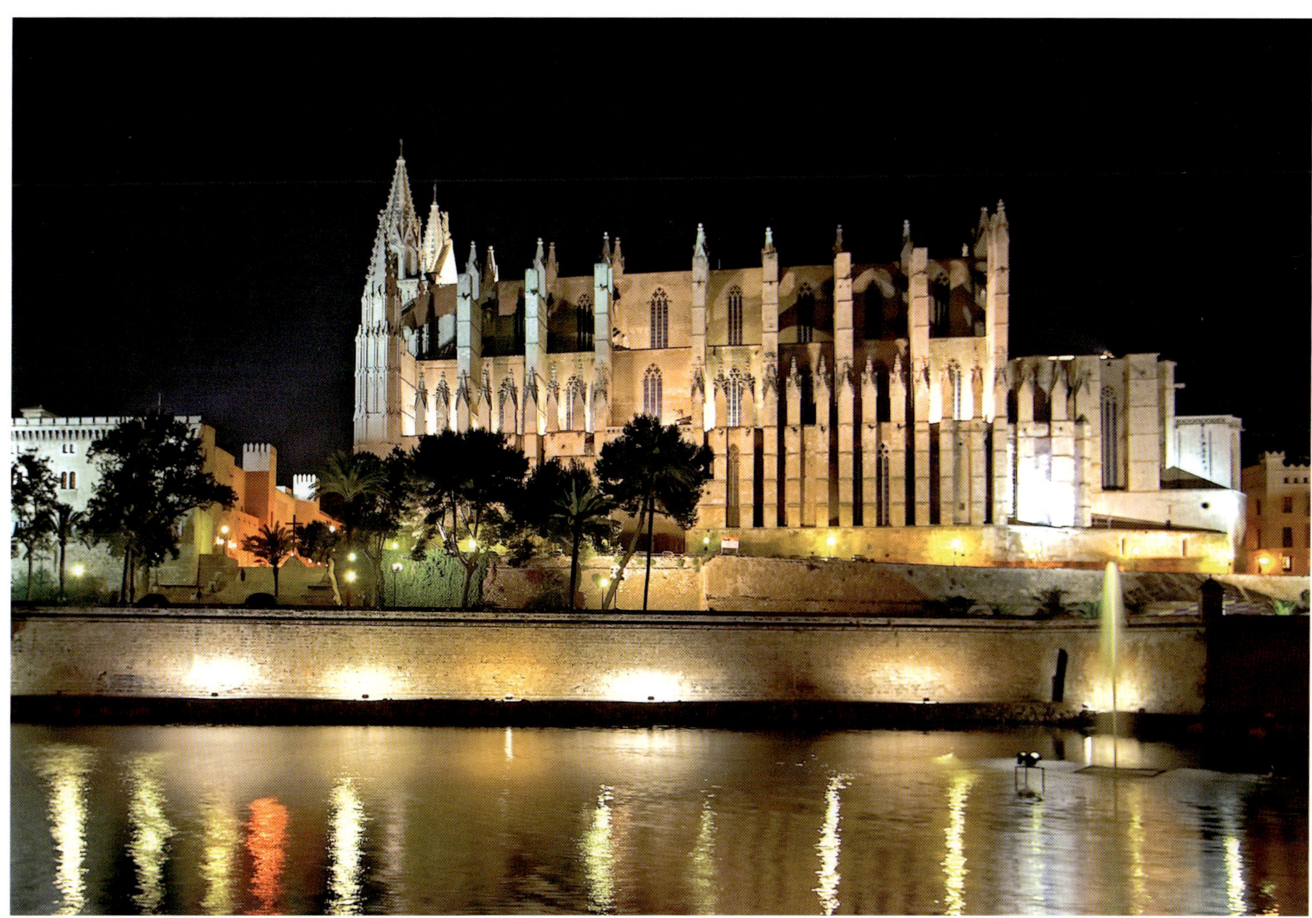

The illuminated cathedral at night.

360° panoramic photo: The Cathedral La Seu towers the port of Palma 2

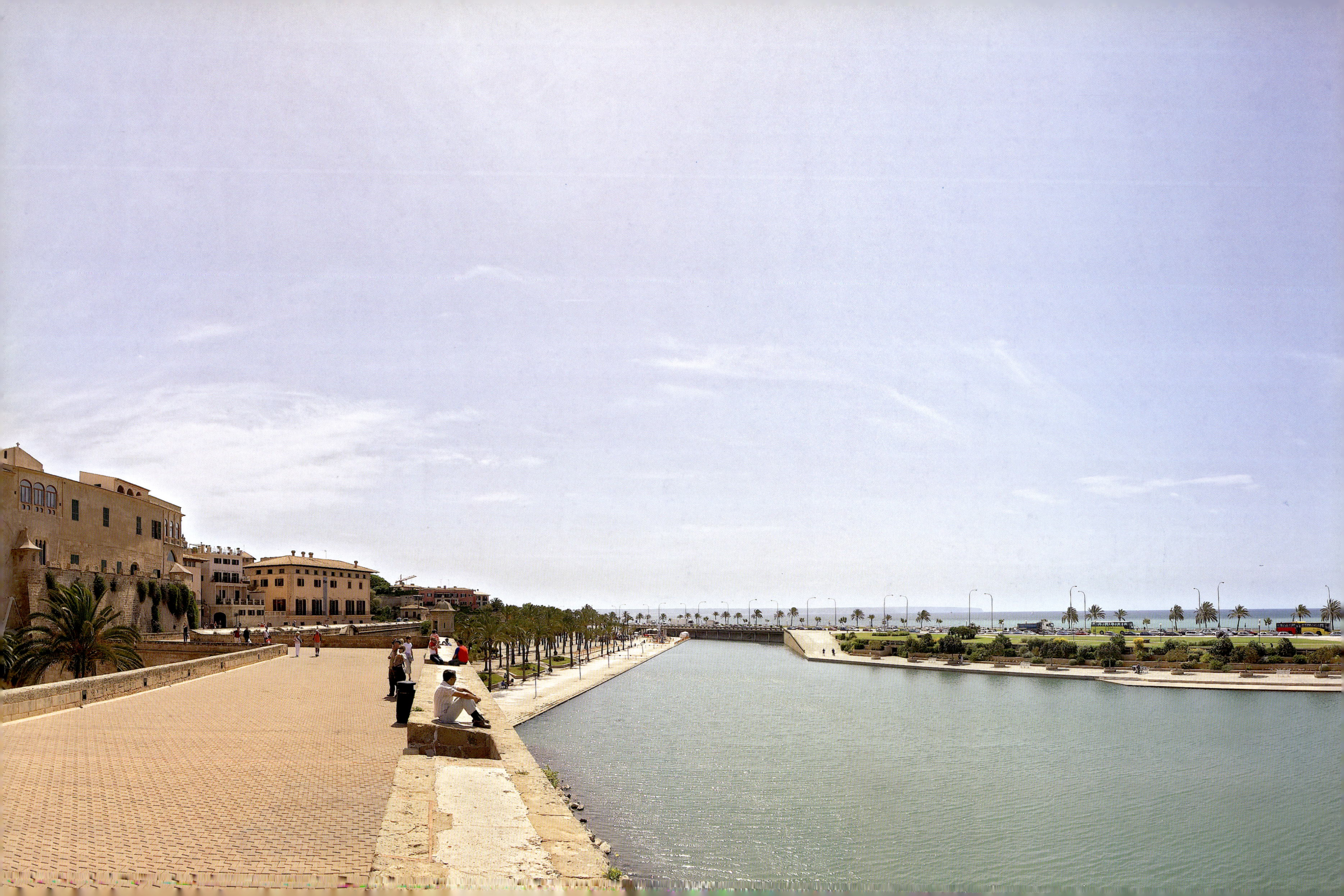

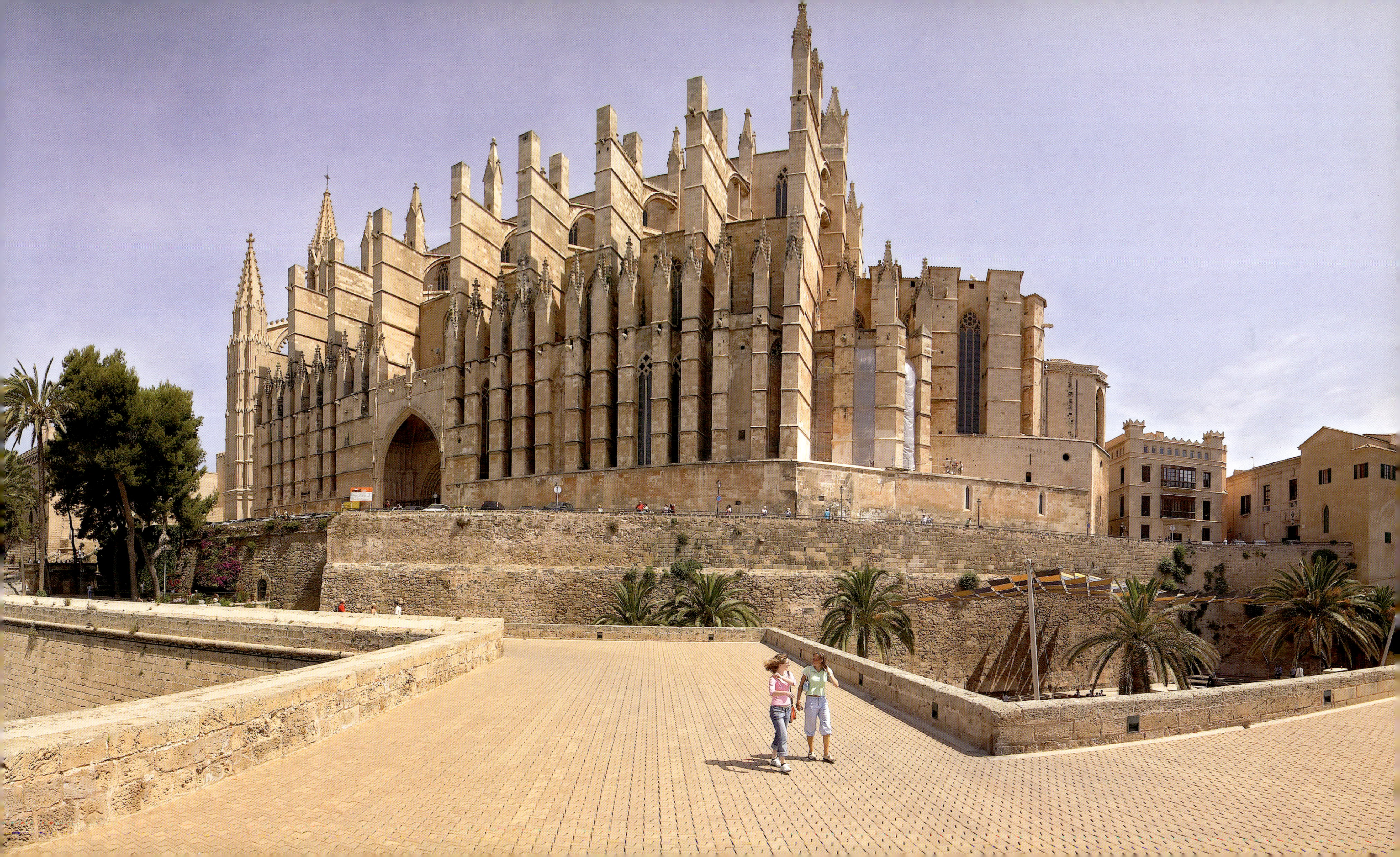

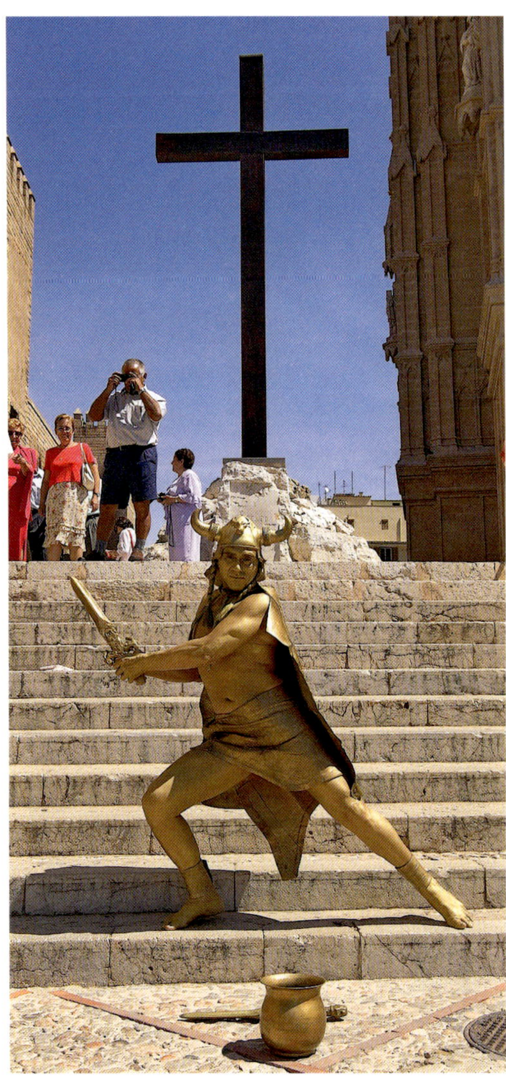

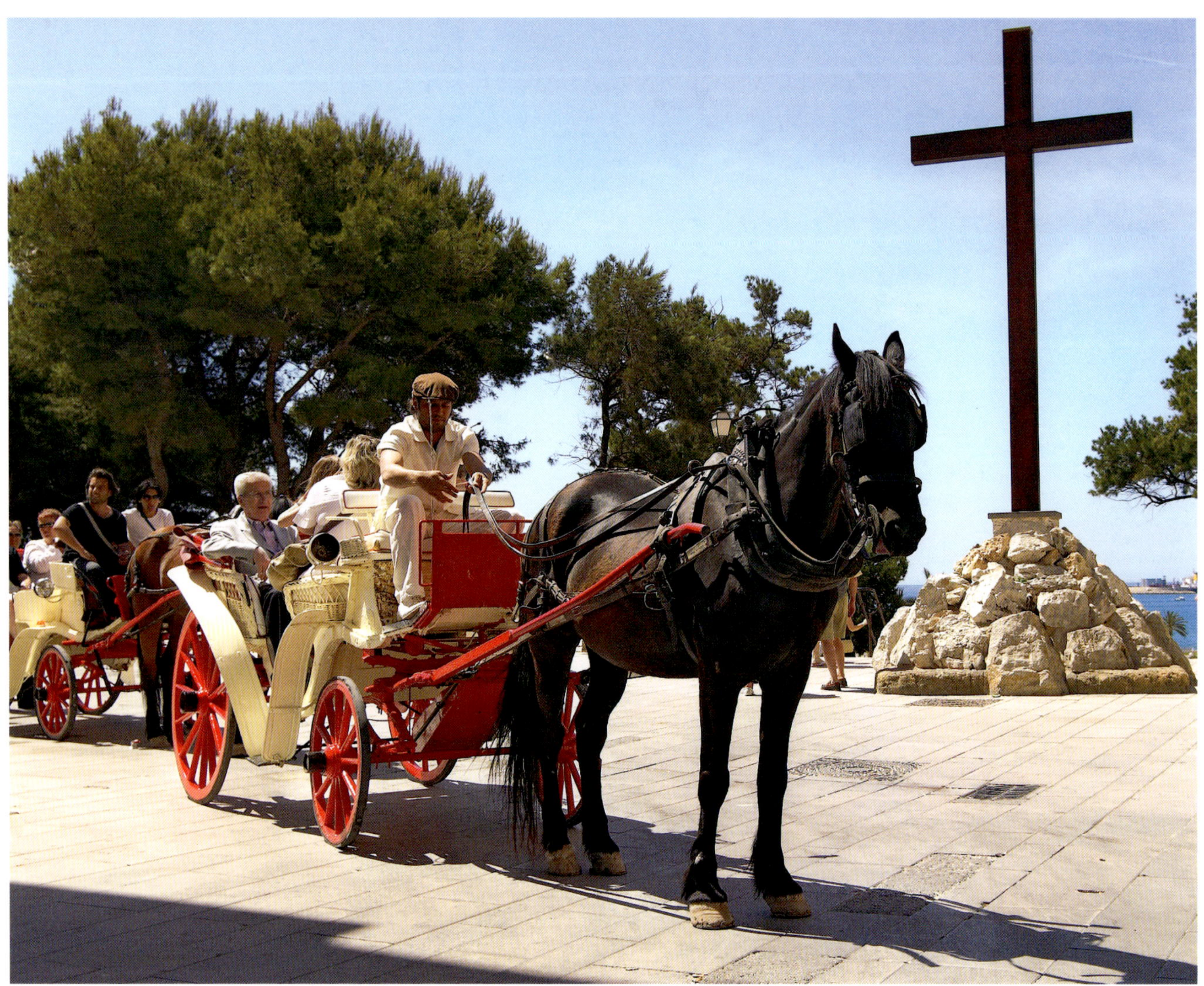

Pantomimes and tourists carriages in front of the cathedral.

Since 1932, the bell tower of the three-naved cathedral houses a museum. The tall side aisles have been cleverly constructed to allow daylight to reach the nave. Seven huge glass rosettes and 60 beautifully designed side windows create an impressive play of light and shadow, from which the church derives its name "Cathedral of the Light".
Many of the side chapels' reredoses feature Baroque elements. The christening chapel was built in a neo-Classic style. During renovation in 1904-14, the architect Antoni Gaudi made several major architectural changes, which did not meet with the approval of all people responsible for the project. The disagreement led Gaudi to finish only one side of the planned heptagonal canopy. The renovation also included the integration of the choir room into the Royal Chapel (next 360° panoramic photo, right).
The square in front of the cathedral is often used by pantomimes for their performances.
Tourists from around the globe go on a sightseeing tour of the city in one of the many carriages offering their services.
In the nearby gardens of "S'Hort del Rei", you can find a bronze sculpture by Llorent Rossello, depicting a Balearic stone thrower with a slingshot. This former art of warfare is a popular sport today.

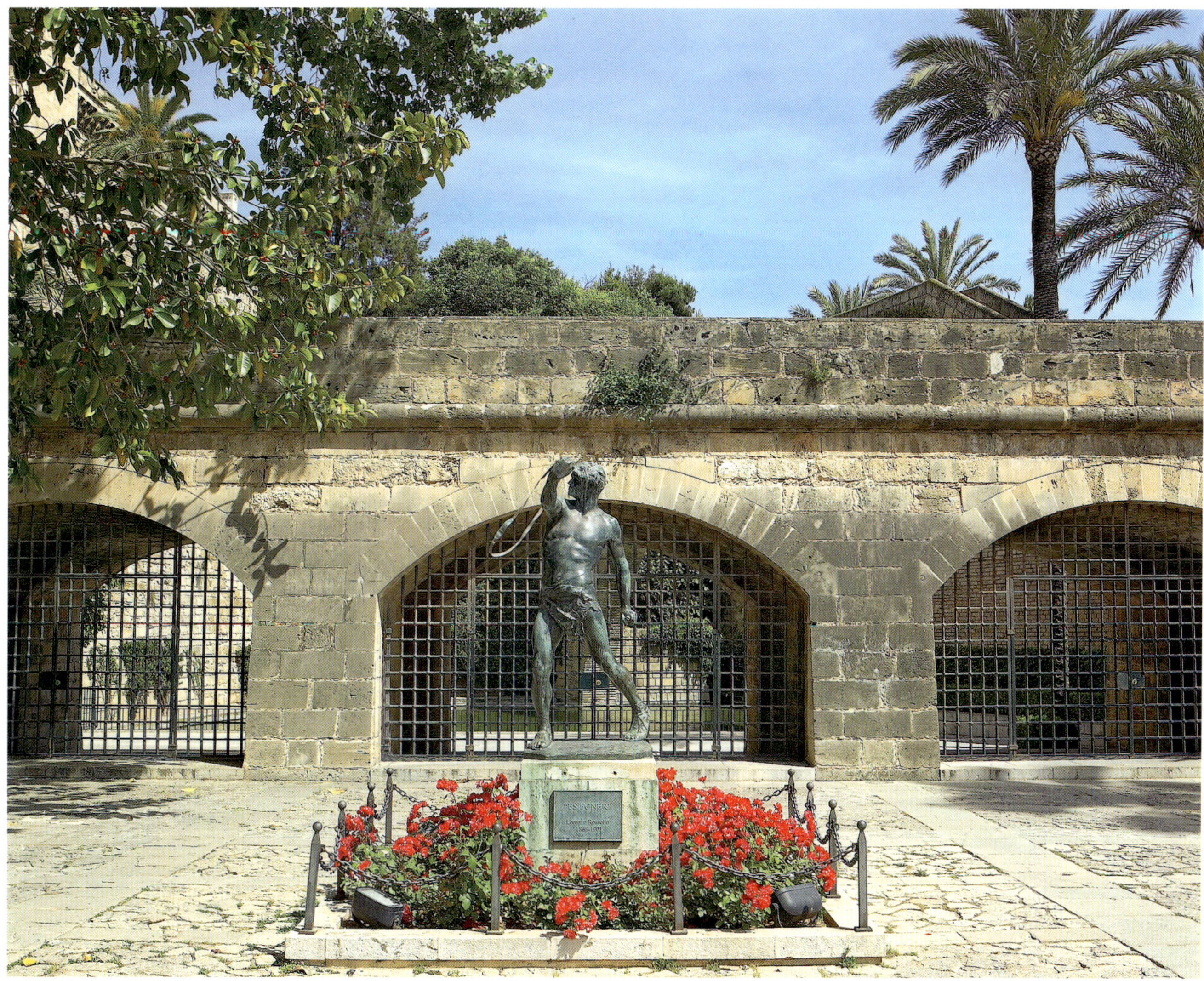

Bronce sculpture by Llorent Rossello in „S'Hort del Rei".

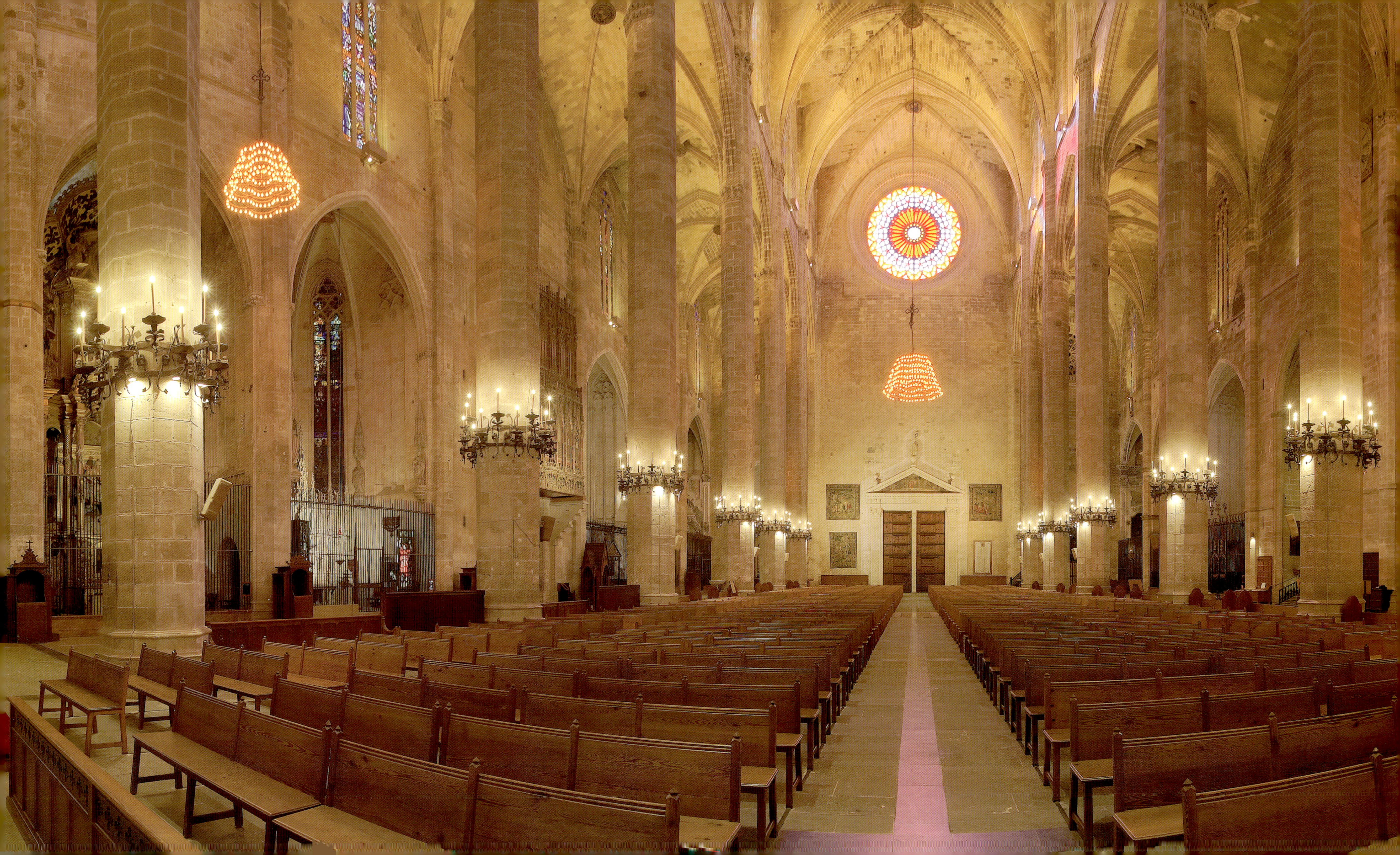

Cathedral La Seu

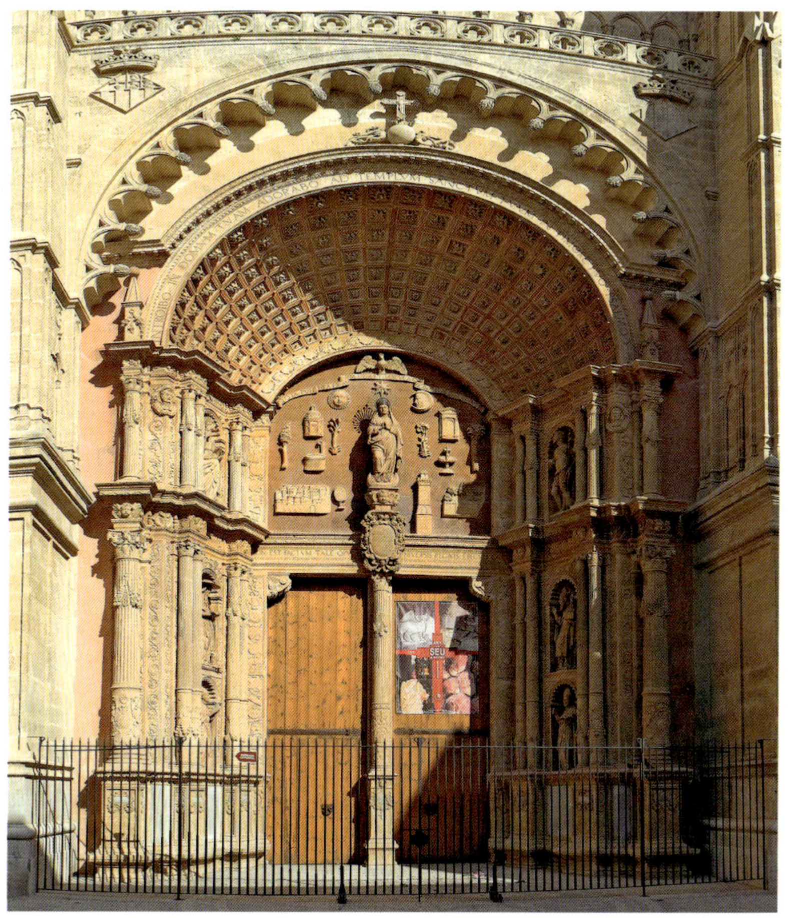

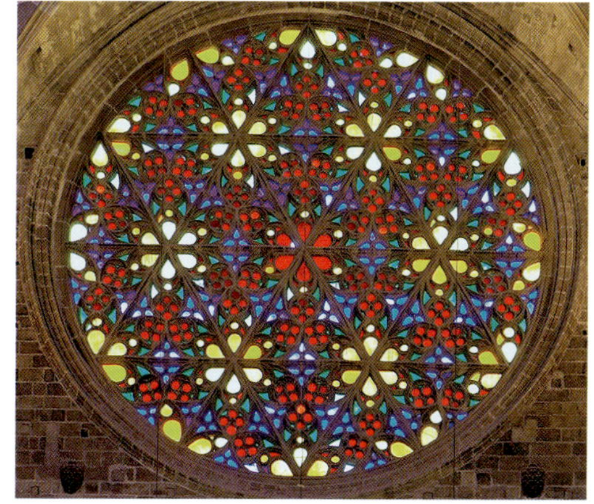

The 7 beautifully designed glass rosettes on the west and east side of the cathedral "La Seu" face each other in a way that allows for the sunlight to flood through both at the same time at certain times. One of the magnificent rosettes has a diameter of 12.55 m, making it the biggest in the world.

The big organ was built in the late 18th century by the Majorcan Gabriel Tomás and restored in 1993.

At the beginning, the cathedral was constructed in a pure Gothic style. A more ornate version of this style can be found on the "Portal de l'Almoina".

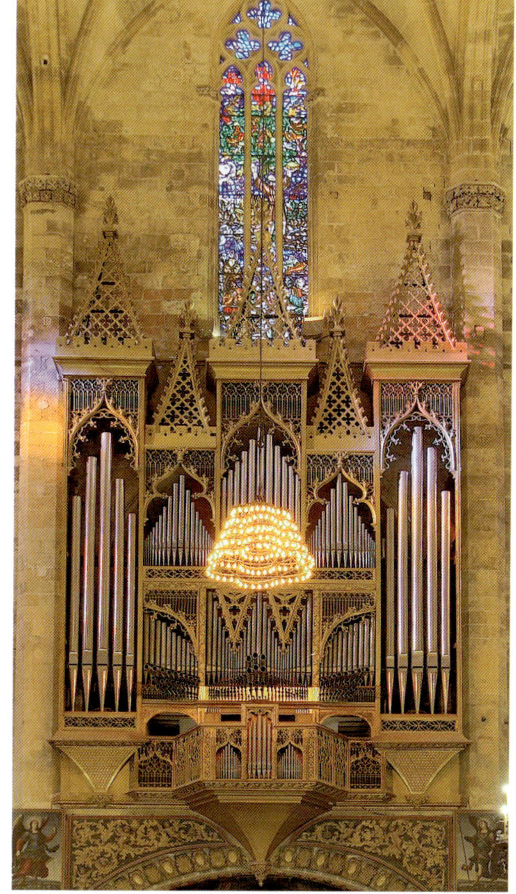

"Portal de l'Almoina"; the biggest glass rosette in the world; Tomás organ.

360° panoramic photo: The magnificent interior of the Cathedral La Seu 3

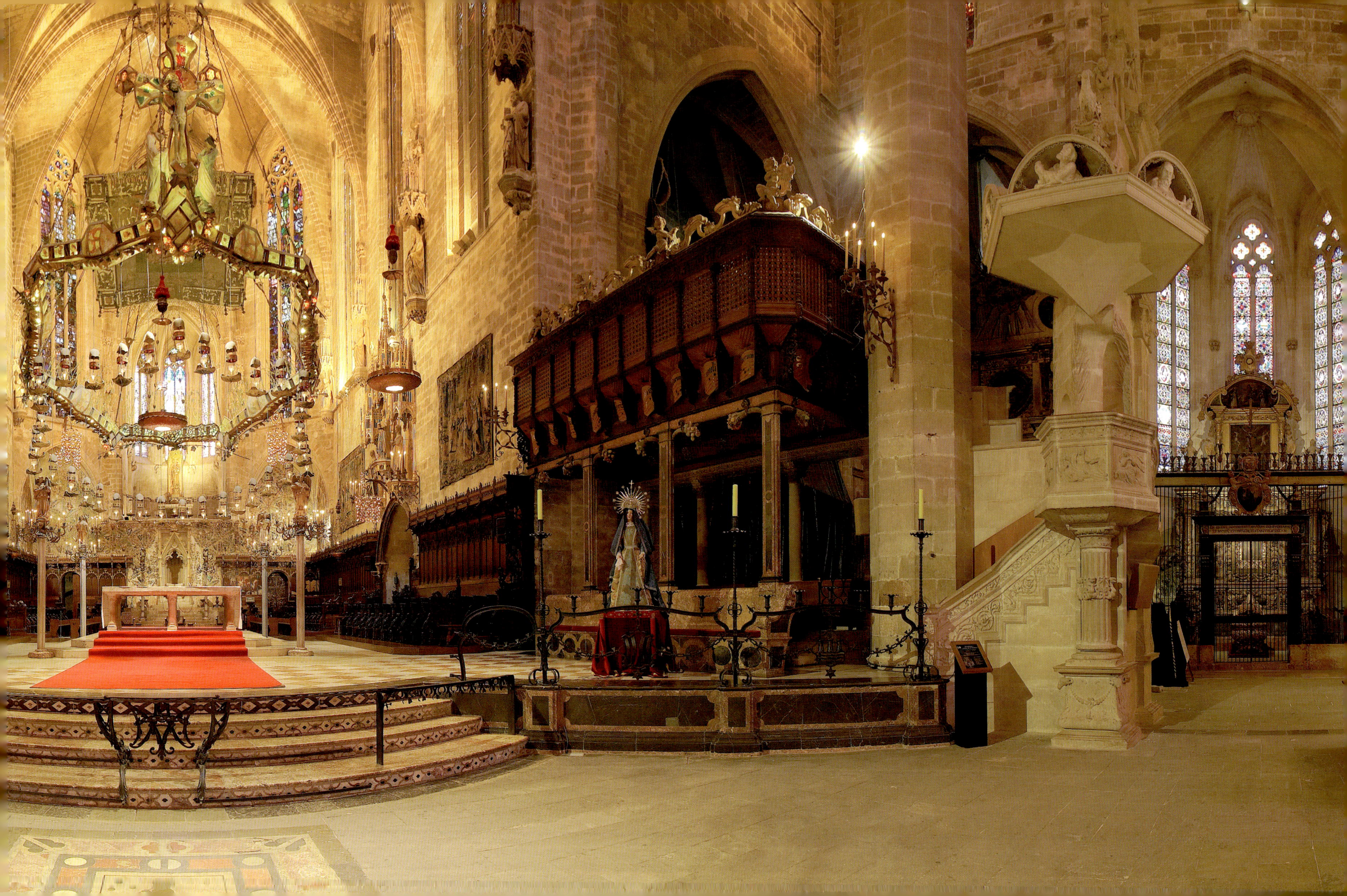

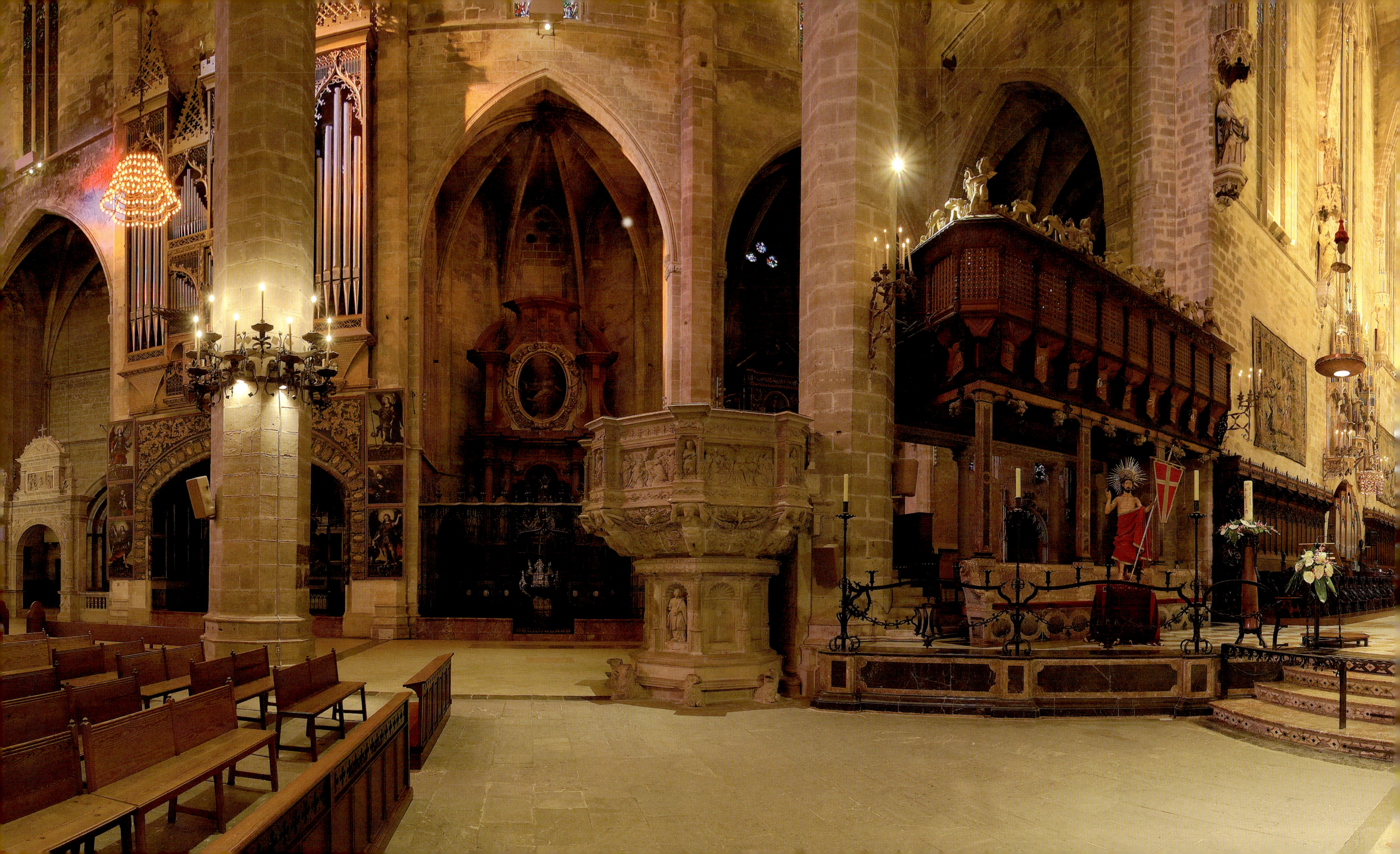

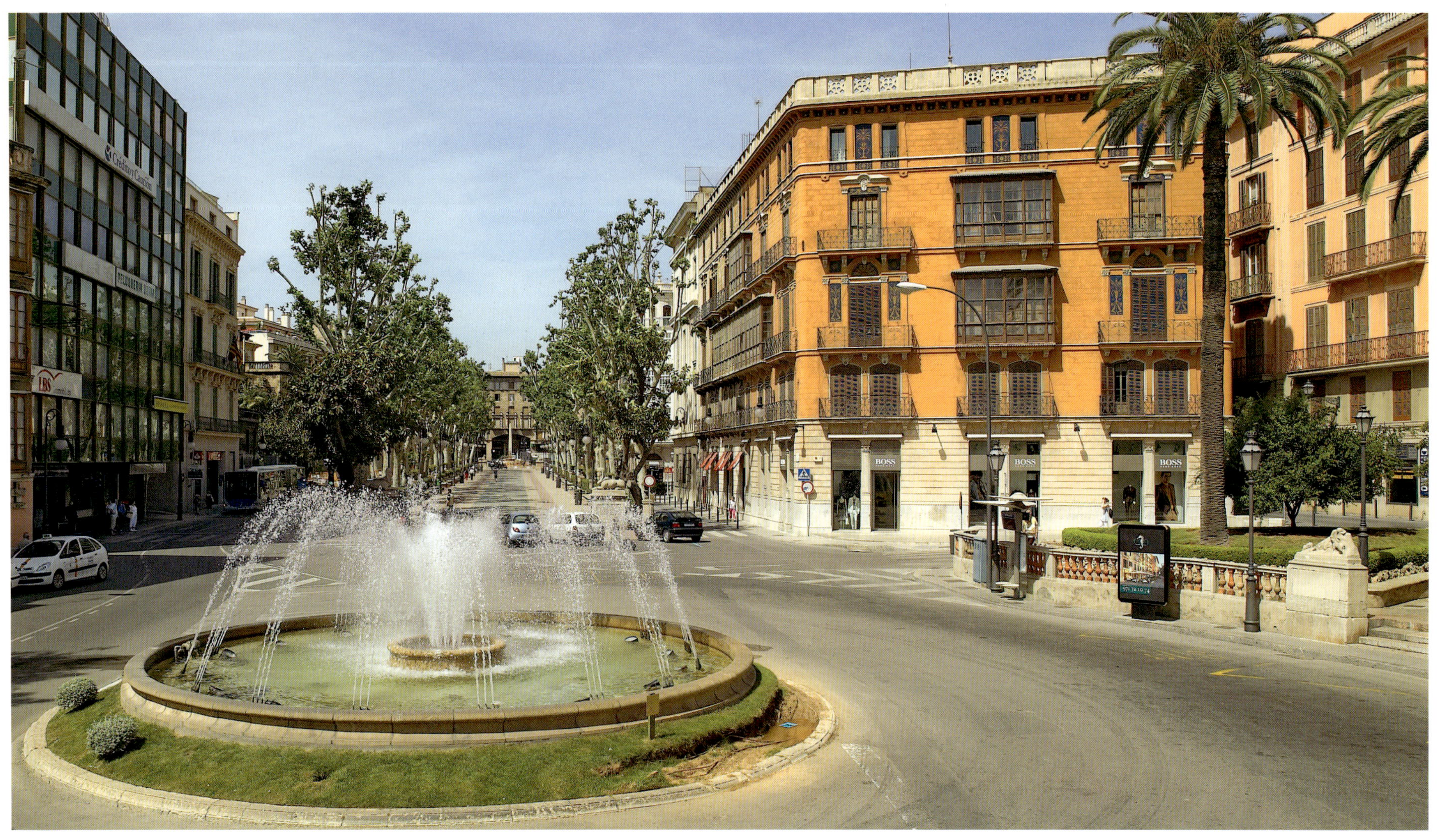

Plaça de la Reina

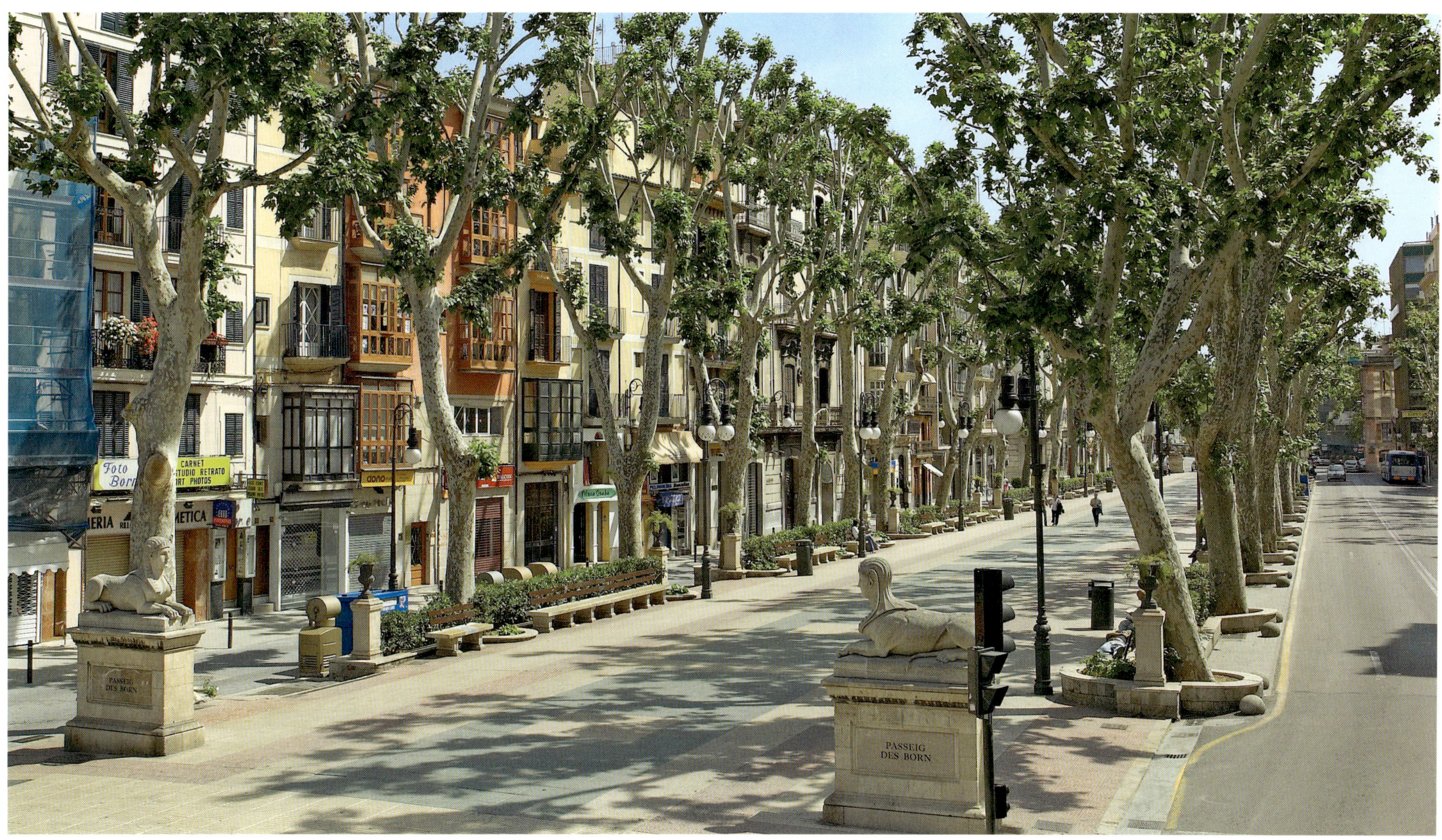

Palma's splendid boulevard Passeig des Born

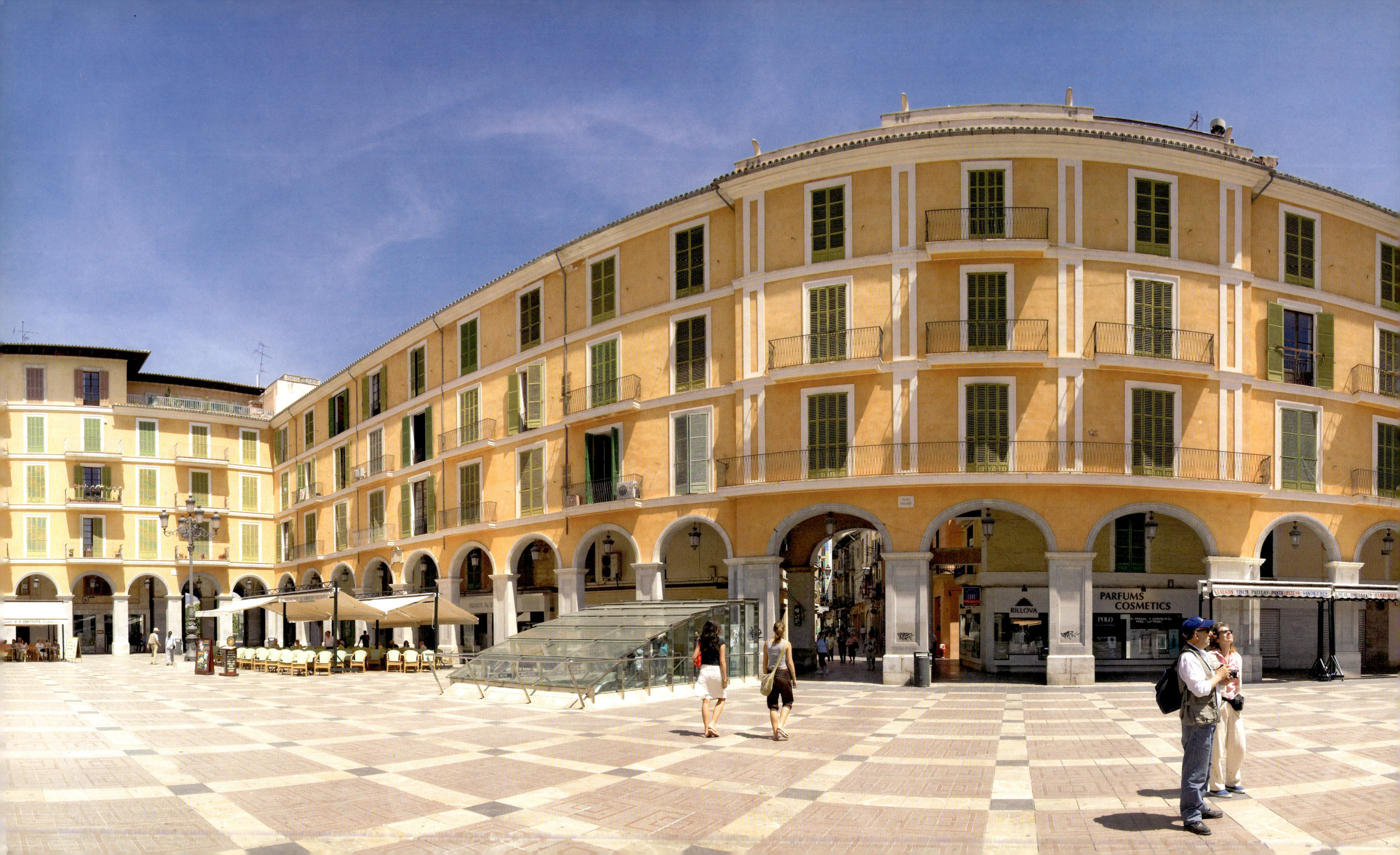
RILLOVA
PARFUMS
COSMETICS
POLO
SALADS FISCH PAELLAS PASTA PIZZAS SANDWICHES

Plaça Major

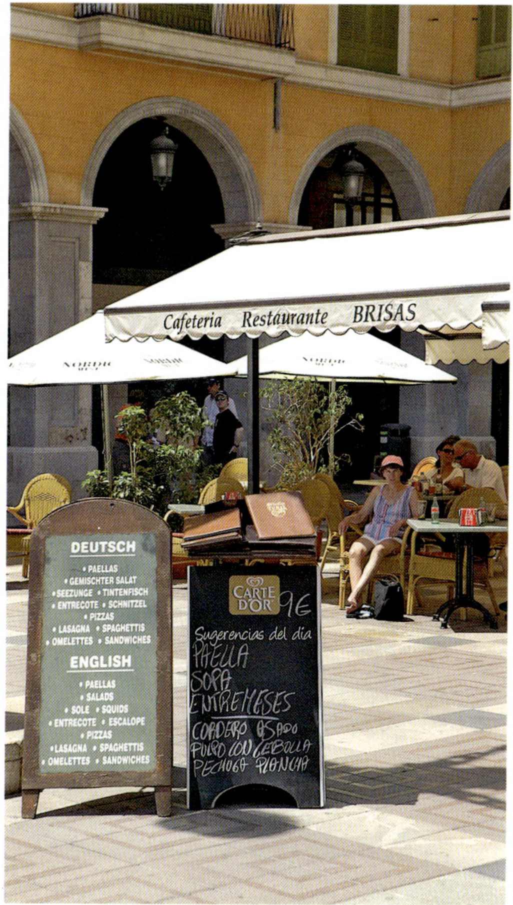

The arcade-lined square (360° panoramic photo) at the centre of the pedestrian area is the meeting point for Palma's major shopping boulevards. It used to be a part of the former city park and presents a perfect backdrop for all kinds of street artists. The square is teeming with life, especially during the summer months. Cafés and restaurants offer more than local specialties. Every Sunday, the square serves as a venue for a weekly market, and the countless shops and boutiques sell leather goods and crafts products. Every other year, a folk dance festival takes place on the square. More than a thousand dancers and musicians participate, and the students from the "Music and Dance School Majorca" perform traditional folk dances.

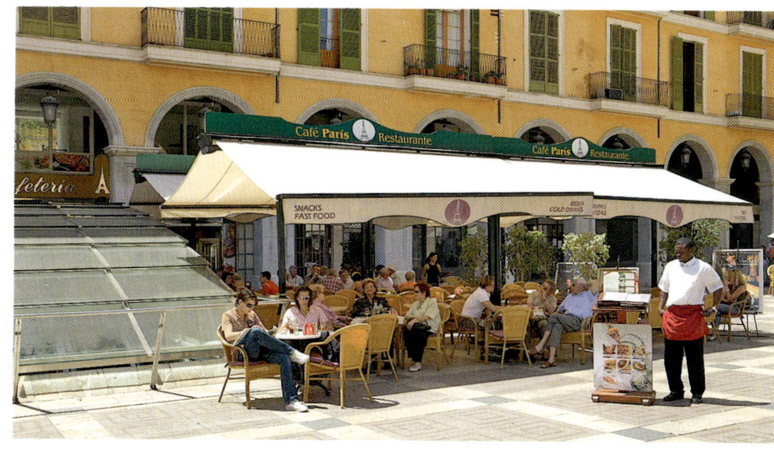

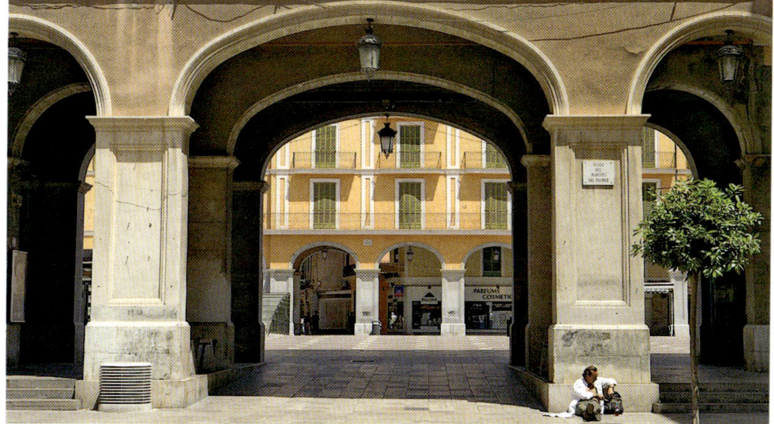

Crossing under a huge archway, you reach the nearby Plaça Marques del Palmer, where you can see the beautiful Art Nouveau buildings "L'Aquila" and "Can Fortesa Rei". Another sight by the square is the museum "Espanyol Contemporani", exhibiting an important collection of contemporary art. The museum also houses the "Collecció March", the art collection of the banker family March.

Plaça Major.

360° panoramic photo: Plaça Major 4

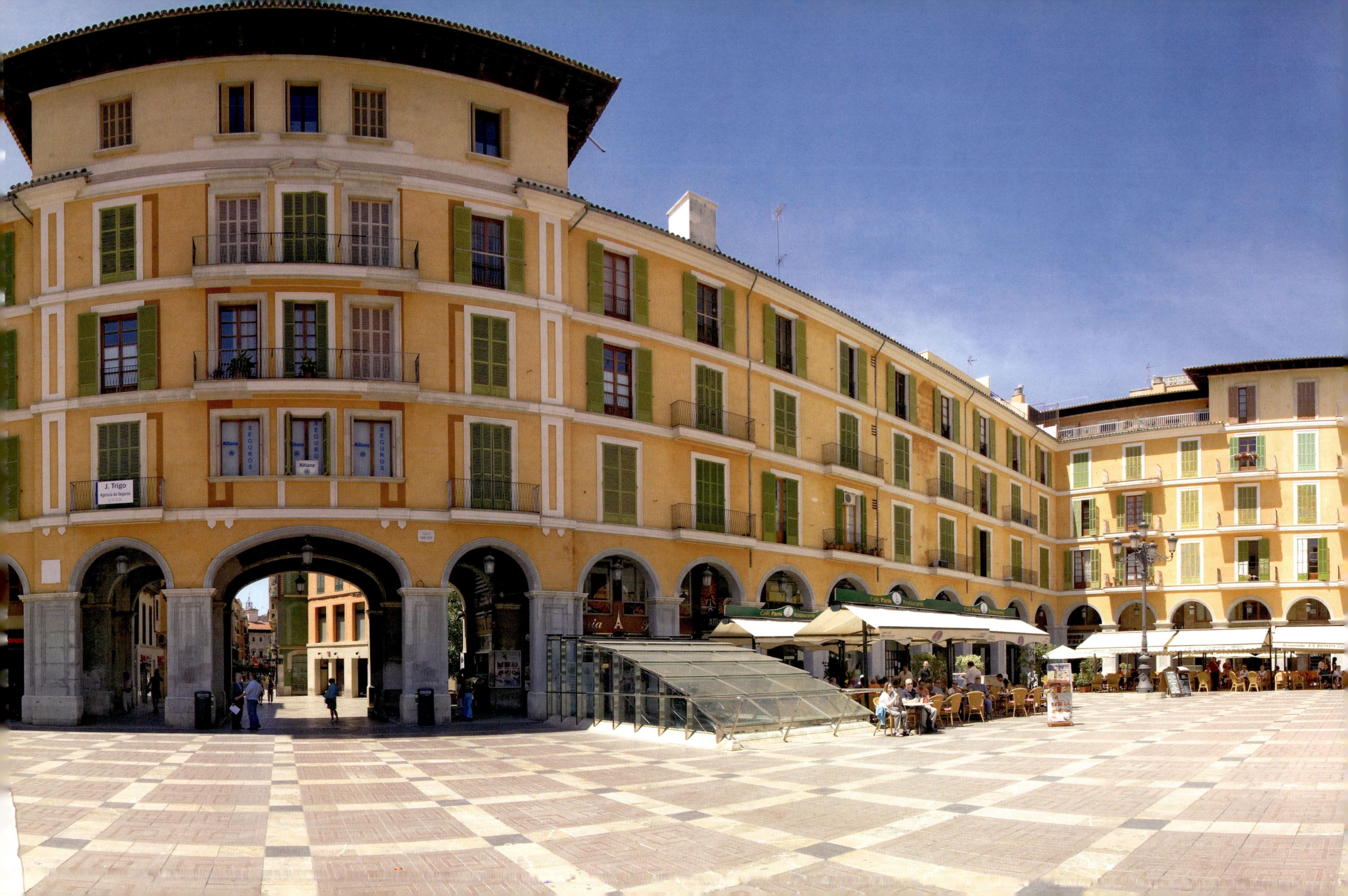
J. Trigo
Agencia de Seguros
Allianz
SEGUROS
Allianz
SEGUROS
Allianz
Allianz
SEGUROS
Café Paris

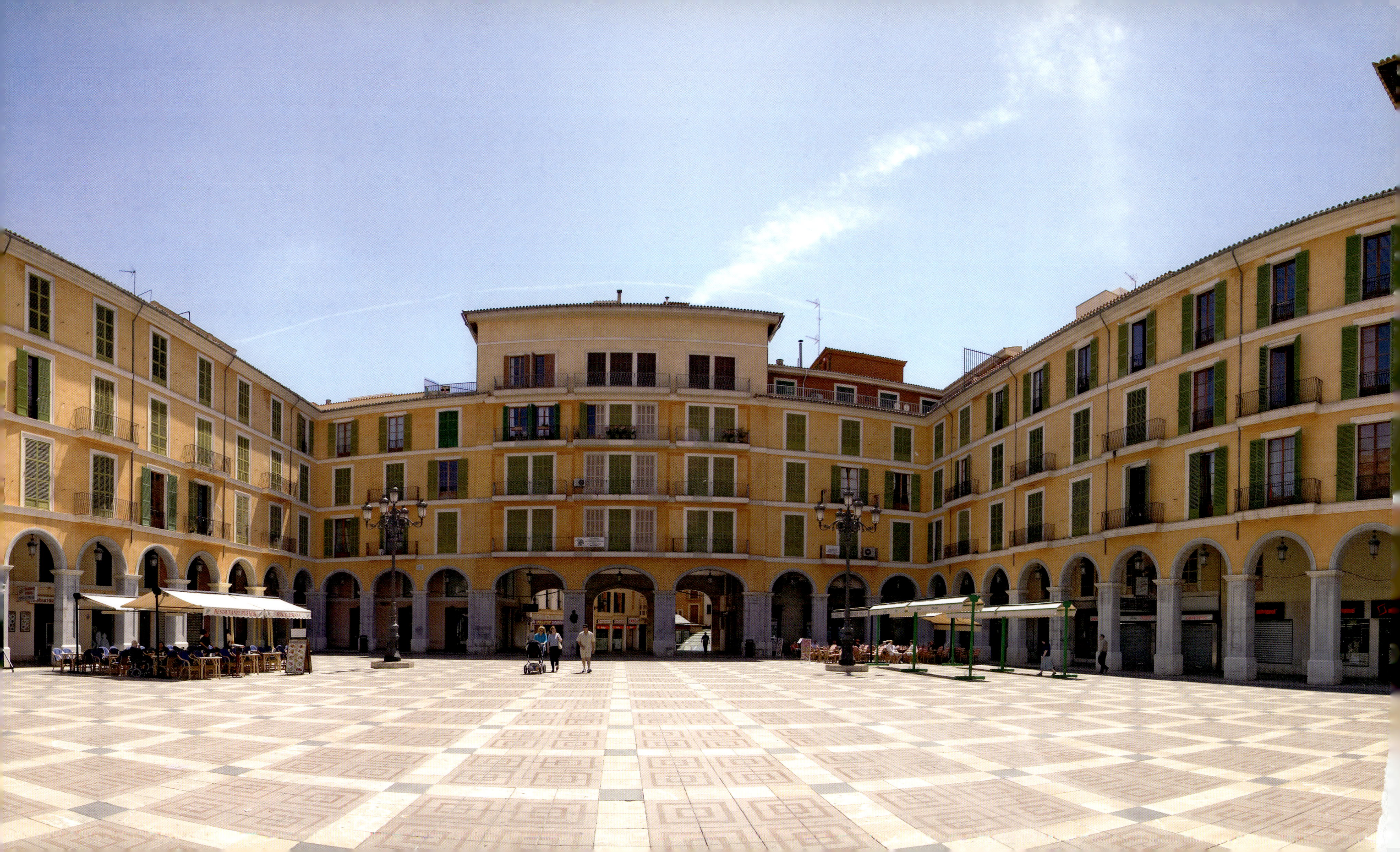

Stairs lead from Plaça Major to Passeig de la Rambla; the idyllic squares of the old part of town are often connected by narrow stairs. The Gran Hotel on the Plaça Weyler, built according to plans by Lluís Domènech, was opened in 1903 and remained open until the Spanish civil war. Today, it is used as an art centre.

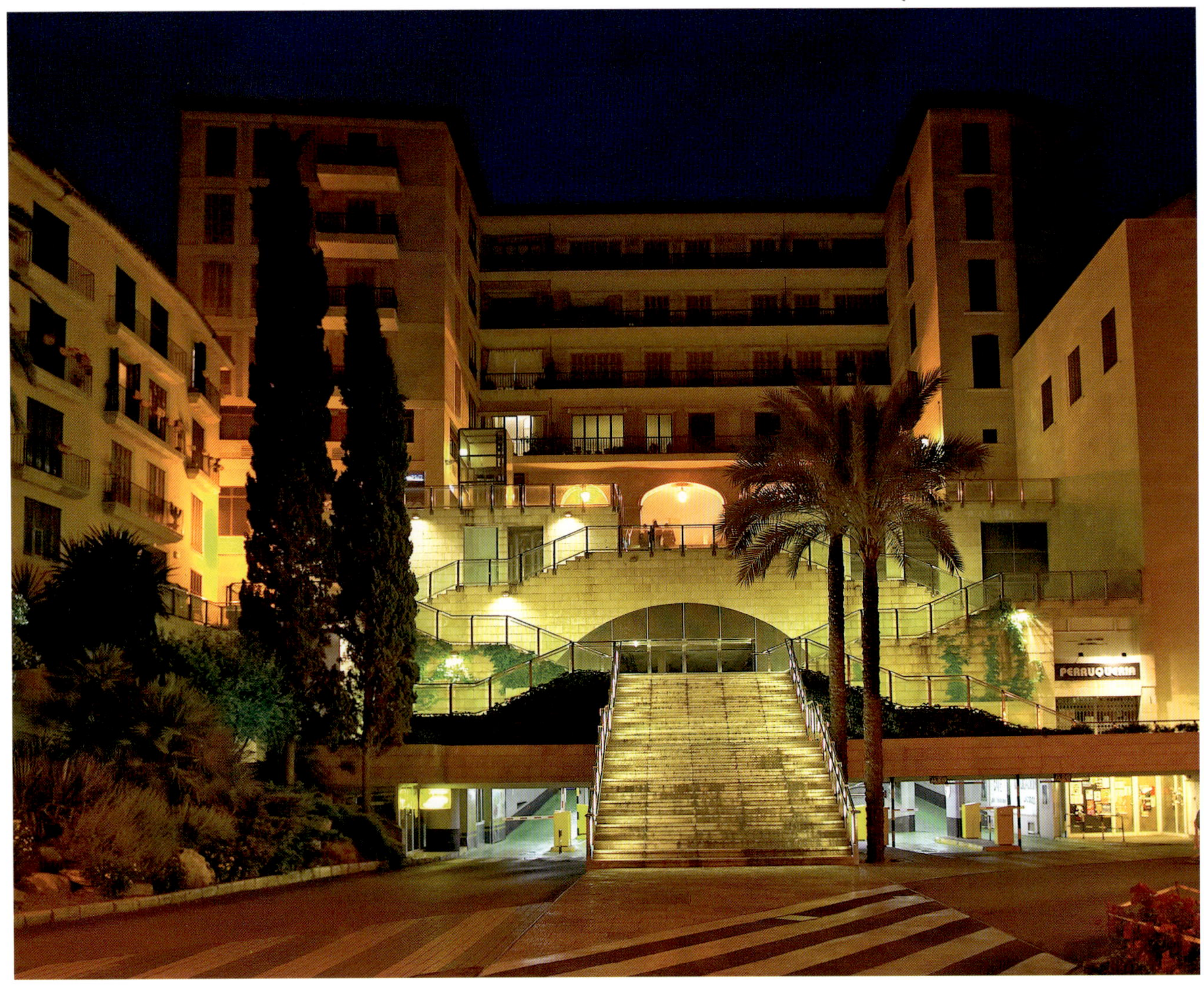

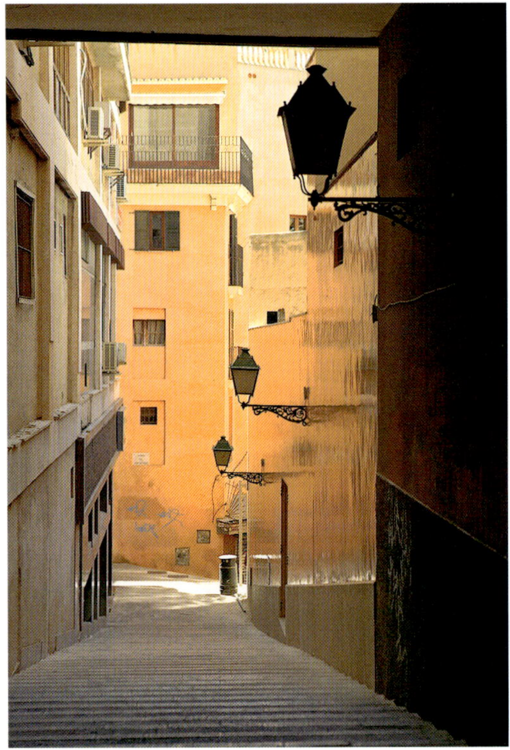

Art centre on Plaça Weyler; one of the narrow stairs in the old part of the town.

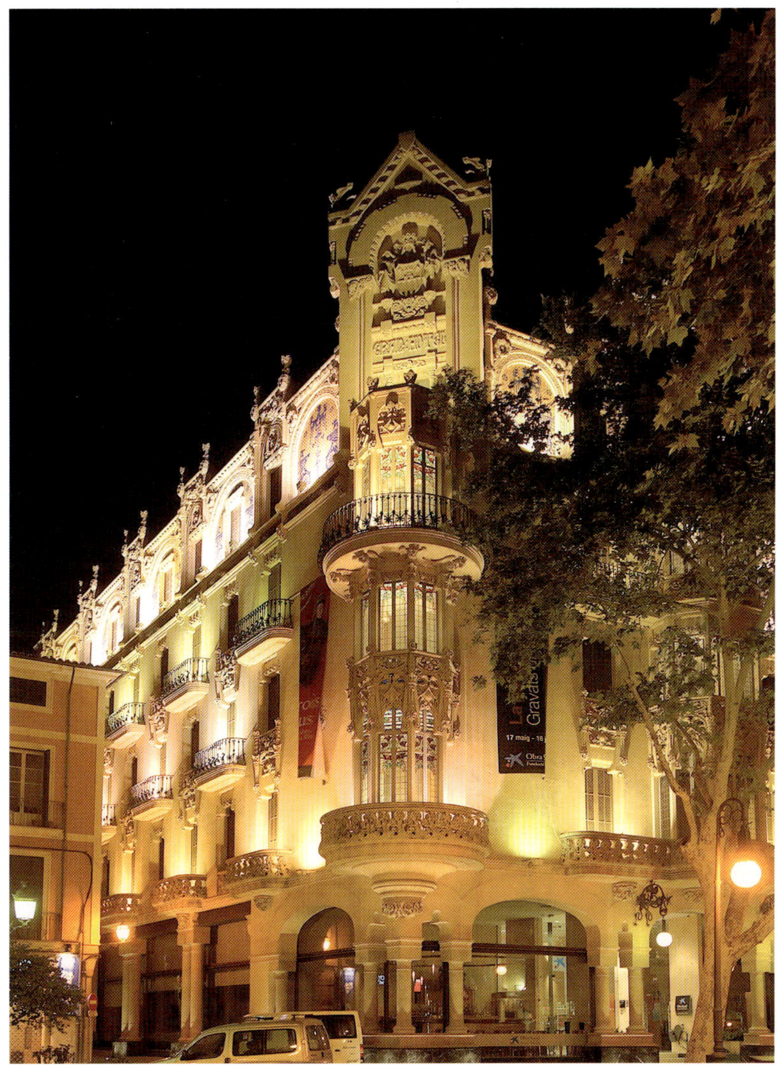

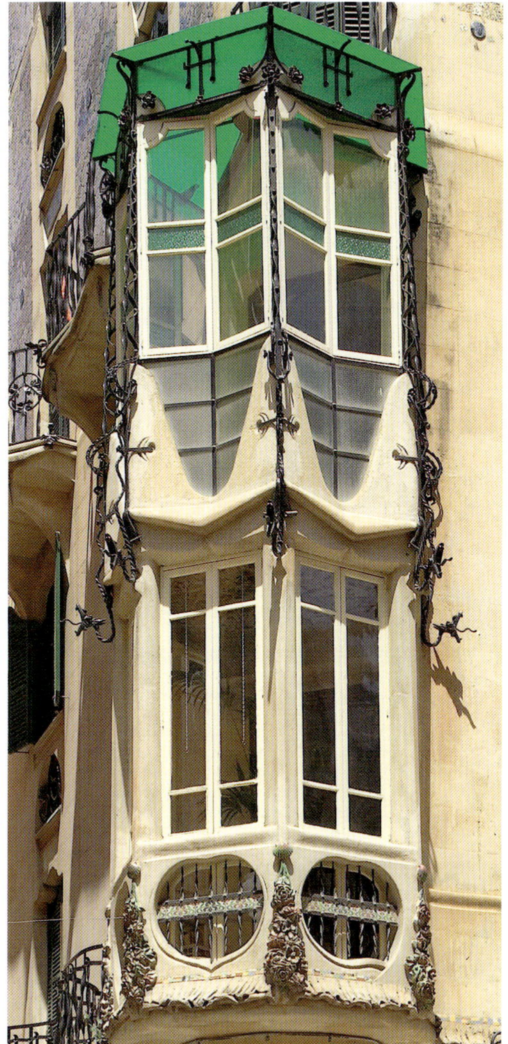

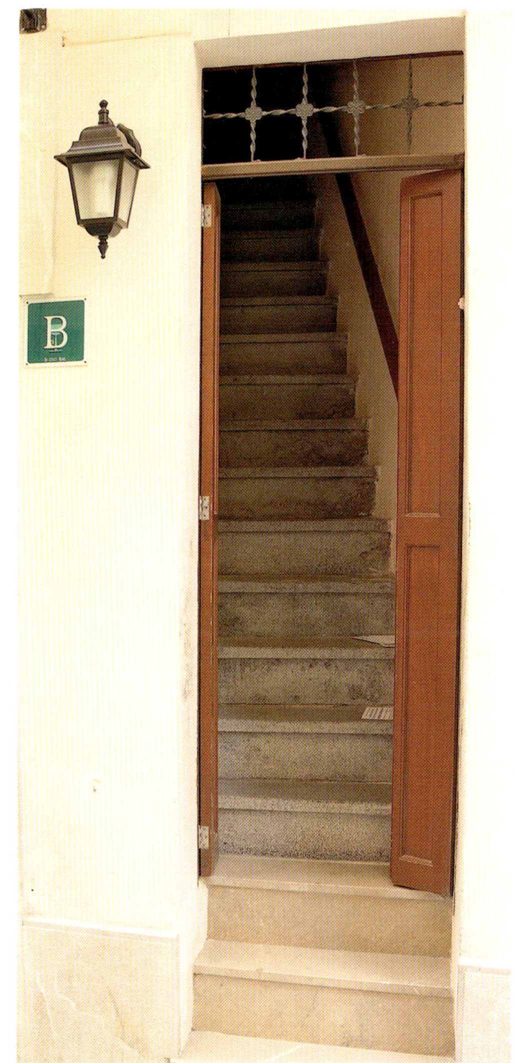

Some of Palma's beautiful old facades and a typical example of the narrow stairs in houses in the old part of town.

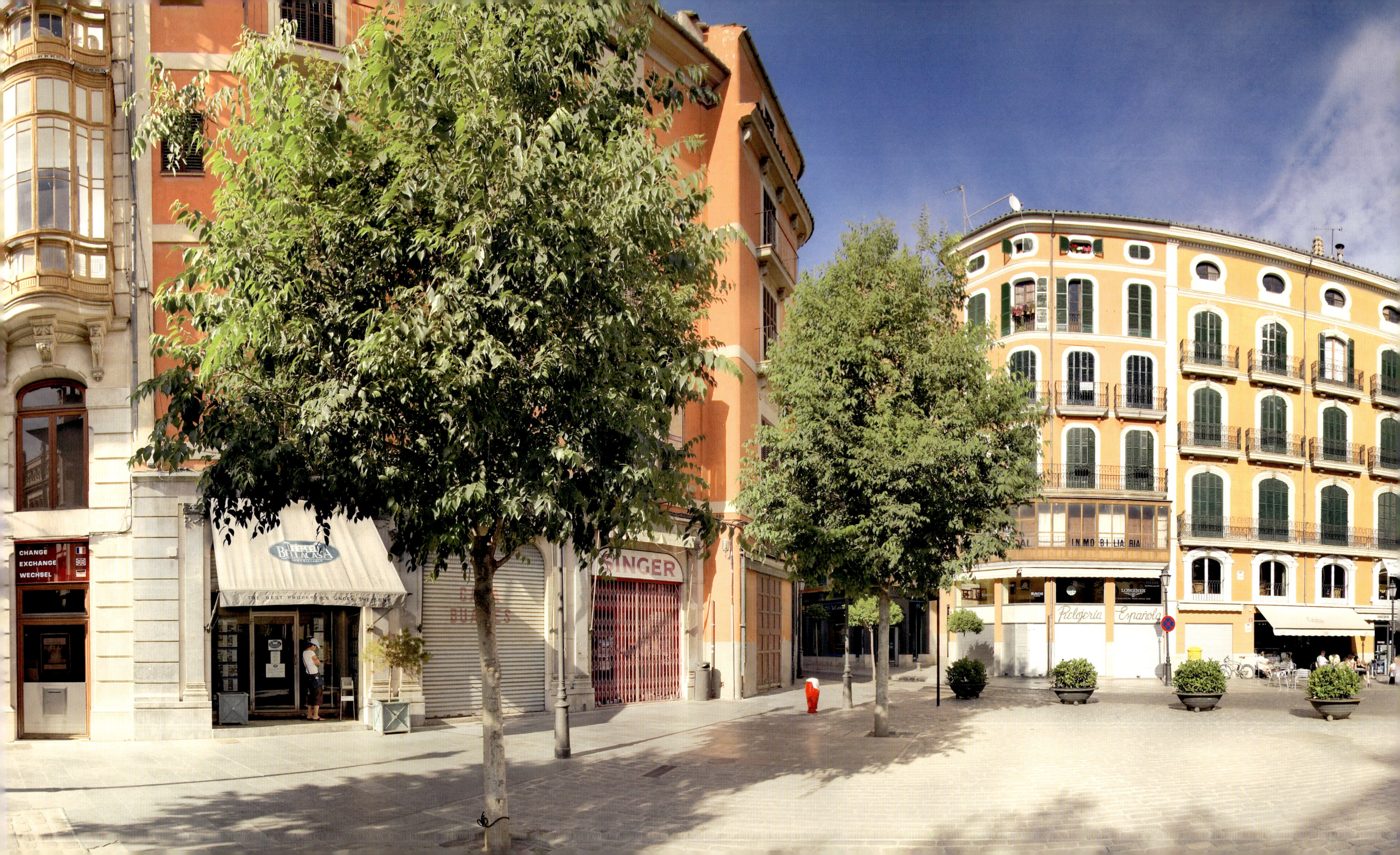
CHANGE
EXCHANGE
WECHSEL
SINGER
INMOBILIARIA
Relojeria Española

Plaça Cort

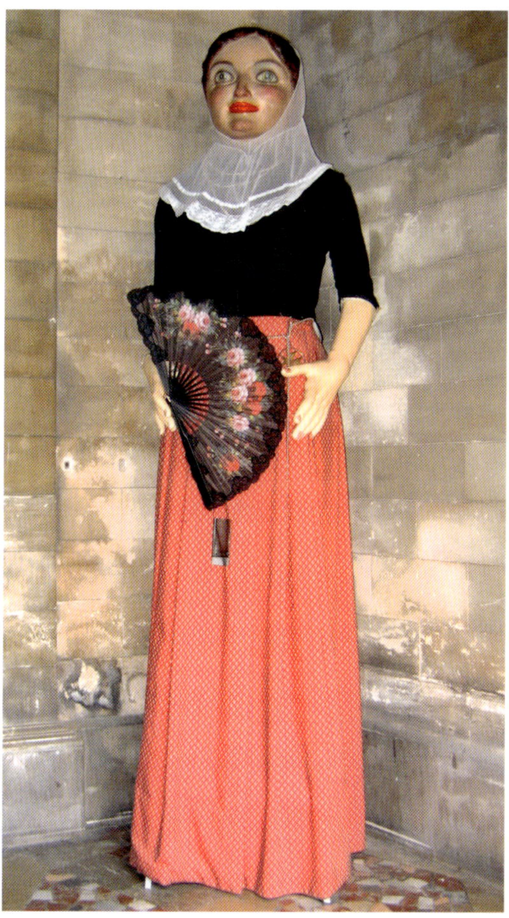

The square is dominated by the city hall (previous 360° panoramic photo, centre) with its ornate facades dating back to the 17th century. The mighty canopy is supported by eleven columns decorated with beautifully carved figures. An old olive tree in front of the building is now as tall as the city hall itself. The interior is decorated with valuable paintings and serves as the venue for permanent and temporary exhibitions. Each Christmas, the famous nativity scene "Misericordia" is displayed in the entrance hall.

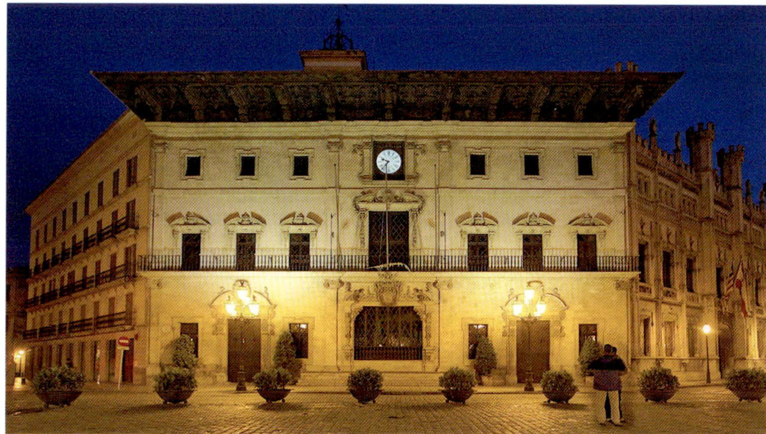

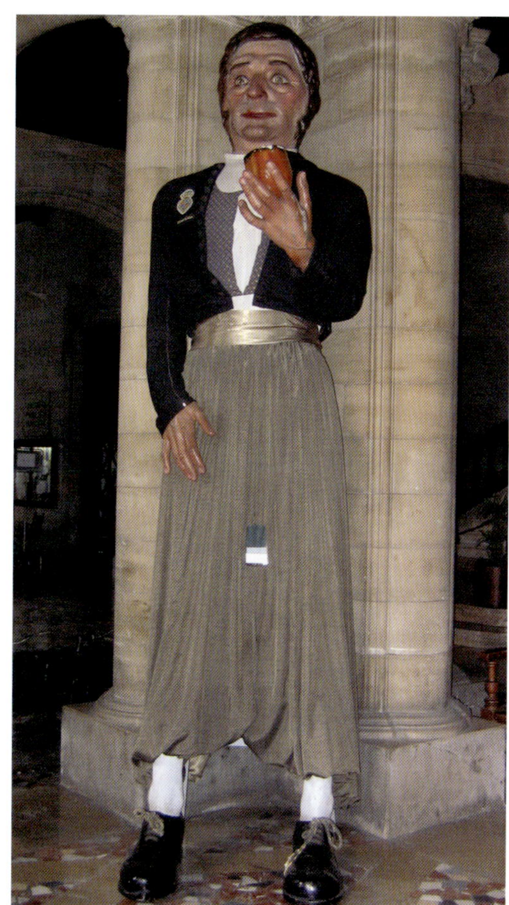

The city hall on Plaça Cort; Figures in traditional Catalan costumes in the city hall's foyer.

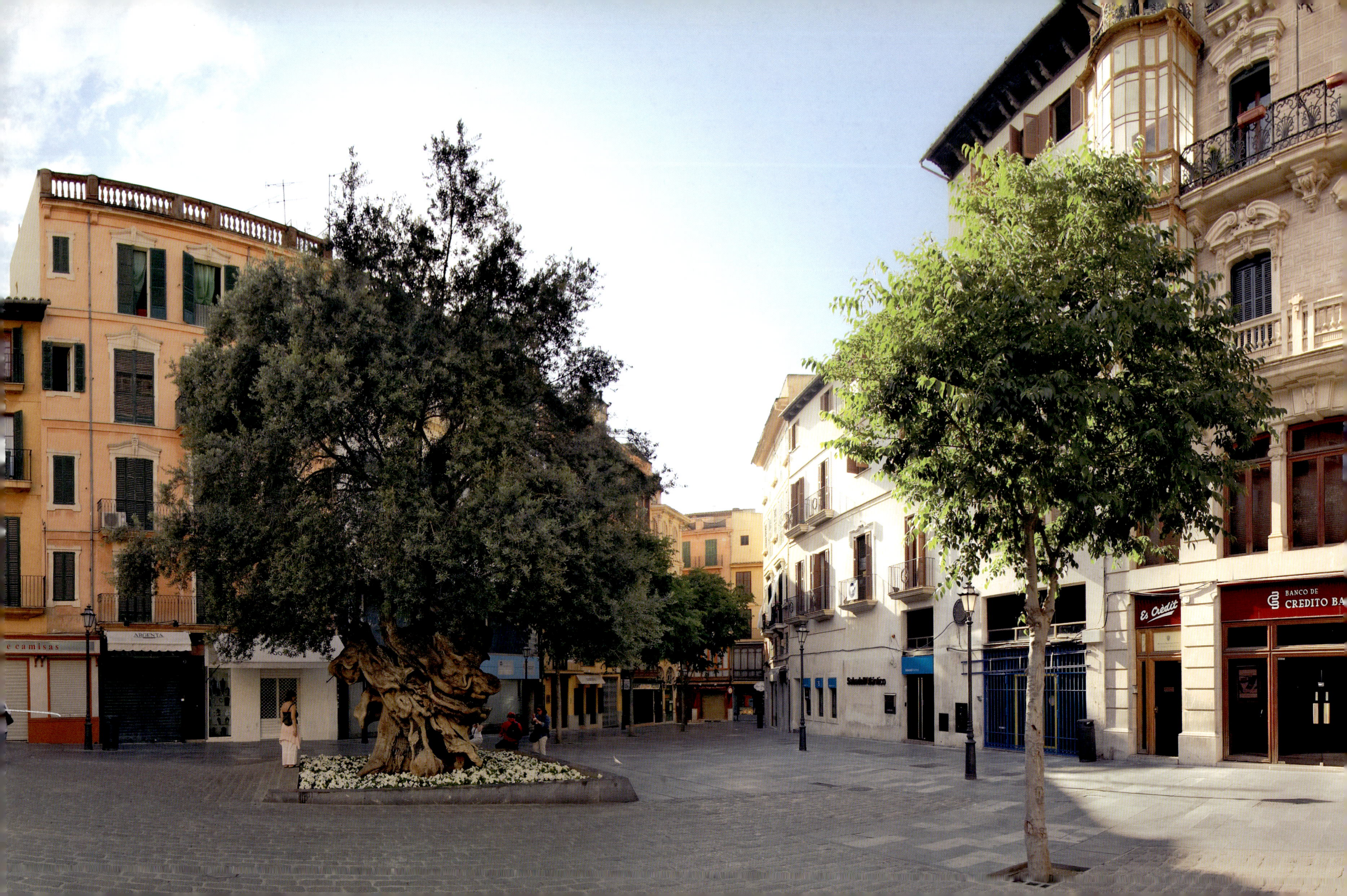
e camisas
ARGENTA
Es Crèdit
BANCO DE
CREDITO BA

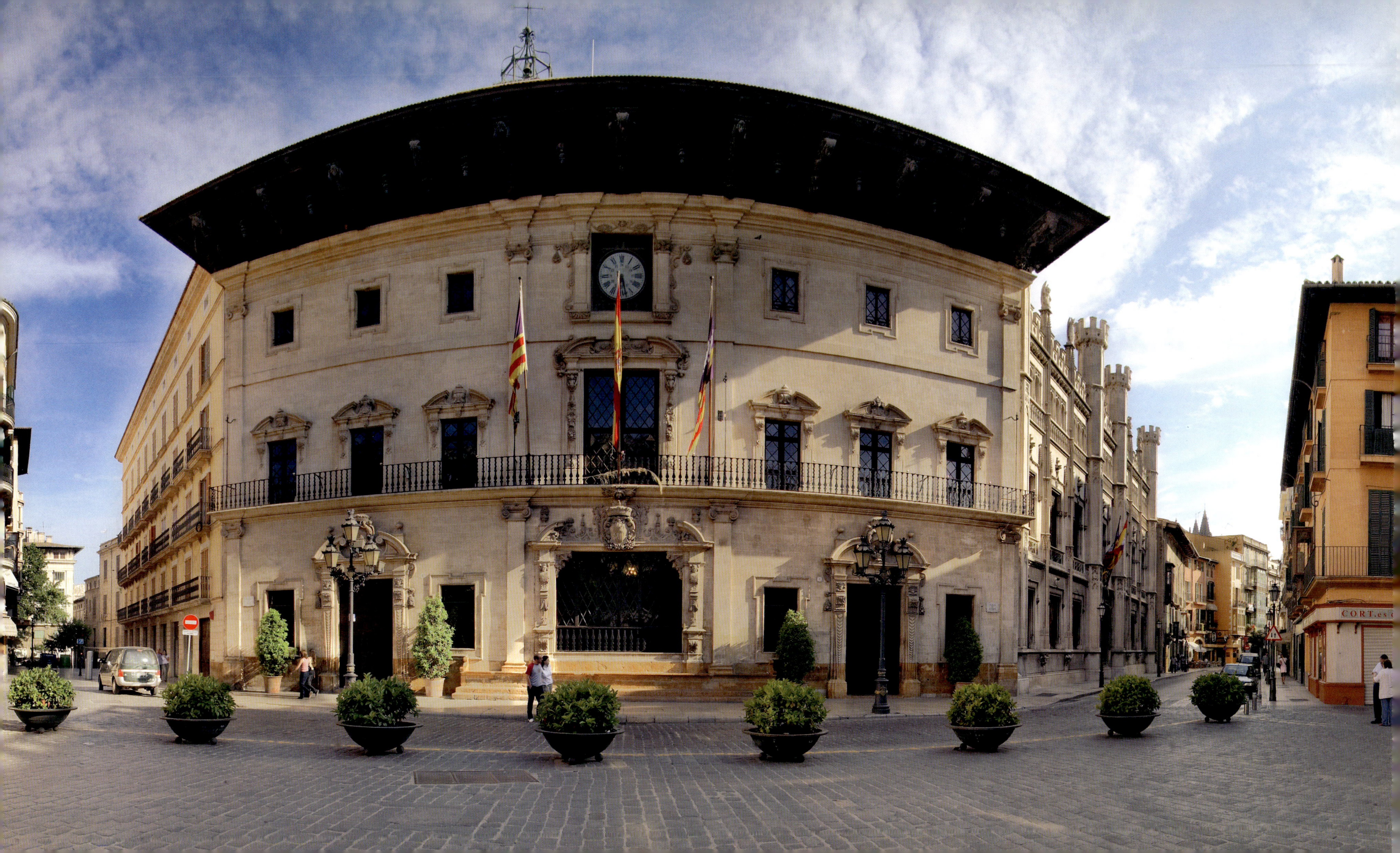
CORT.es

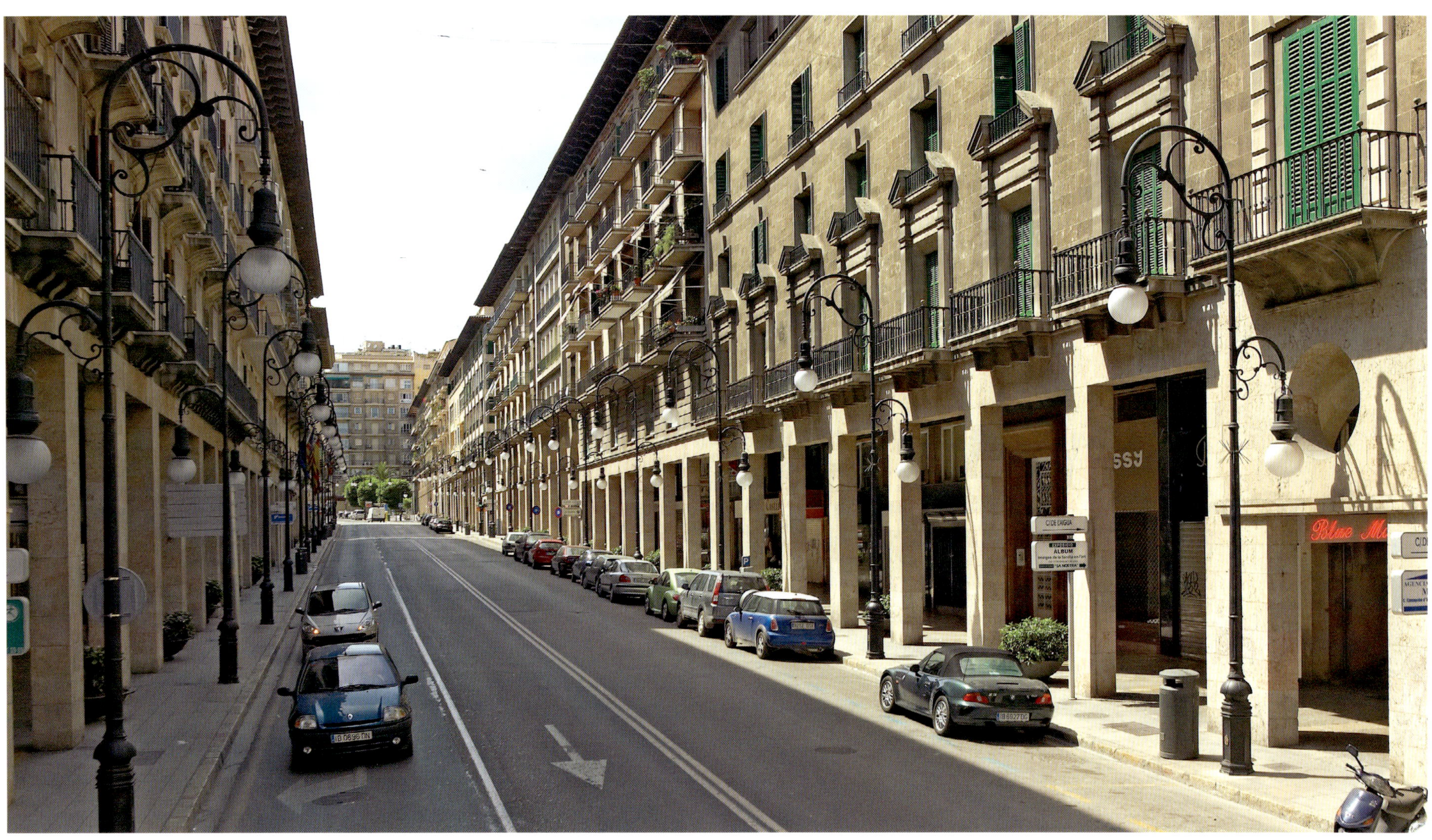

The Avenida Jaime III is one of the most elegant shopping venues of Palma.

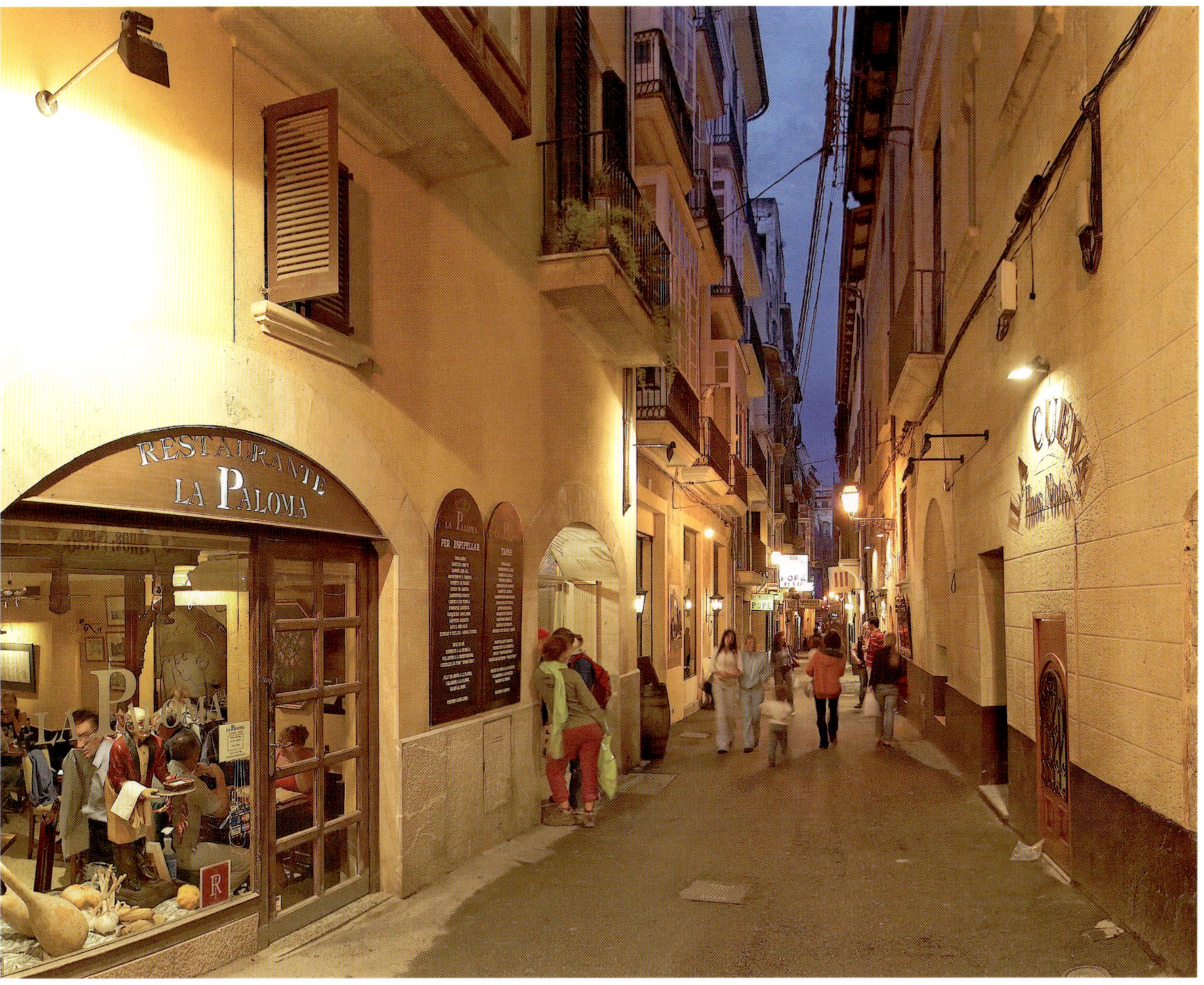

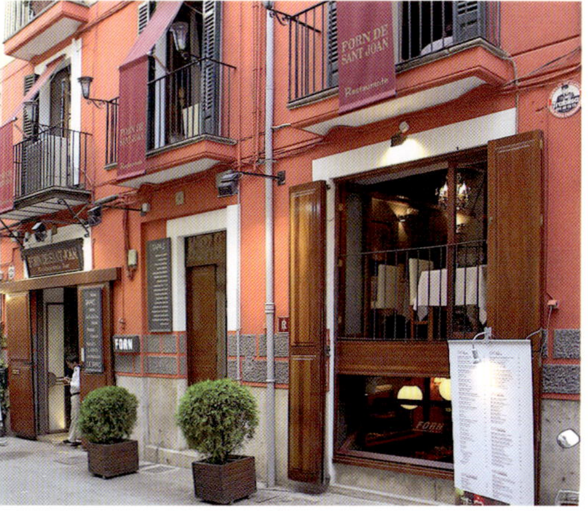

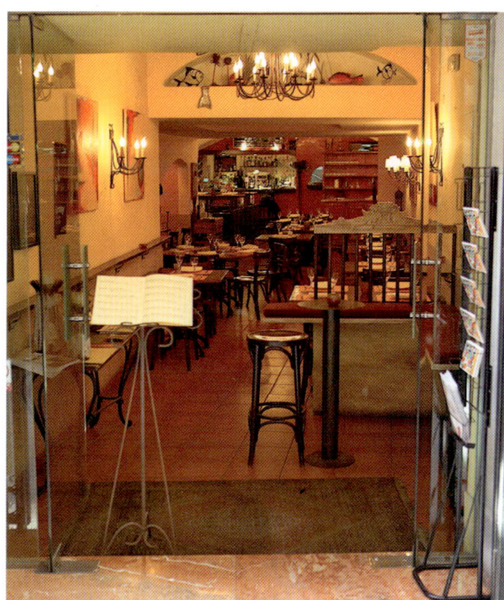

Countless idyllic restaurants (top, in the Apuntadores) offer typical Majorcan specialties and international dishes.

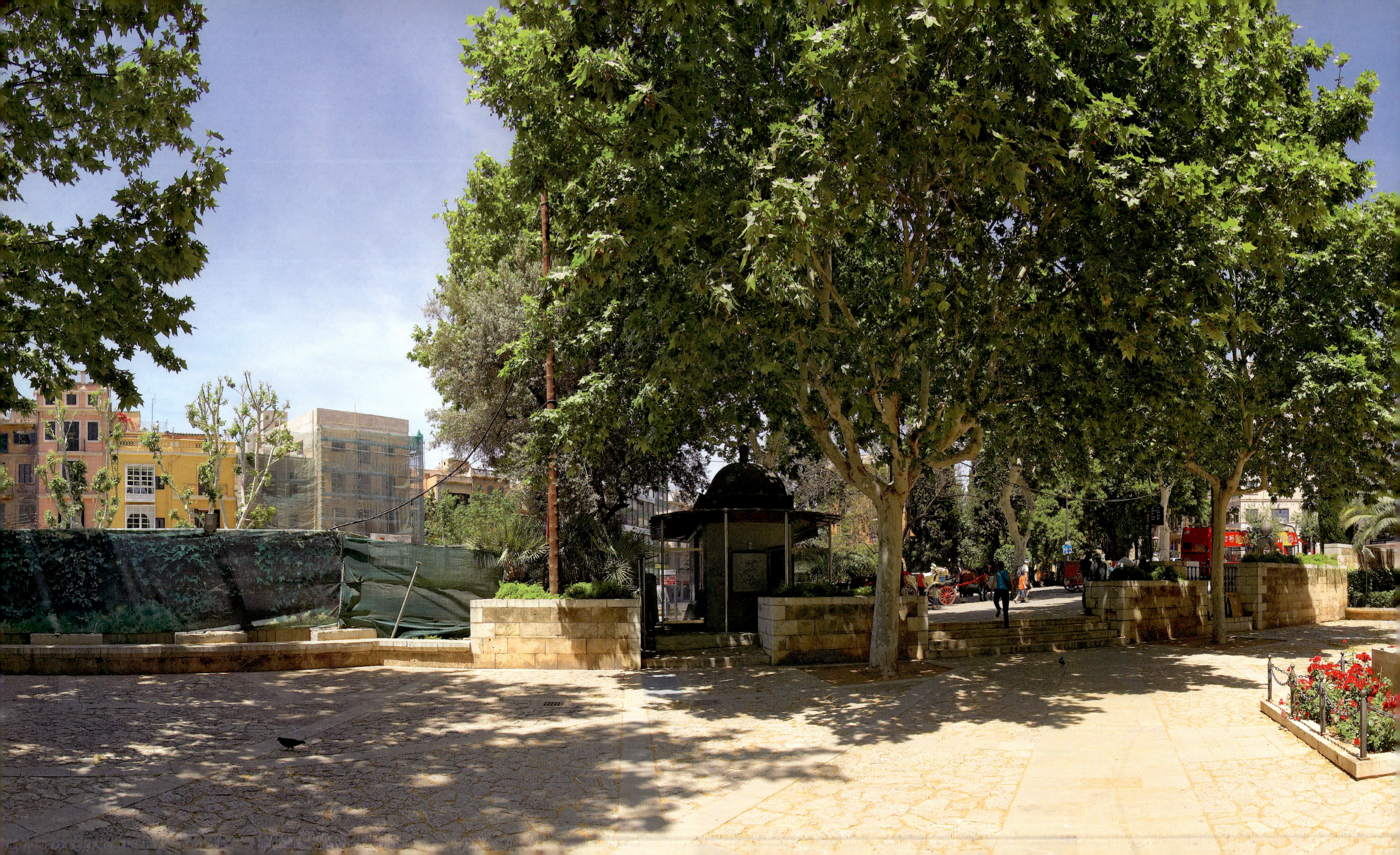

S'Hort del Rei

Facing the cathedral lies the "Palau de l'Almudaina" (previous 360° panoramic photo, centre). It was once the seat of Moorish viziers and houses a national museum today. The official audience chambers of King Juan Carlos are also located in the building. The Islamic palace was built within the first roman settlement in Palma, erected by Quintus Metellus in 123 BC. Under Jaime II., major reconstruction began in 1309, giving the building all the luxury and amenities expected by the Majorcan court. The additions included four towers with battlements, an archway on the side facing the sea, and an open lancet loggia. One of the towers displays a revolving statue of an angel, created by the artist Antonia Camprodon. Other contemporary creations include the magnificent throne room and the Gothic chapel St. Anna's, built in 1432. Only parts of the palace are open to the public.
In front of the palace lie the royal gardens "S'Hort del Rei" with its many fountains, sculptures, colourful flower beds and shady trees. The park's main attraction is the sculpture "Personality" by Joan Miró.

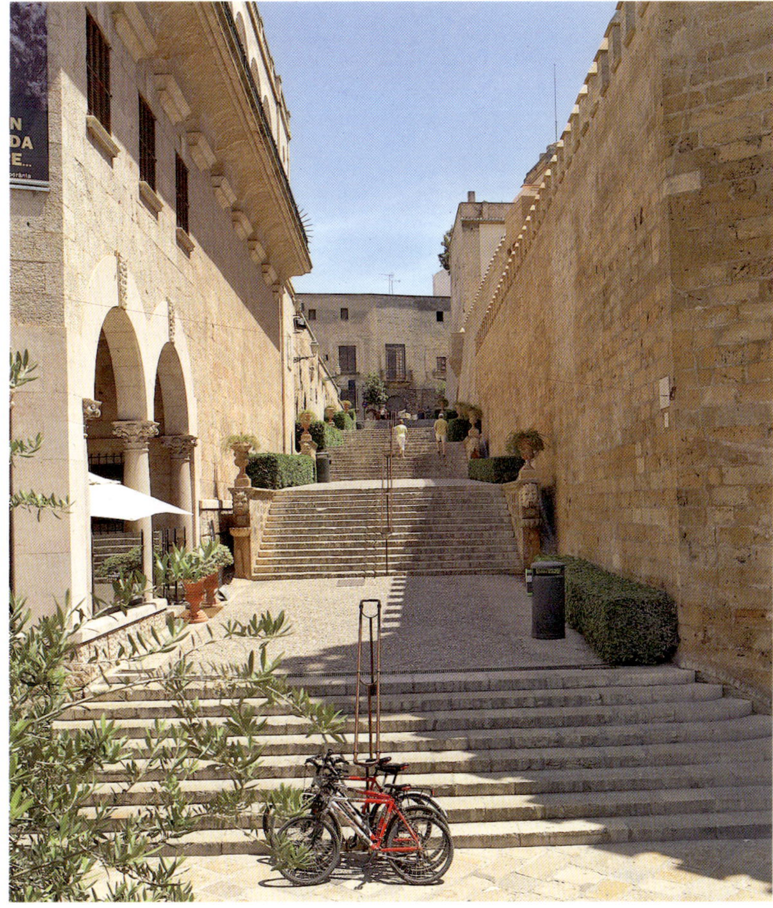

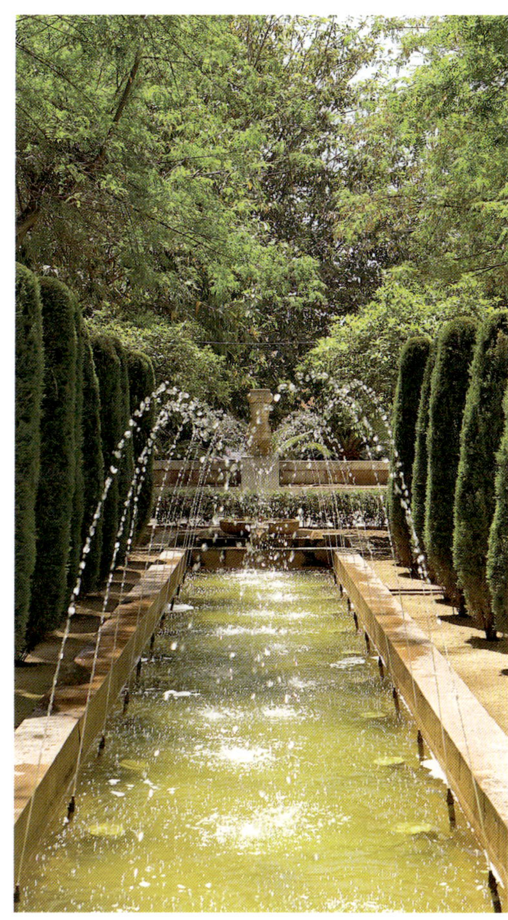

The royal gardens „S'Hort del Rei"

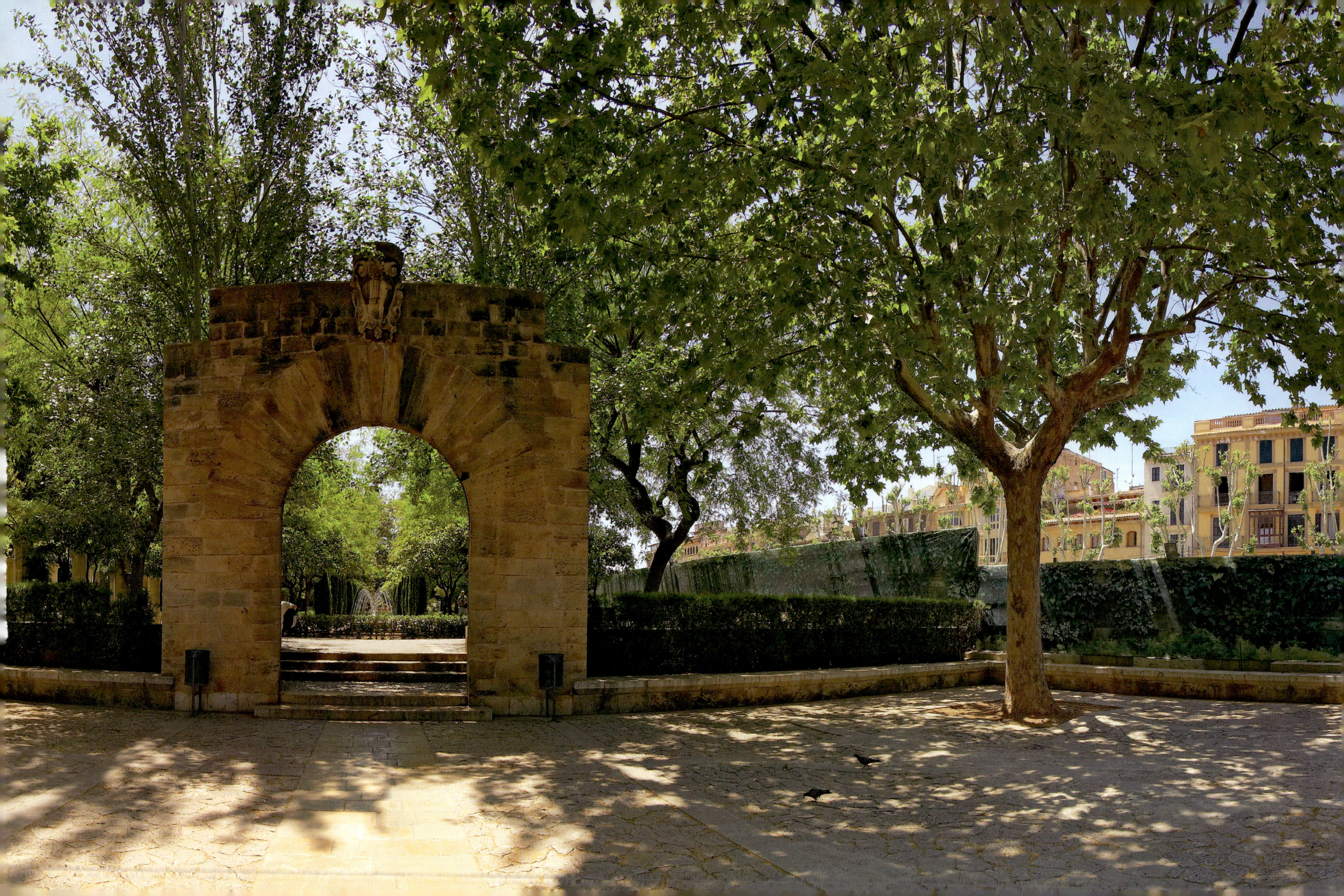

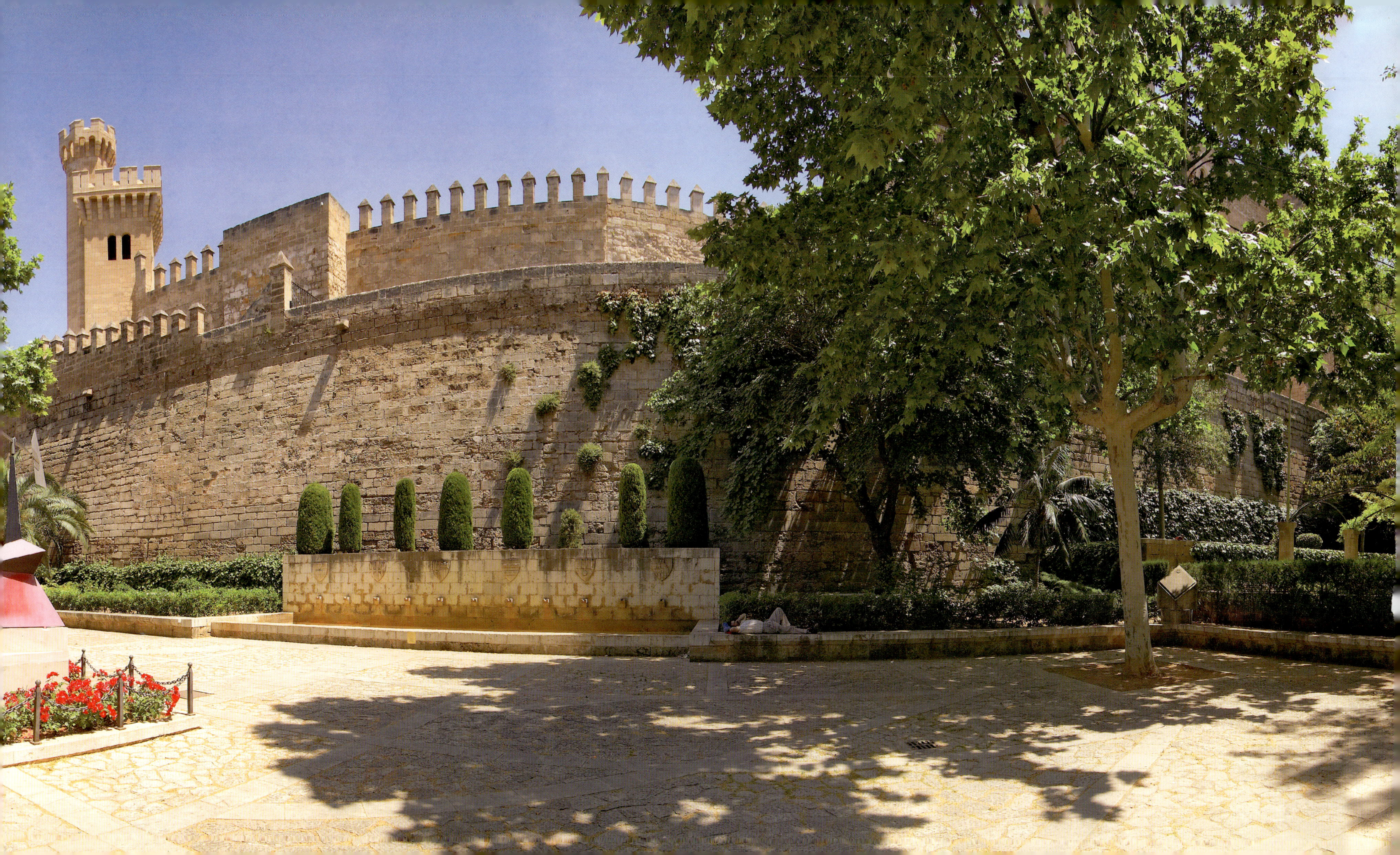

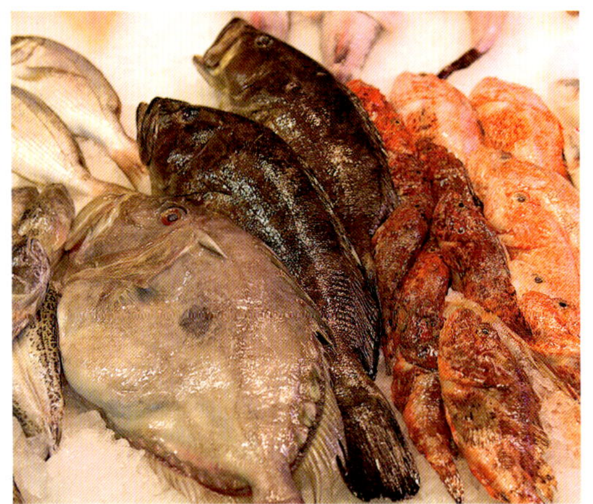

Apart from the well-known market halls of Plaça Olivar or Santa Catalina, Palma has many small markets, where vendors sell fresh fruit and vegetables, but also fish, ham, cheese and many sausage varieties. The enticing fragrance of fresh herbs and the wide variety of olives and capers can persuade anyone to buy something. In the smaller towns on the island, you can still find typical Majorcan markets; goods for sale there include bantams, emus, thoroughbreds and mongrel dogs.

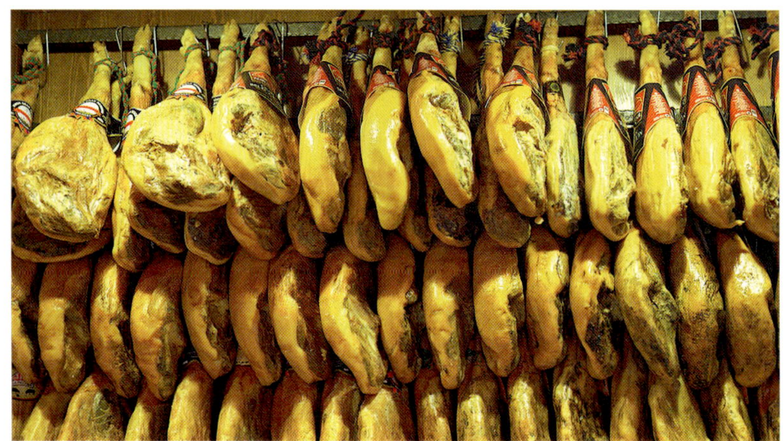

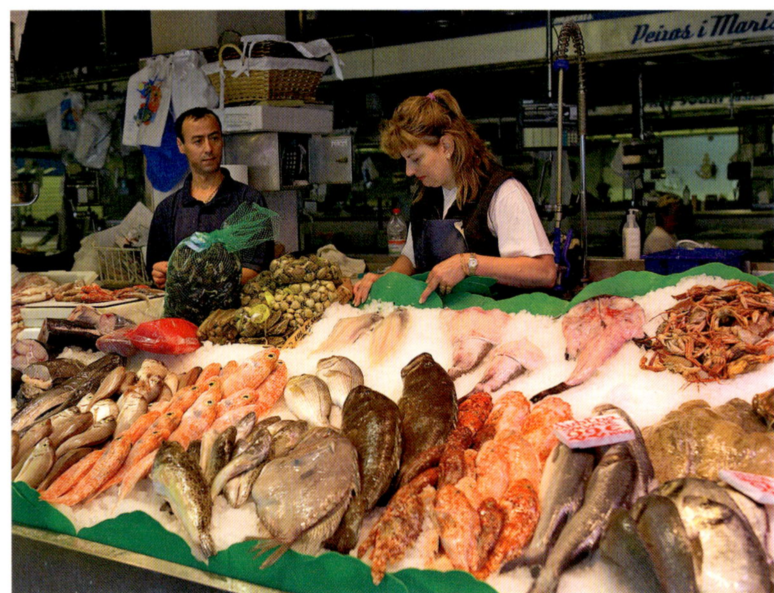

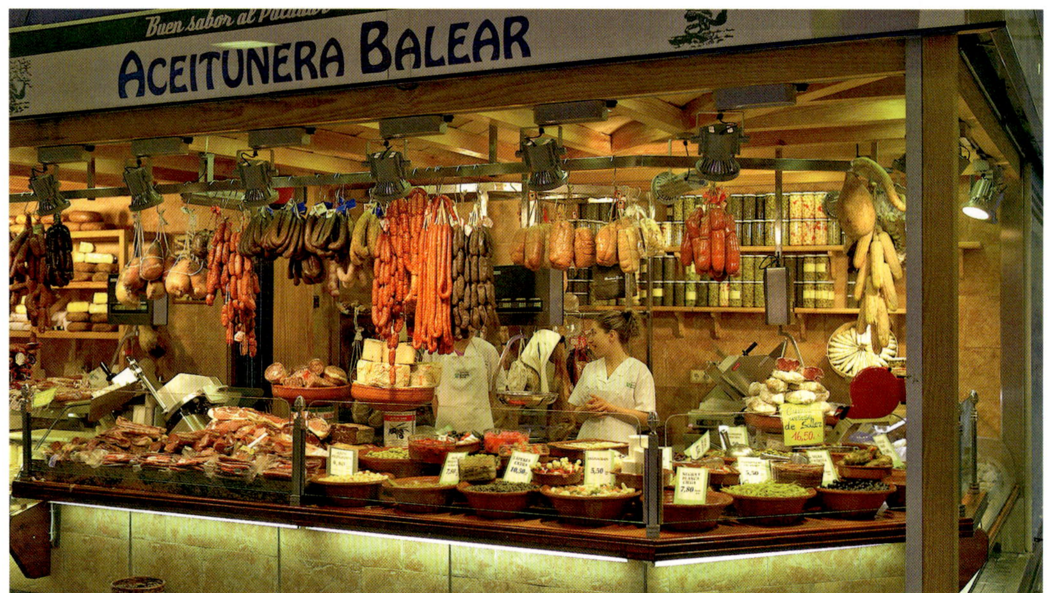

Market scenes in Palma

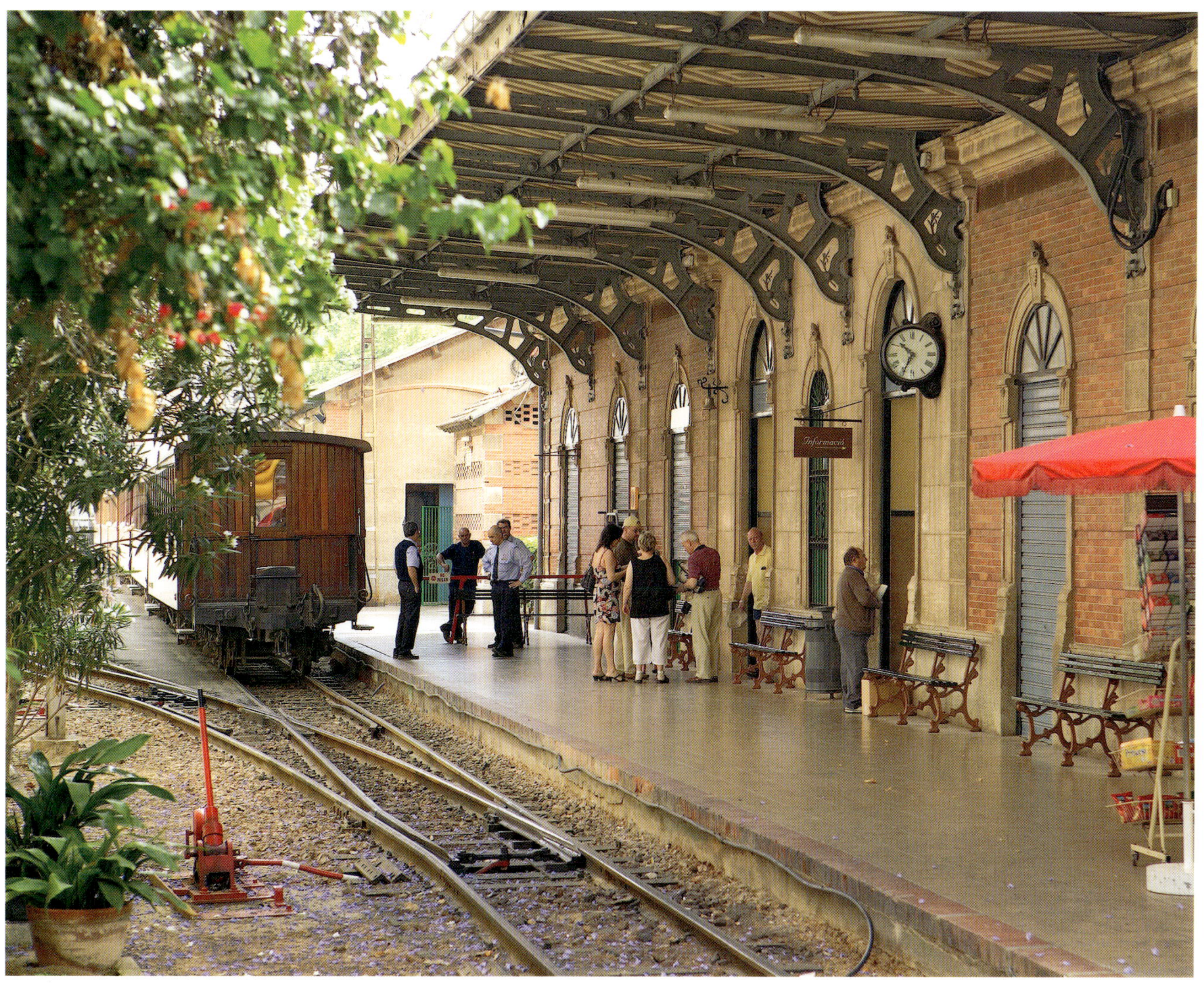

Palma and Sóller are connected by a 27 km panoramic railway line for the narrow-gauge railway "Red Lightning". The railway line with 13 tunnels was opened in 1912, mainly for transporting citrus fruit. Before that, the fruit had to be transported around half the island by ship. The "Red Lightning" making its way through the mountains of the Tramuntana with peaks of more than 1,000 m is one of the island's biggest tourist attractions. One of the highlights of the 1-hour trip is a viaduct with a length of 52 m, offering a wonderful view.

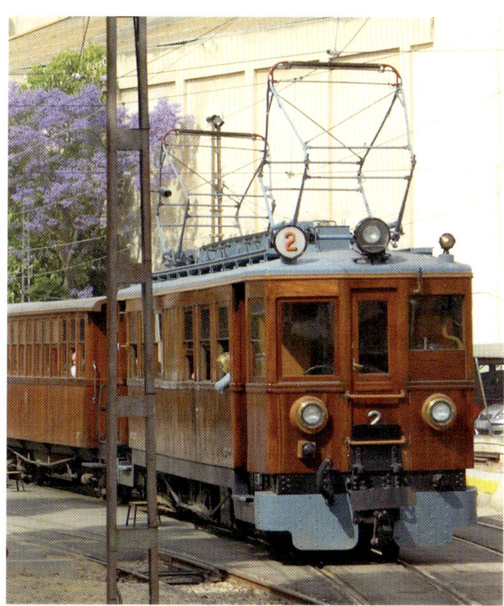

Station in Palma; Narrow-gauge railway Palma-Sóller

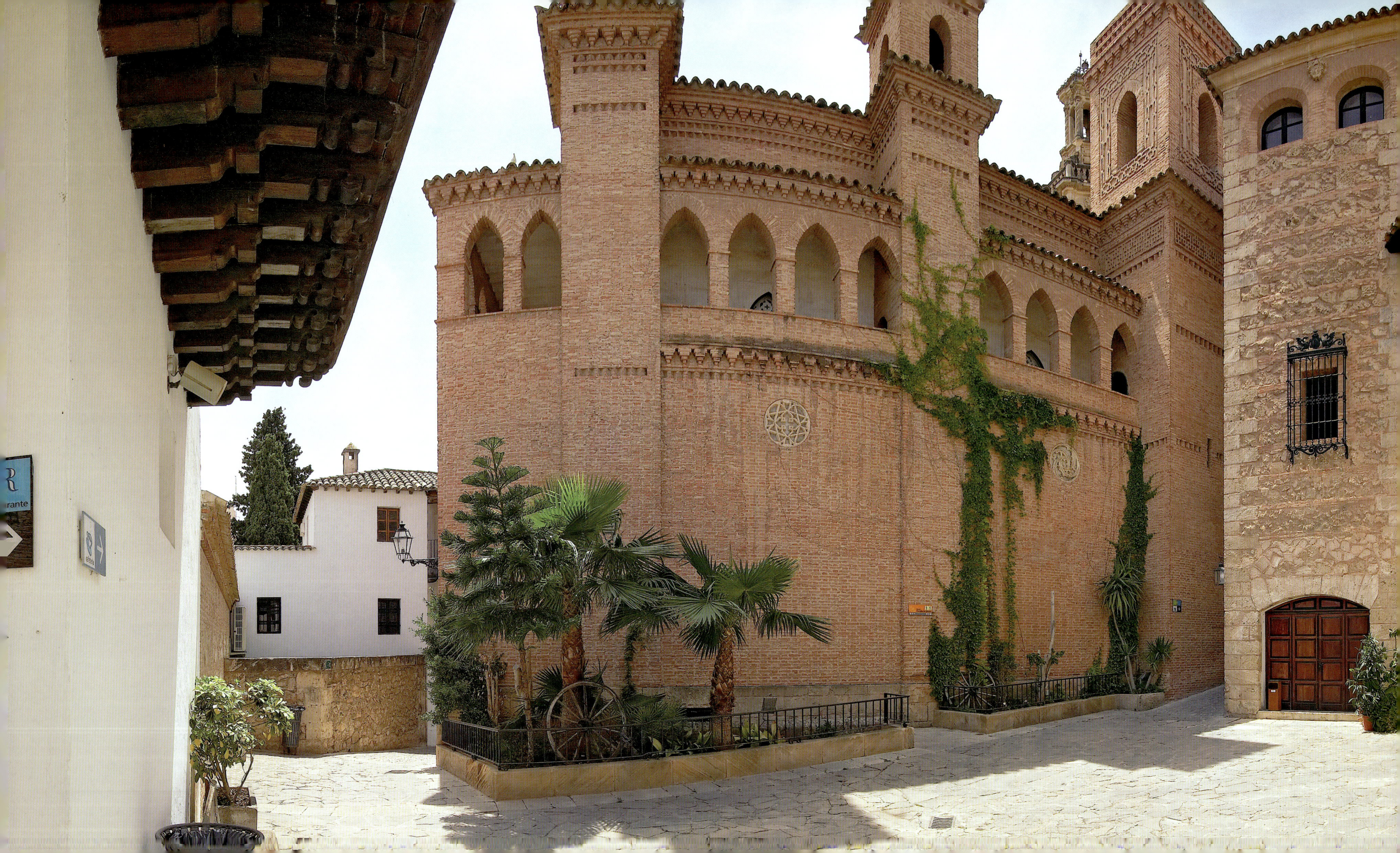

Pueblo Español

"Pueblo Español" with an area of 26.000 m² (previous 360° panoramic photo) is a walled-in reconstructed mediaeval city. It consists of 22 buildings, palaces, churches and squares. Spain's most important buildings from various cultural eras and regions were scaled down to house restaurants and artisans' workshops. A number of shops in the narrow cobblestone streets offer crafts products and souvenirs. There are regular folkloristic performances, which are always popular with tourists. A part of the compound is the location of Palma's neo-Classical congress building, which was extensively restored over the past few years.
The reproductions include the "Patio de los Arrayones", a part of the "Al Hambra", the "Palacio de la Diputatión" and others.

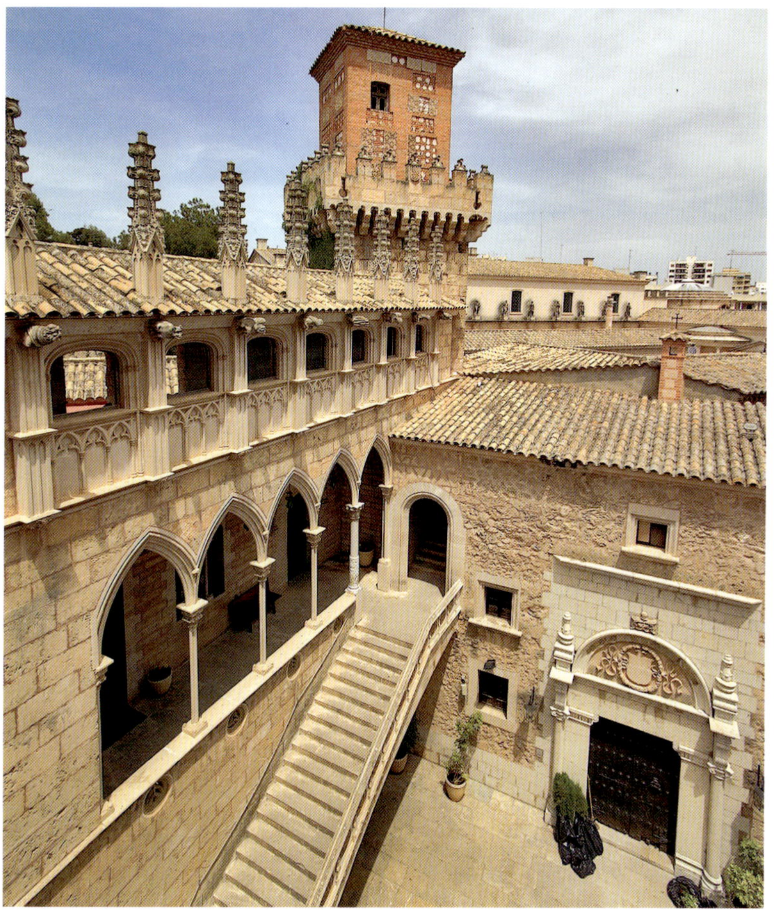

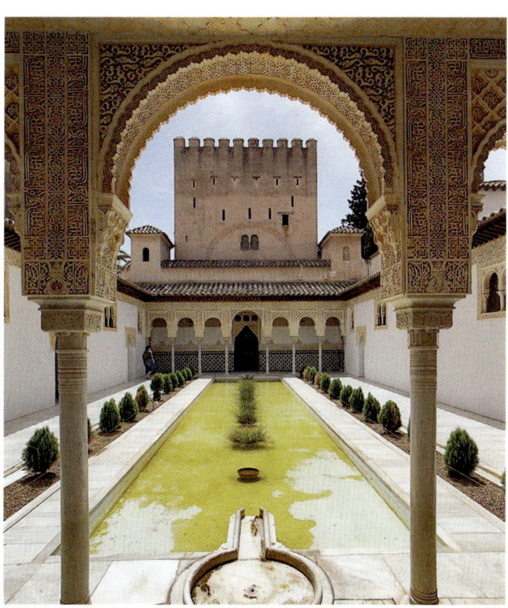

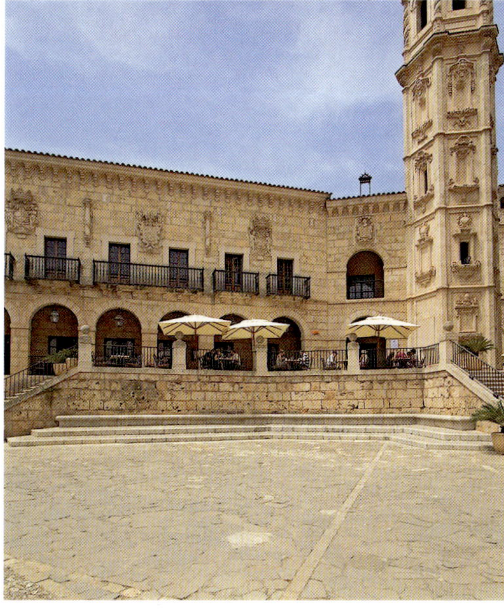

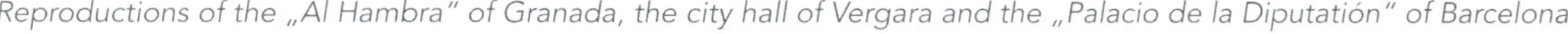

Reproductions of the „Al Hambra" of Granada, the city hall of Vergara and the „Palacio de la Diputatión" of Barcelona.

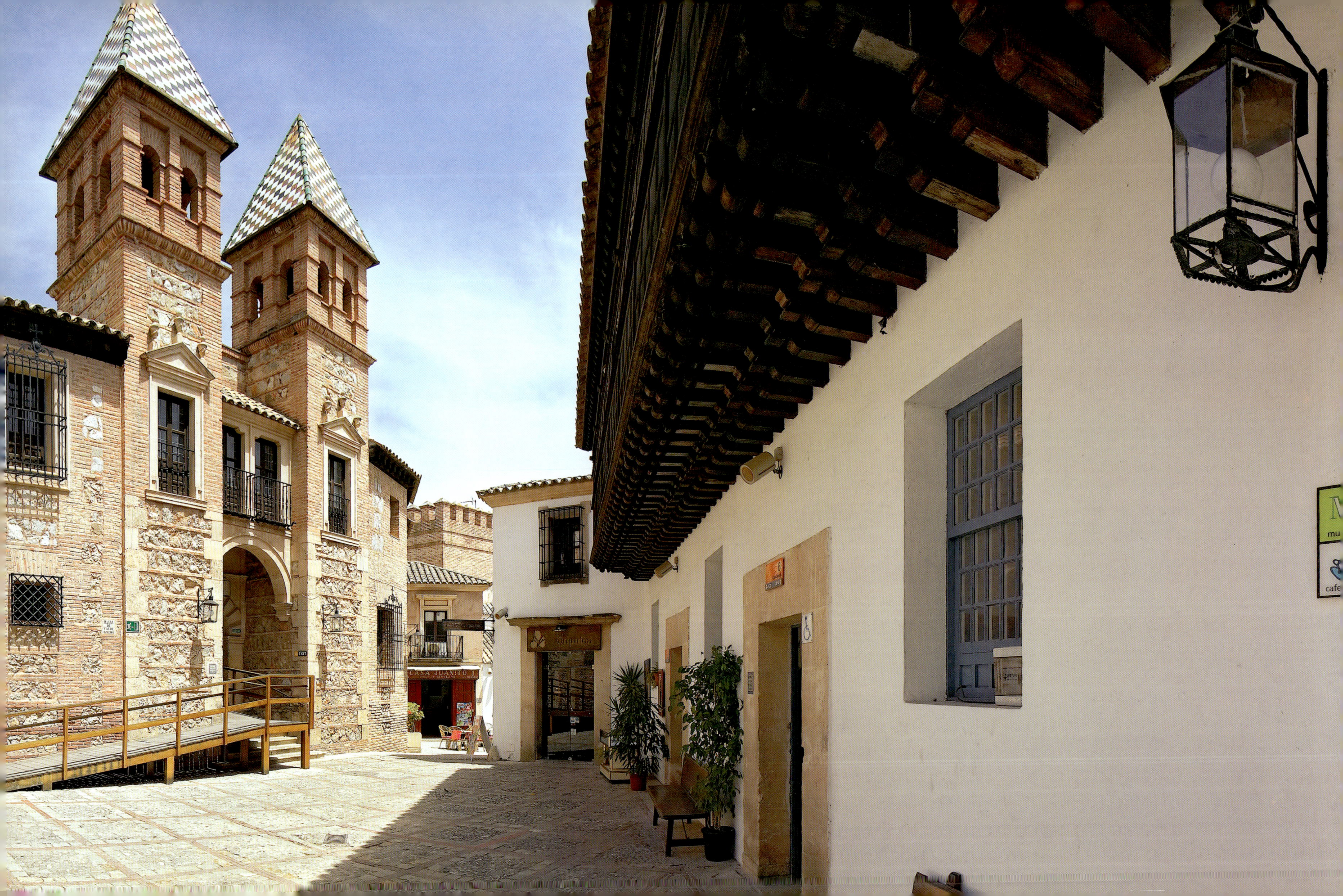
CASA JUANITO

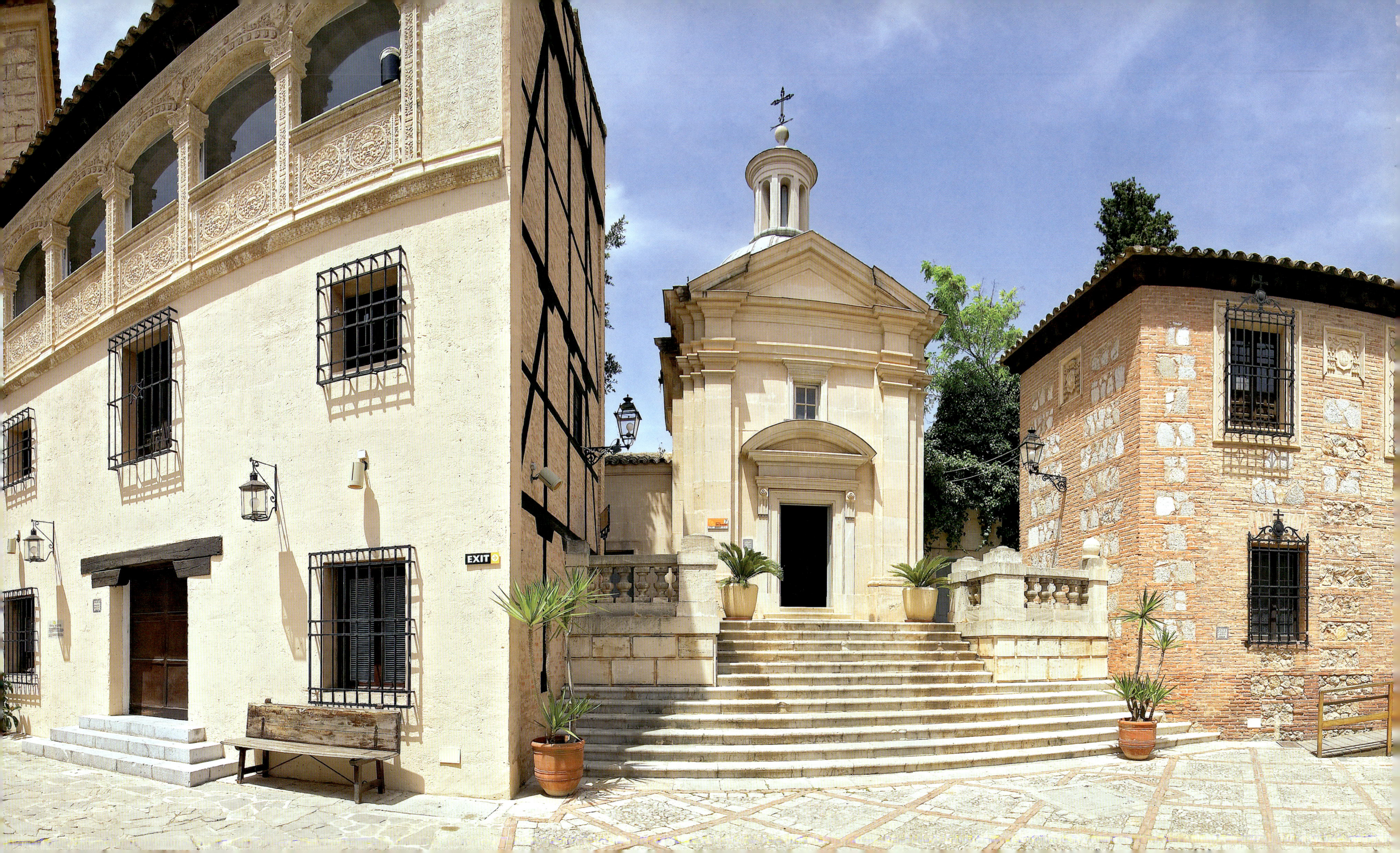
EXIT

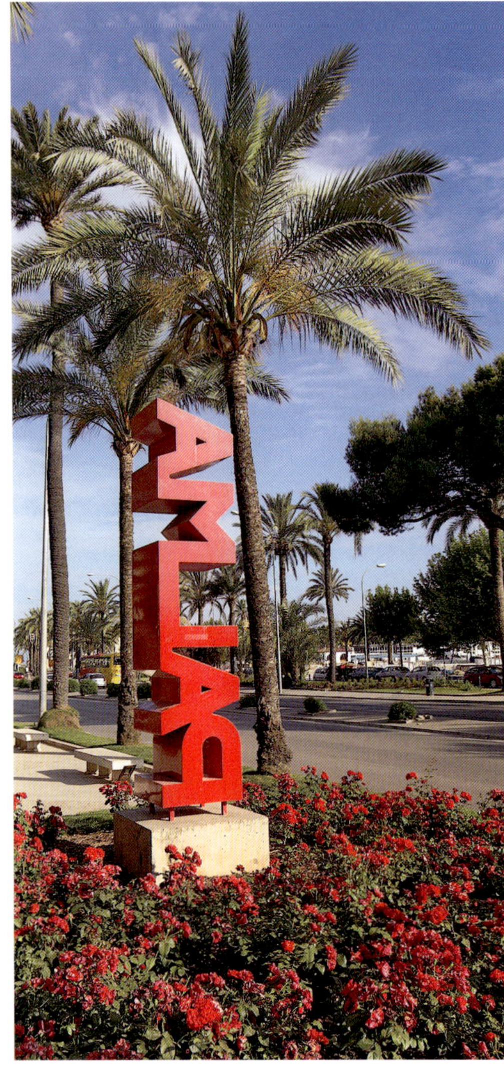

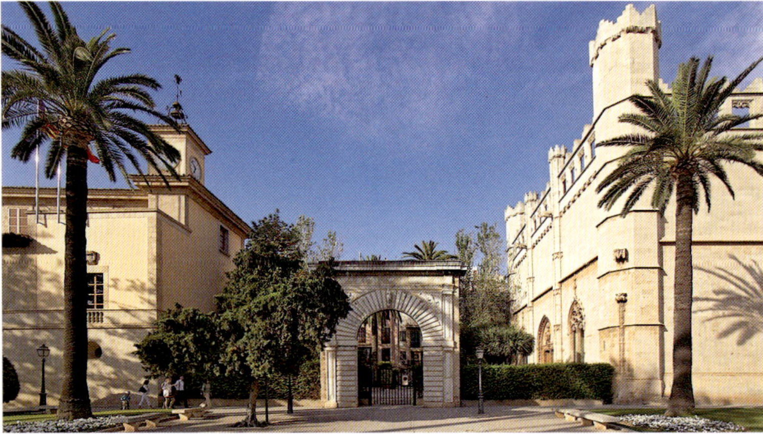

The spacious area of the port of Palma is a great place to take a long walk. It is lined by historic buildings and sculptures. The former sea trade market on Plaça de la Llotja, built in the 15th century, is said to be one of Spain's most beautiful Gothic buildings. It has become a venue for exhibitions. The "Consulat del Mar" was built in 1325. The esplanade is the location of a monument depicting the famous Catalan philosopher, logician and theologian Ramon Lull. The founder of Catalan literature lived in 1232-1316 and wrote no less than 260 works.

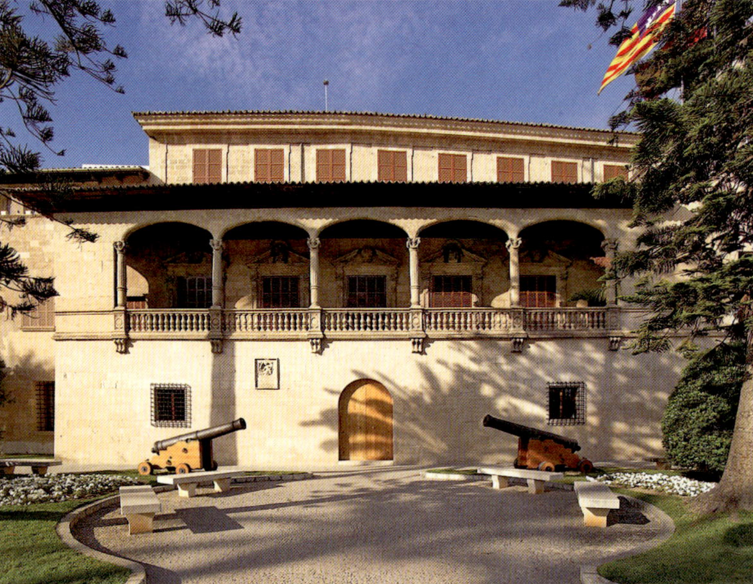

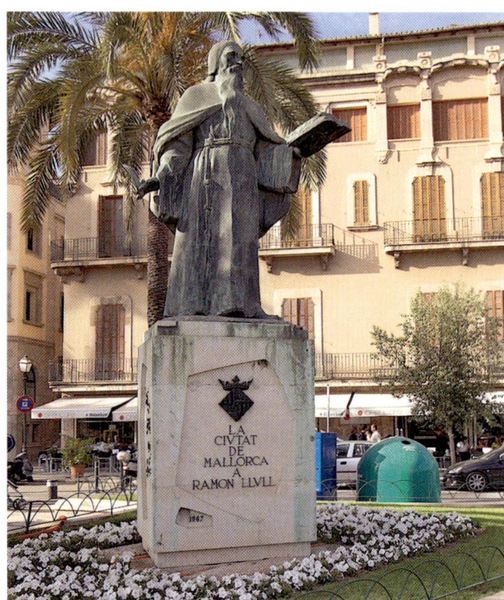

Harbour promenade of Palma; Plaça de la Llotja; the „Consulat del Mar"; Ramon Lull statue

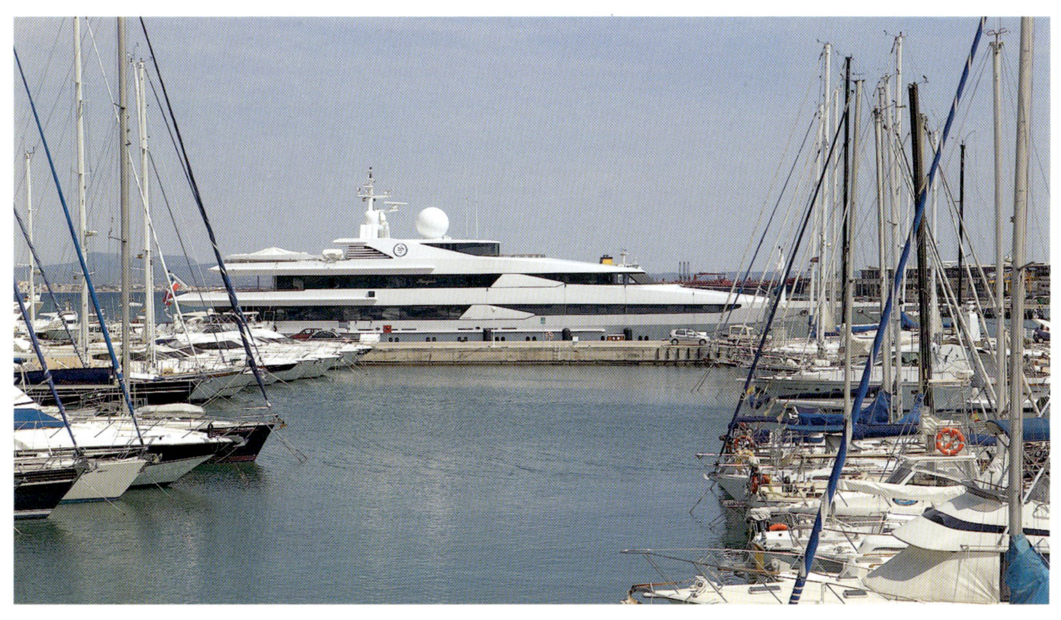

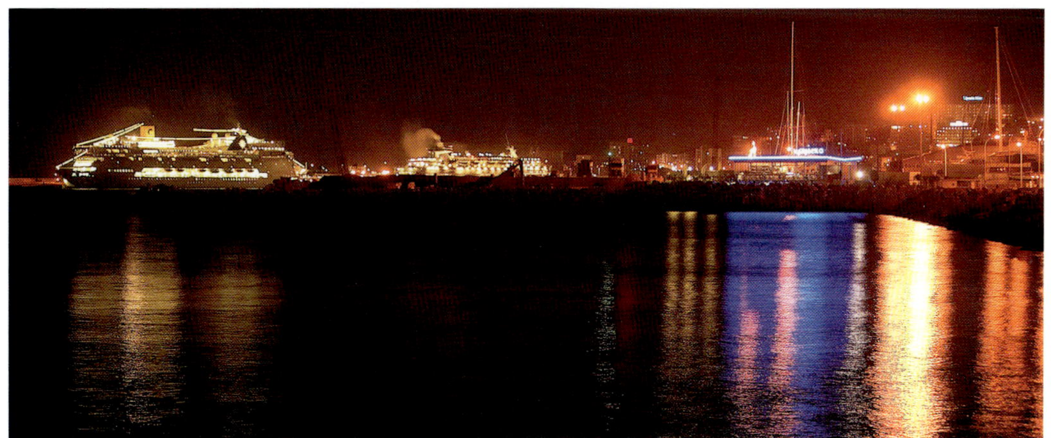

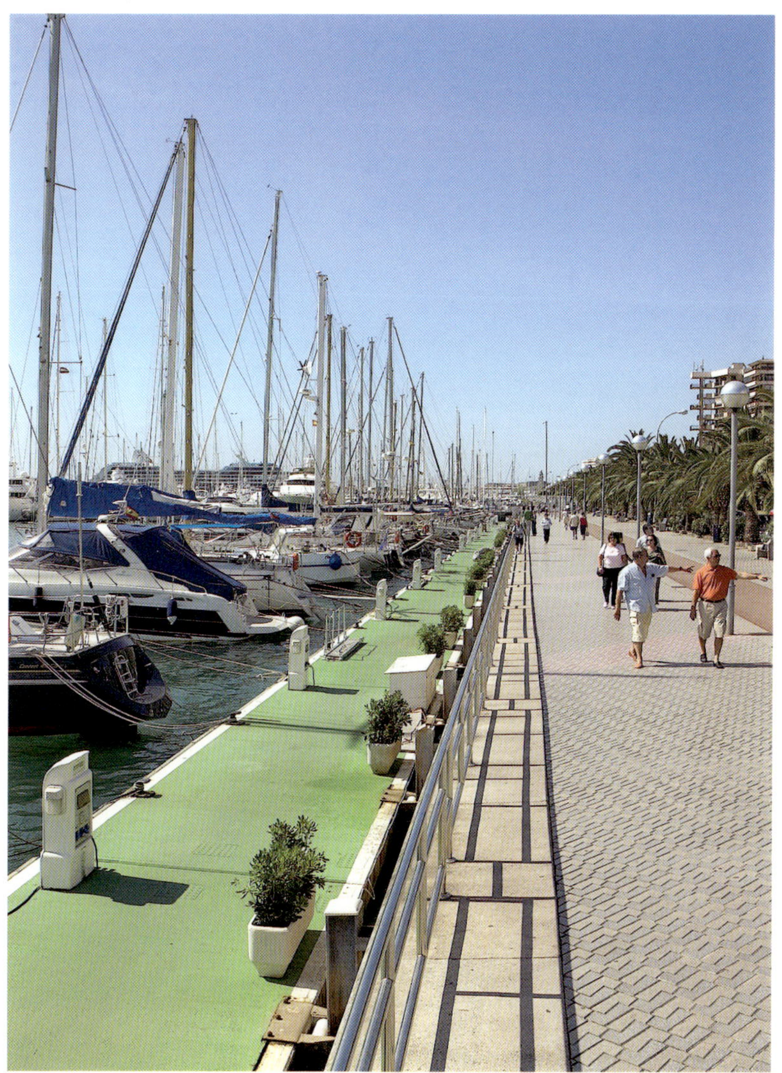

Port of Palma

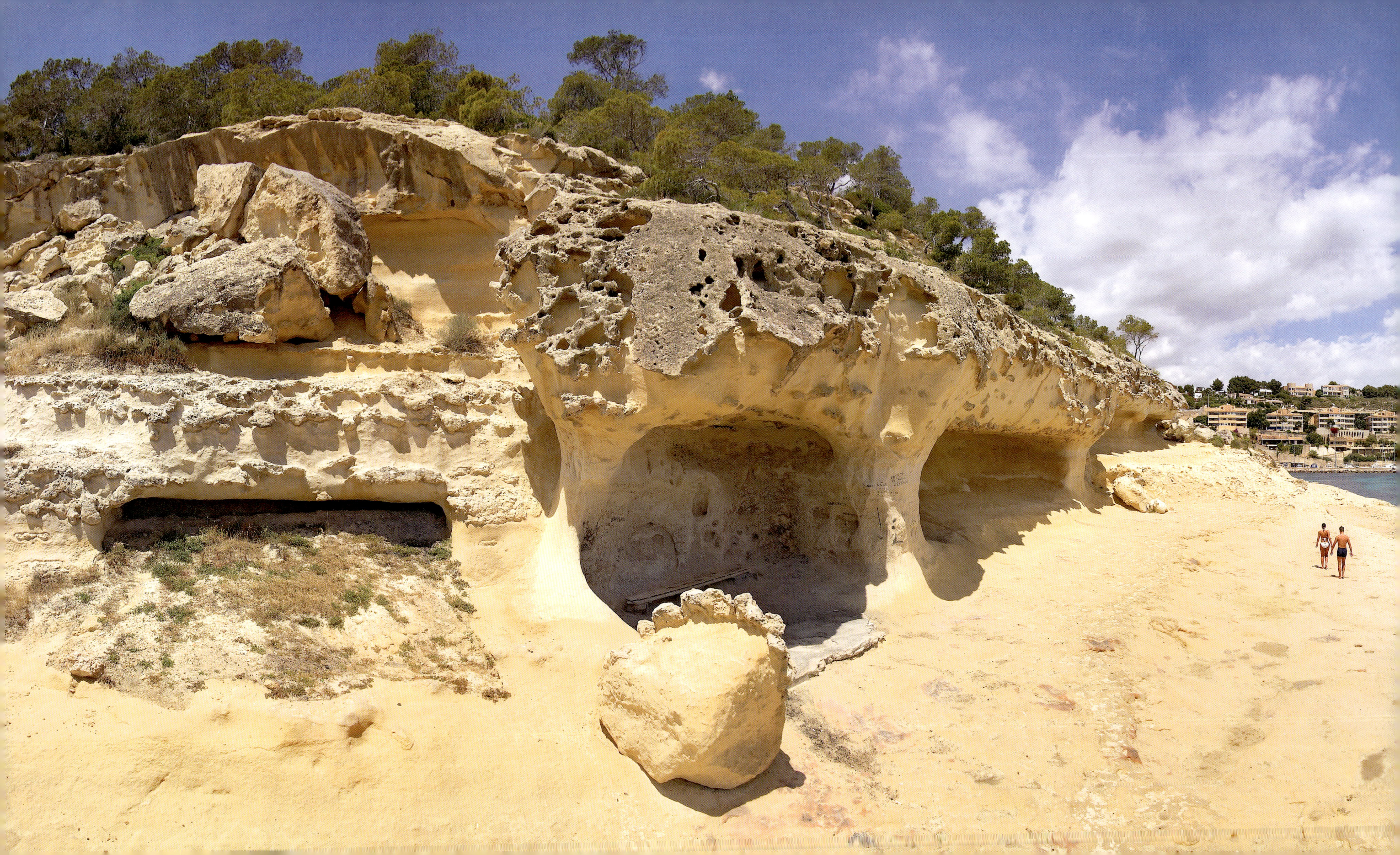

Cala Portals Vells

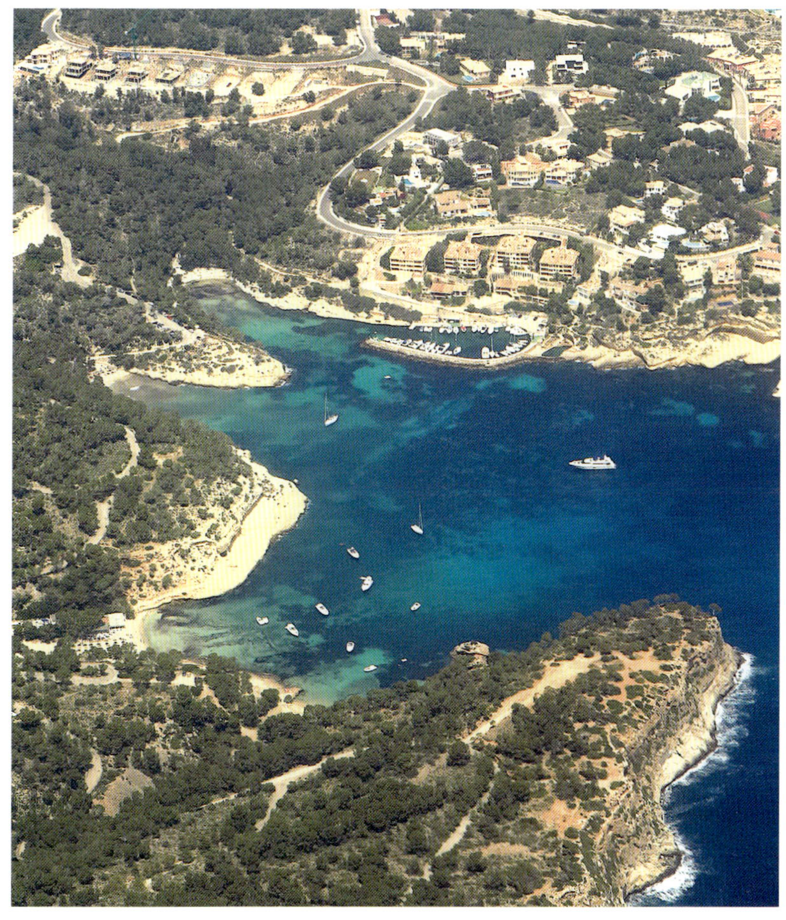

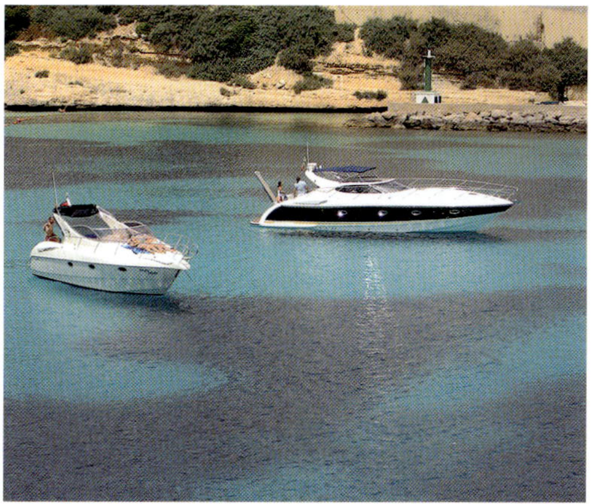

The protected bay with a length of 110 m (previous 360° panoramic photo) is also called "Three-Finger Bay". Many seabirds use the surrounding area for nesting. The three small sandy beaches have crystal-clear water, thus being perfect for diving, snorkelling and swimming. One of the coves, Cala Mago, is designated as a nudist beach. The way to the bay leads through a wonderful pine forest, passing the golf course of Poniente. Idyllic little beach restaurants offer refreshments and delicious food.

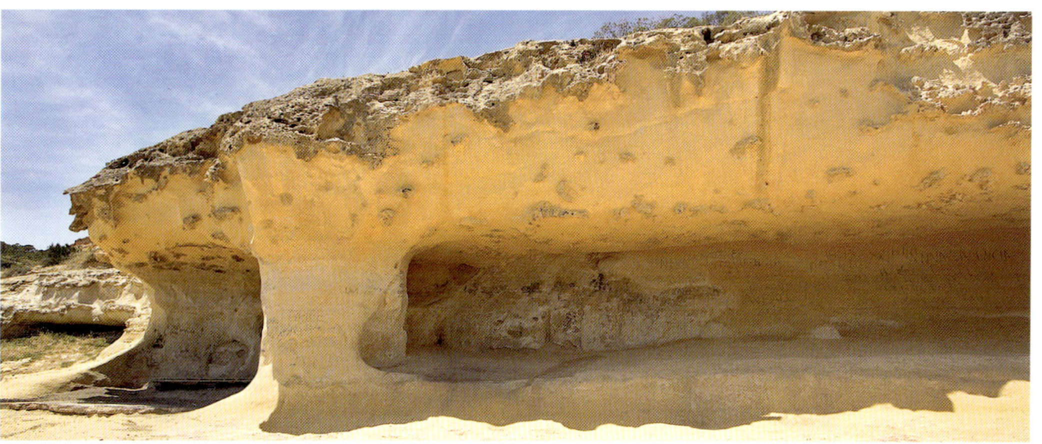

Cala Portals Vells

360° panoramic photo: Cala Portals Vells 8

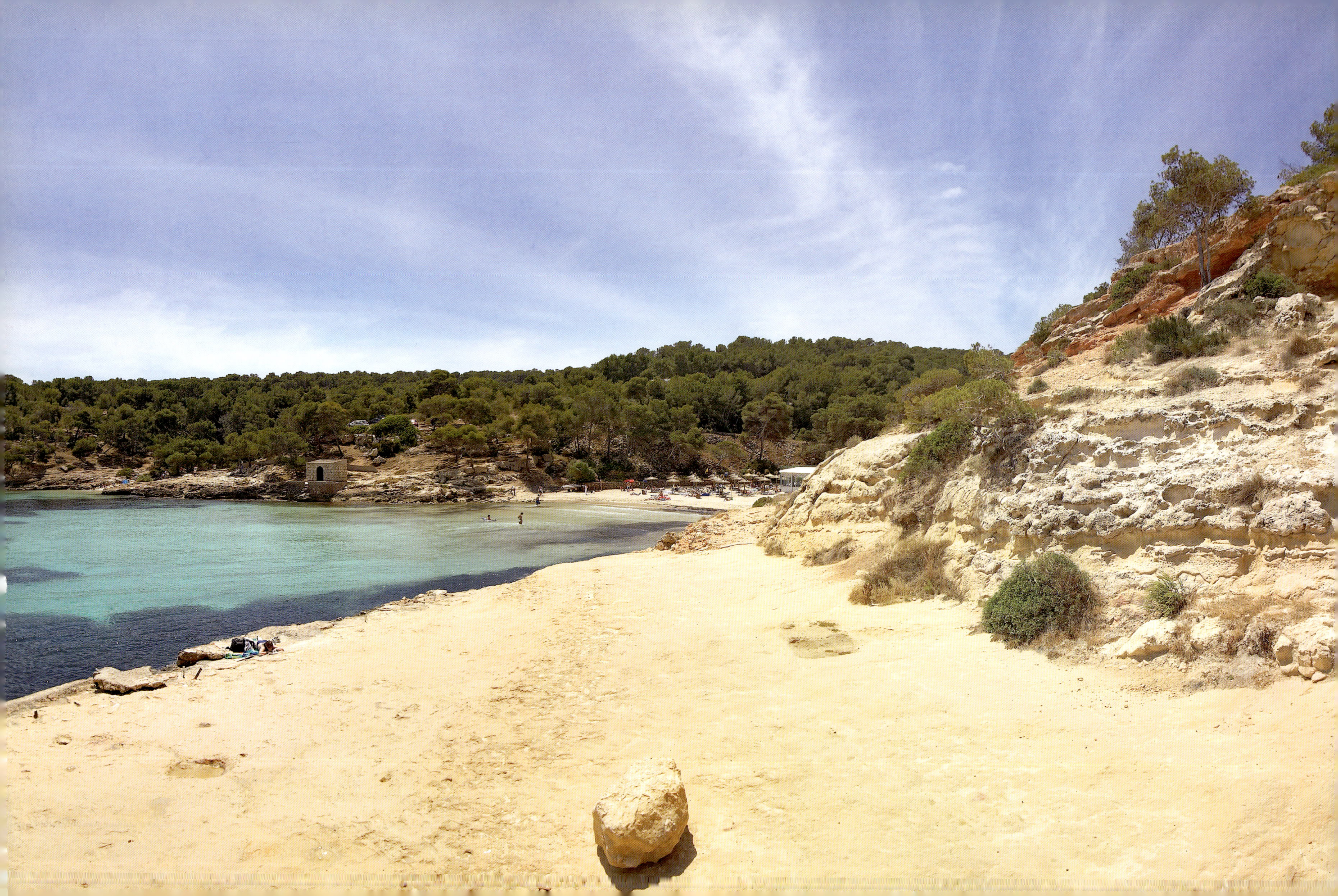

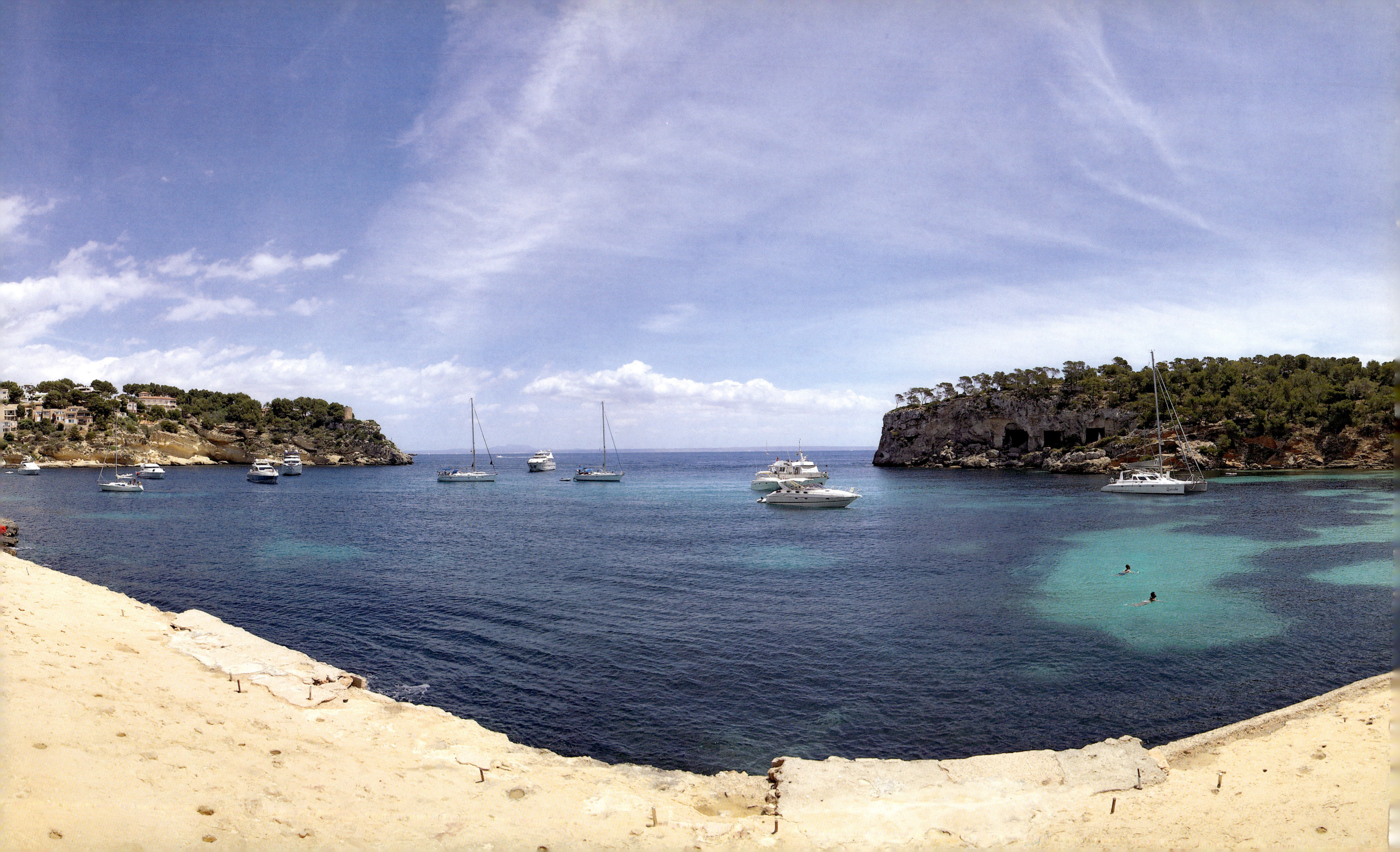

One of the major tourist places on the island is Peguera. The great location of this fantastic bay, surrounded by green hills, offers everything you could desire from a holiday destination. However, you won't find historic places and Majorcan flair. A long palm-lined esplanade, pools with surrounding greenery and planted terraces were carefully integrated into the landscape. The mixture of private properties, numerous pubs, restaurants and hotels created a town with a casual flair.

During the summer months, the small town is populated, and sometimes crowded, mainly by German and British tourists. Tennis courts and a stable are available; the hinterland offers great opportunities for hikes and bike tours. Not far from the town lies the bay of Cala Fornells with a beautiful sandy beach, from which some of the holiday complexes on the west side of the bay derive their names. These complexes have evolved into small villages with restaurants and pools.

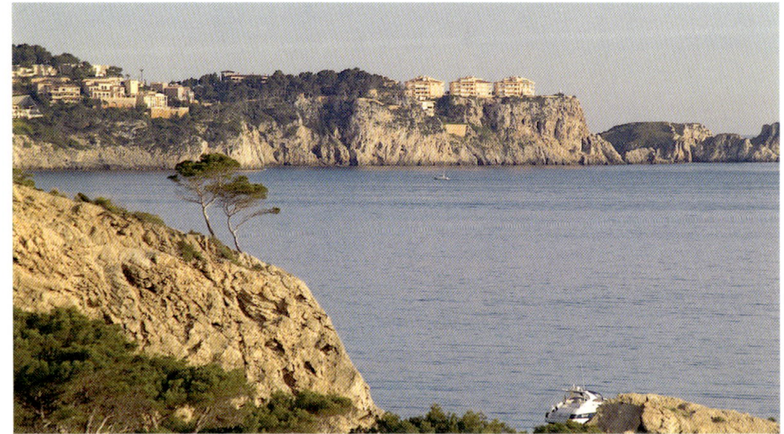

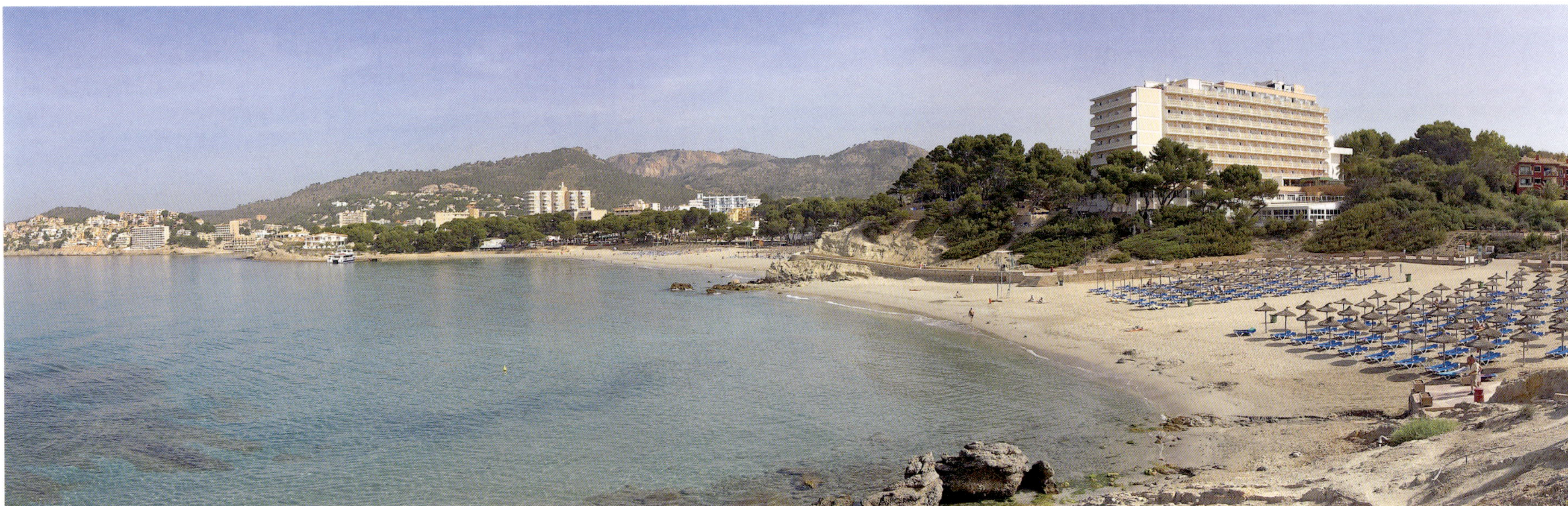

Peguera

There is another beautiful beach in the holiday village of Camp de Mar, attracting nature enthusiasts, as well as families with children, golfers or tennis players.

The small holiday village of Sant Elm in the far west of Majorca is first spotted when the island is approached by ship. Just off the fantastic sandy beach with a length of 180 m, lies the island "Sa Dragonera" (dragon's island). It is a natural reserve and the home of endemic lizards, Eleonora's falcons and Audouin's gulls.

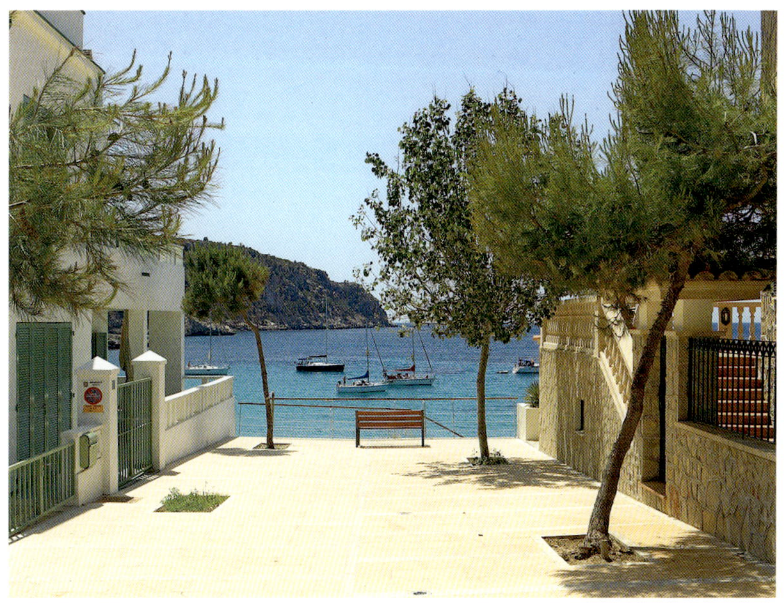

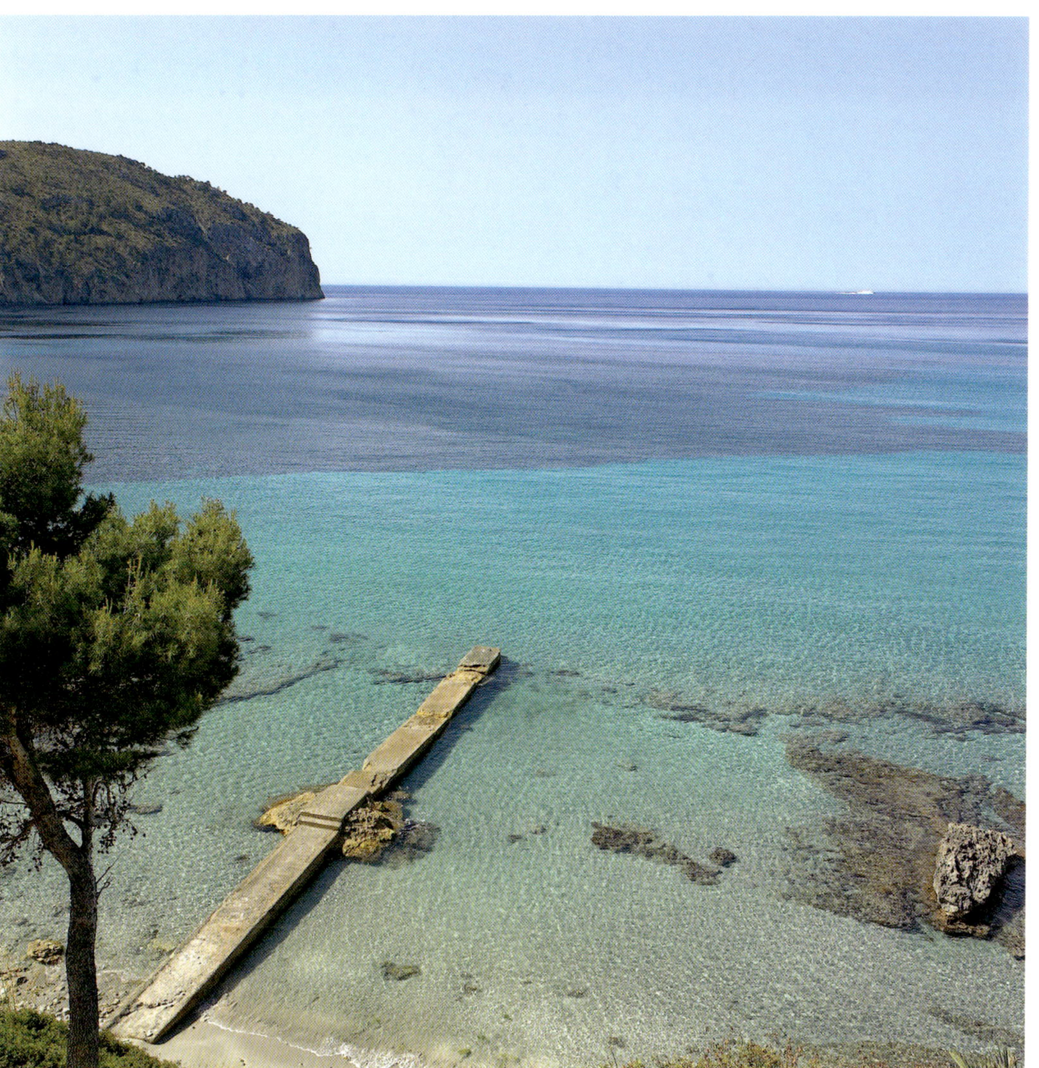

Sant Elm; Camp de Mar

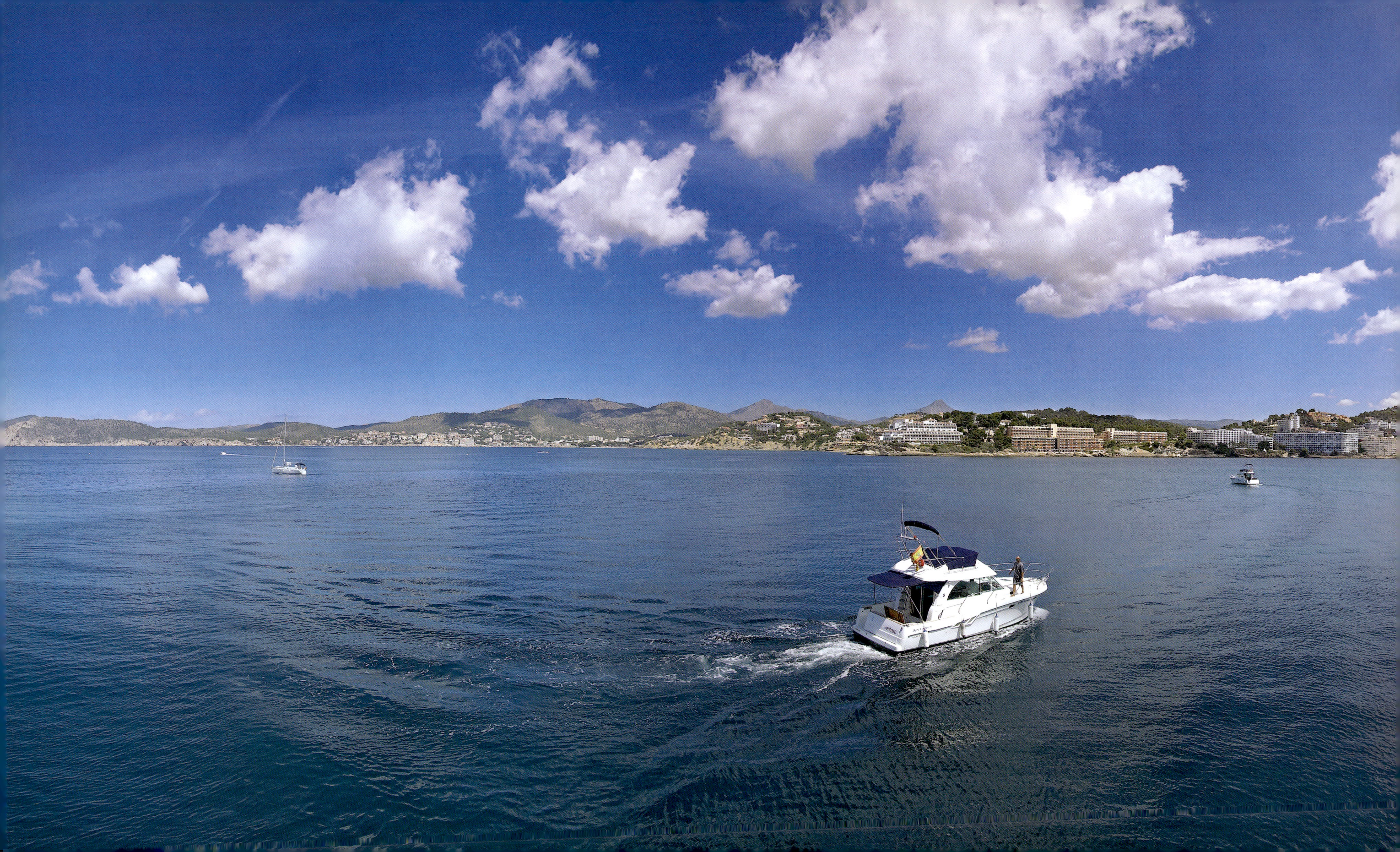

Cala de Santa Ponsa

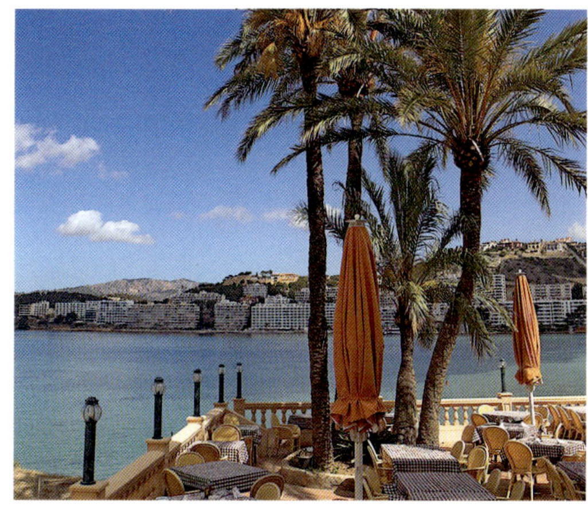

The very wide and 300 m long beach of Santa Ponsa (previous 360° panoramic photo) is lined by hills with magnificent villas. Many Germans have their second residence here. Close to the beach, you can find numerous hotels, as well as a small idyllic marina just outside of town. The centre is the location of many bars, restaurants and clubs.
Only 2 km away, there is another popular tourist destination – the white beach of "Costa de la Palma", meaning "calm coast". From there you can hike up a hill for a breathtaking view of the area.

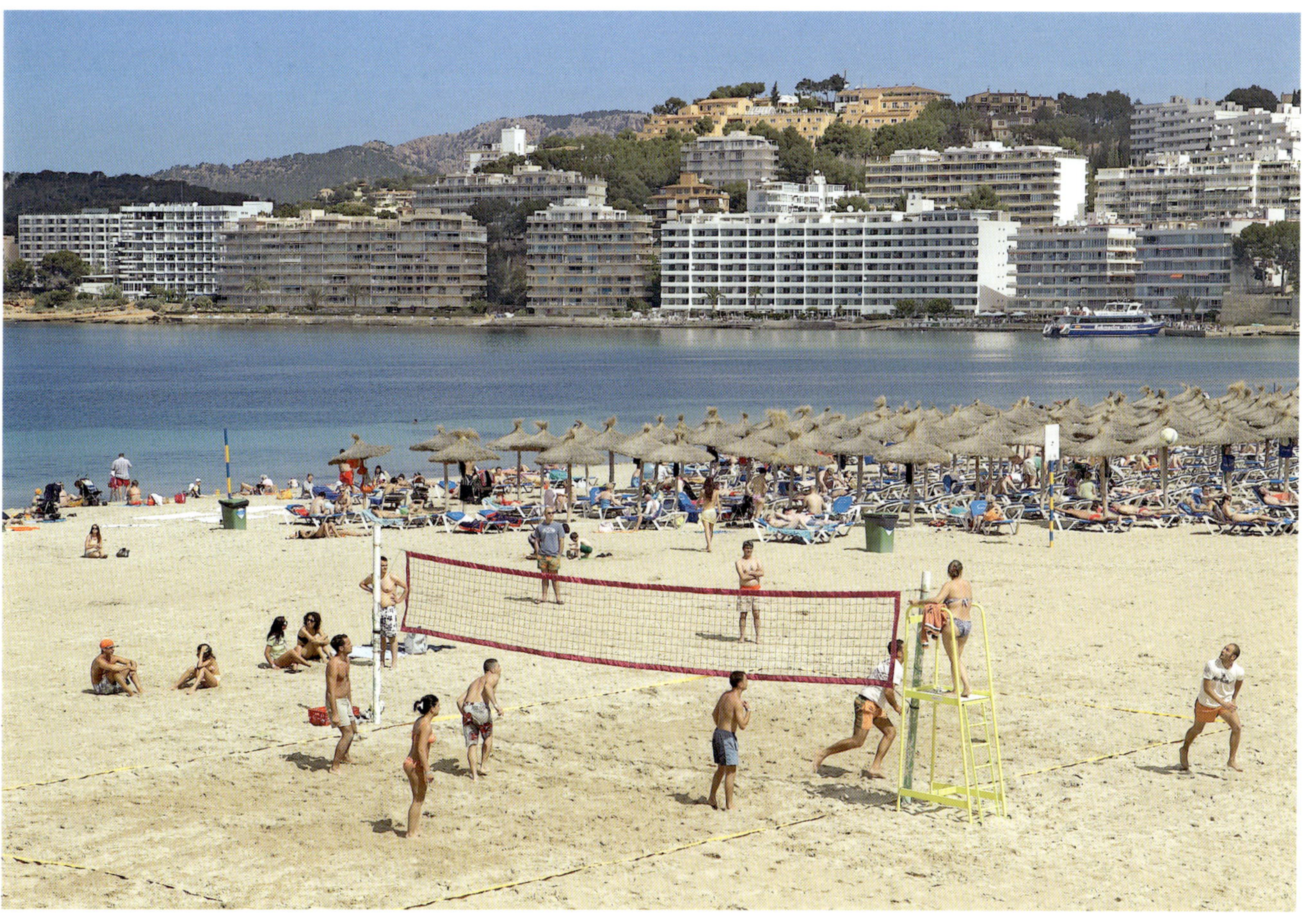

Cala de Santa Ponsa

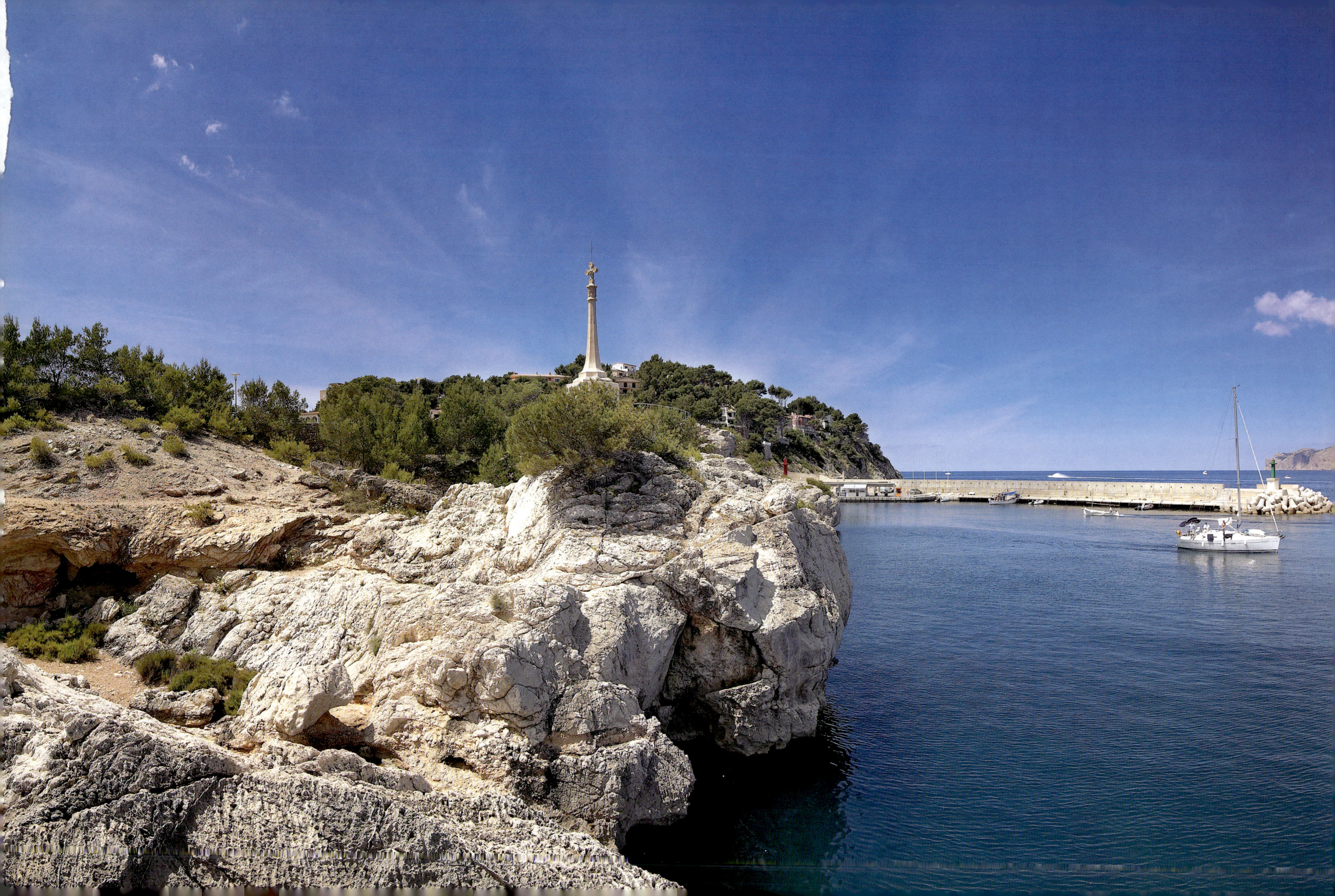

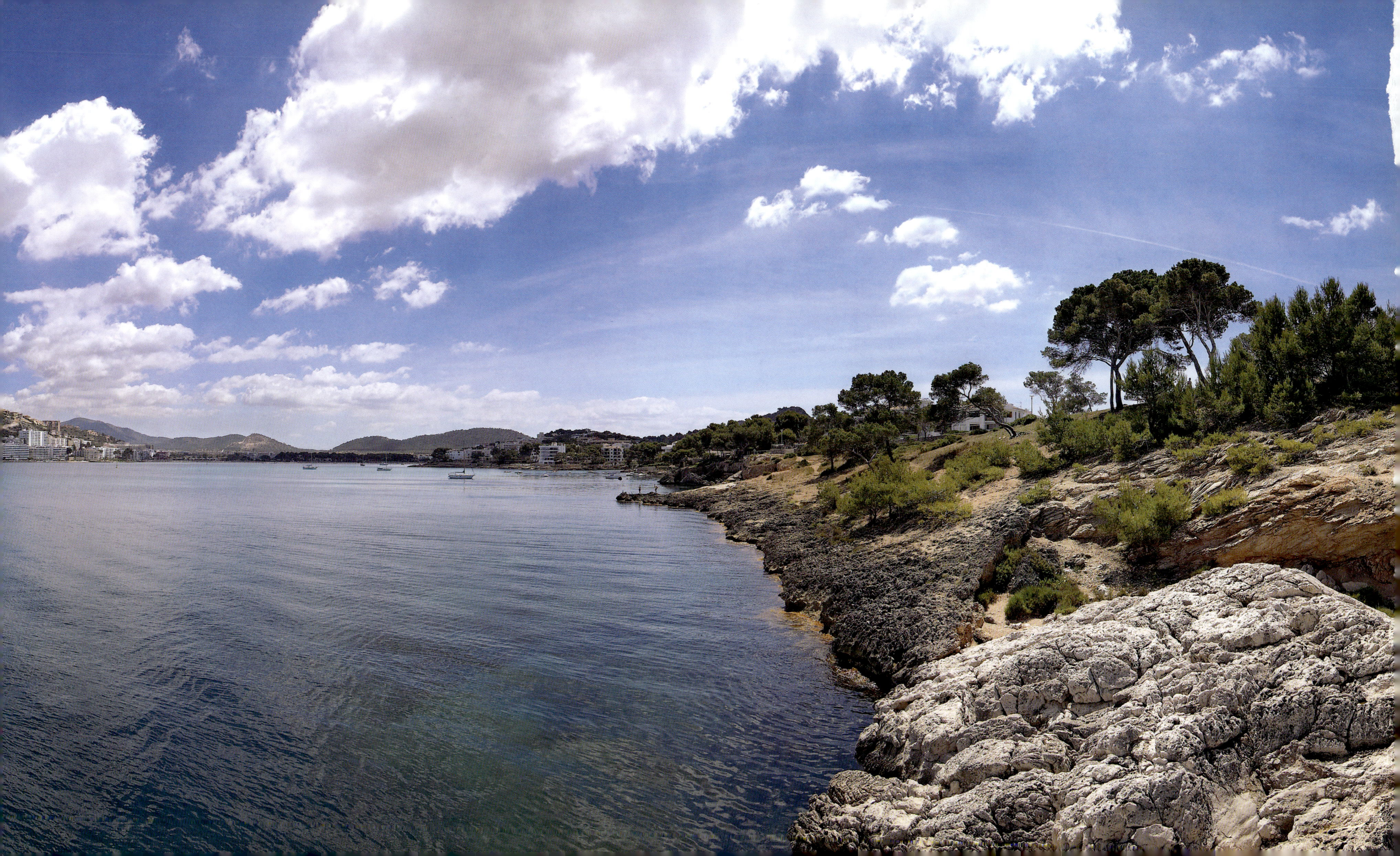

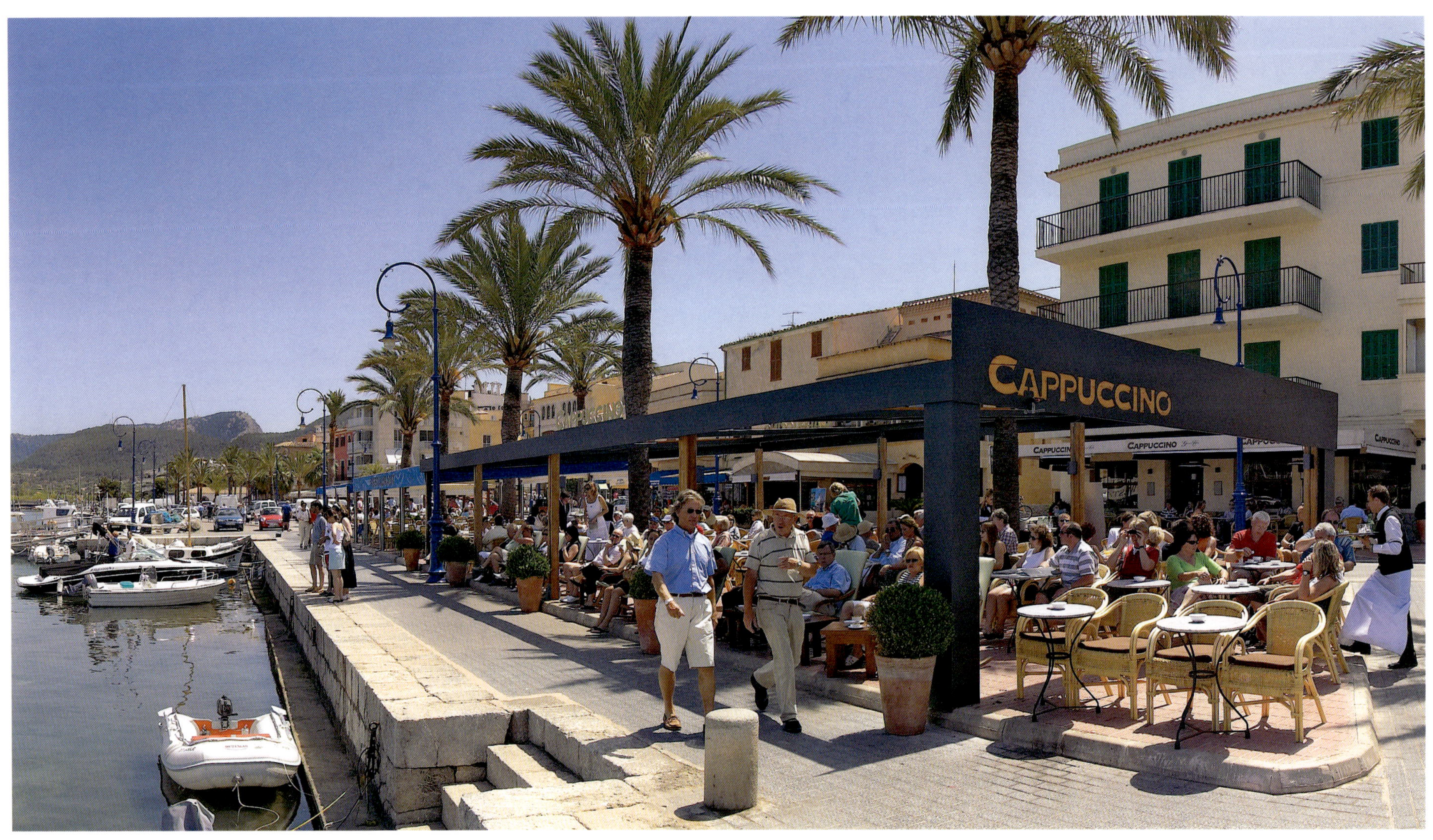

One of the many restaurants in Port Andratx, which offer a lovely view of the sunset.

The port of Andratx is said to be one of the most beautiful ports in the Mediterranean. In Roman times, it was used to ship supplies for the troops, but today it is a mooring spot for many luxury yachts. Its good weather makes it a favourite with sailors, and there are great opportunities for divers as well. The small village was first documented in 1236. It was founded by persecuted Christians, a little further inland for protection against pirates. Every Wednesday, a market is held in the village, which is very popular with tourists. The port is surrounded by a row eight green mountain peaks with heights between 300 and almost 1,000 m. The hike to the ruins of a Trappist monastery at a height of 380 m is one of the island's most beautiful tours.

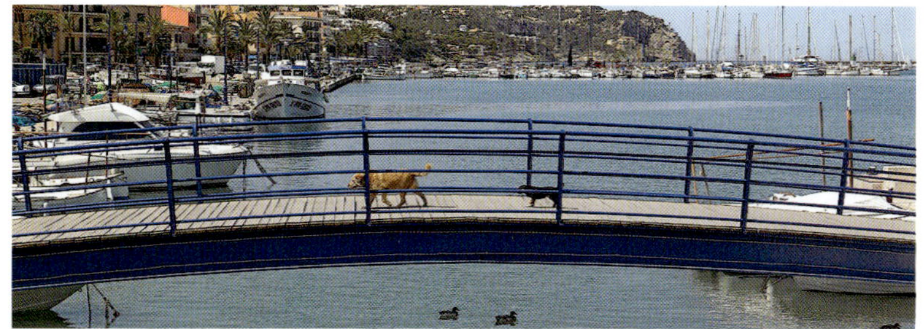

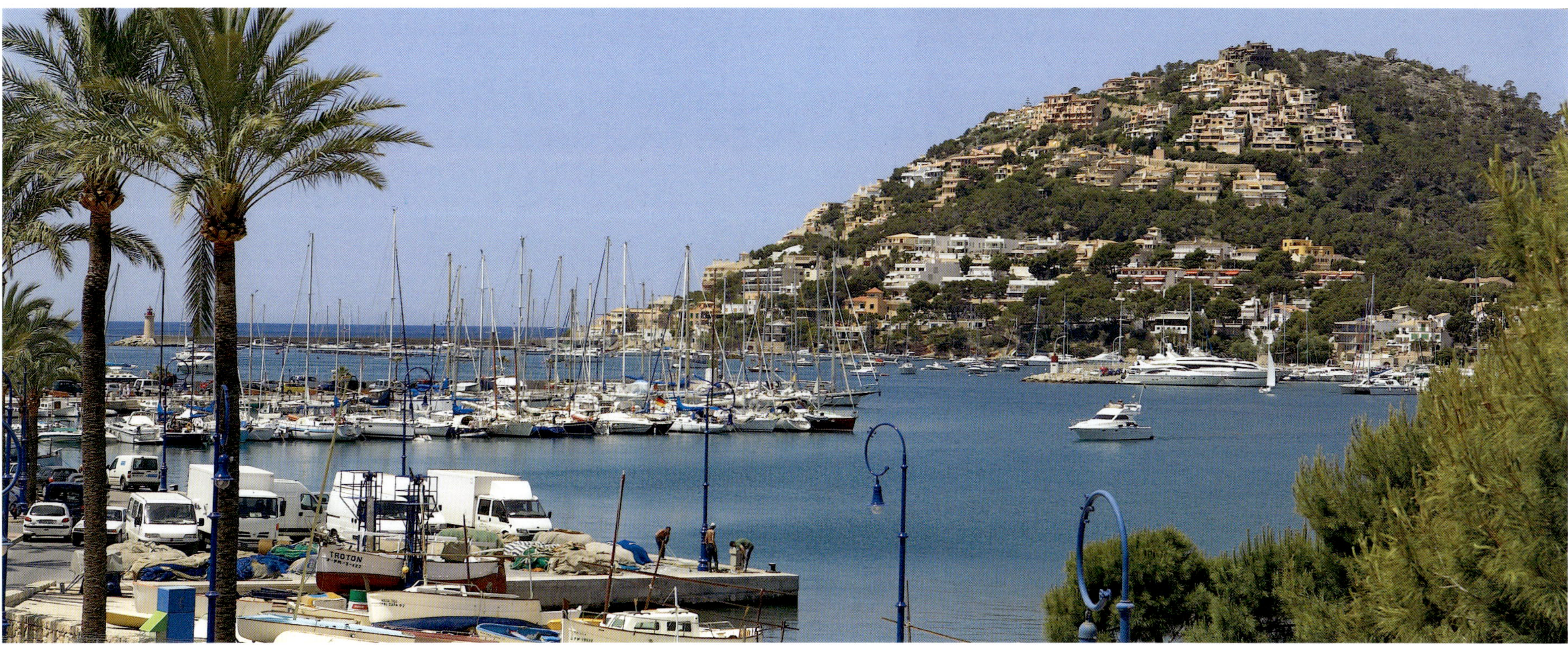

The port of Andratx and the Puig de S'Espart.

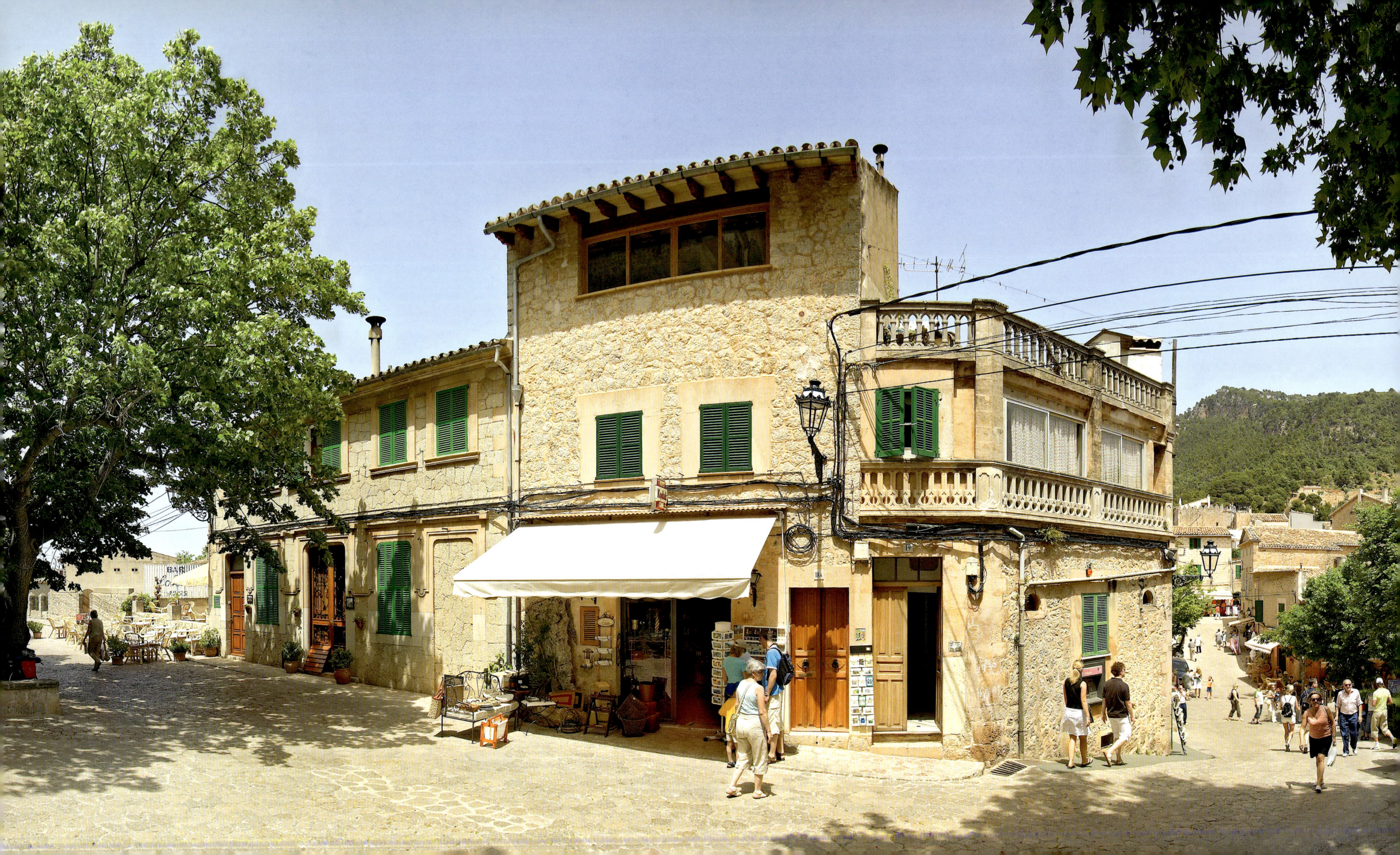

VALLDEMOSSA

Plaça de la Cartoixa

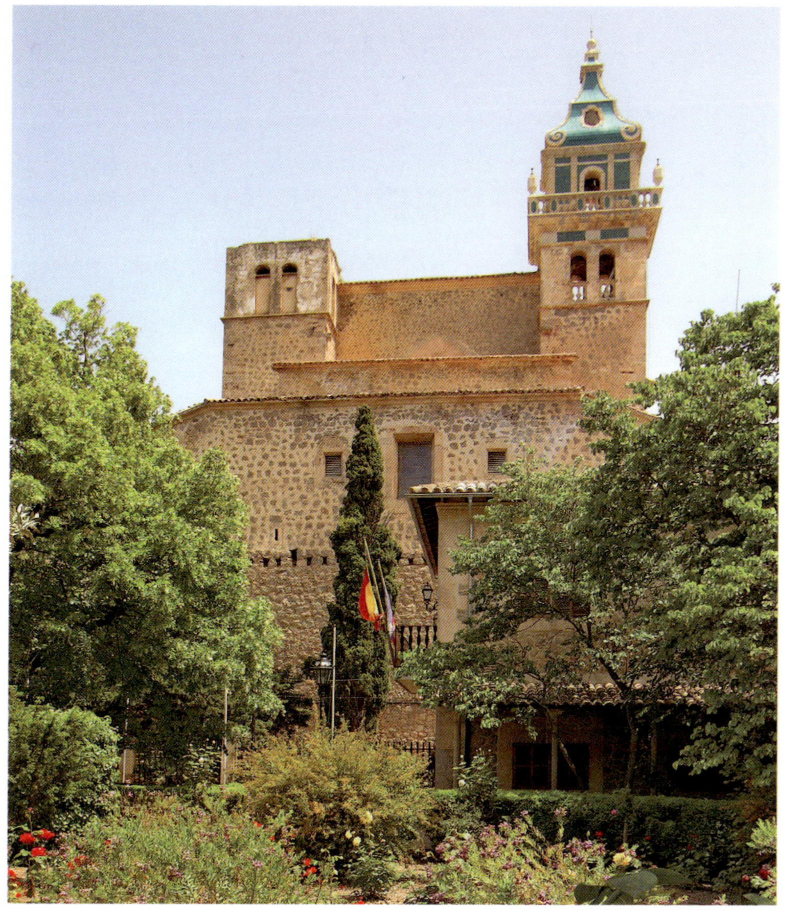

The small community north of Palma, at a height of 420 m, derives its reputation from the fact that the famous composer Frédéric Chopin and his lover, French writer George Sand, spent the winter of 1838/39 at the former local Carthusian monastery (previous 360° panoramic photo). The sojourn served as the inspiration for Sand's travelogue "A winter in Majorca". Today, the monastery with its well-kept gardens is used as a venue for exhibitions. Valldemossa is the place of birth of Catalina Thomás, who was canonized in 1930 by Pius XI. The local cultural centre "Costa Nord", offering information about the natural life of the Serra de Tramuntana, was founded on the initiative of actor Michael Douglas. A beverage made from almonds is one of the specialties of the mountain village.

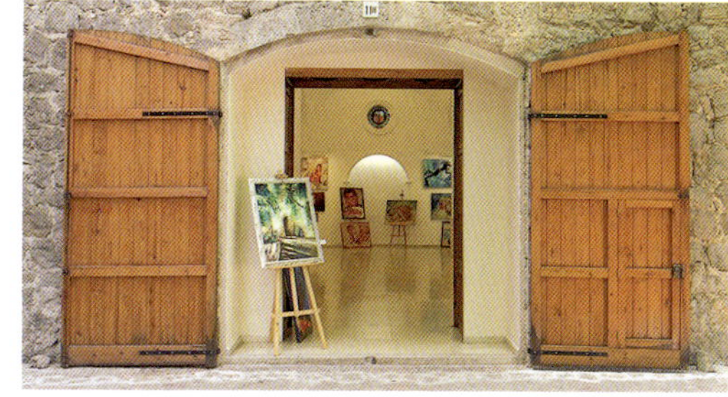

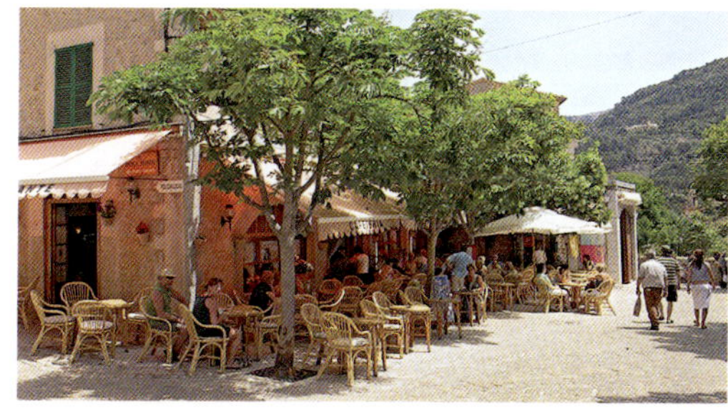

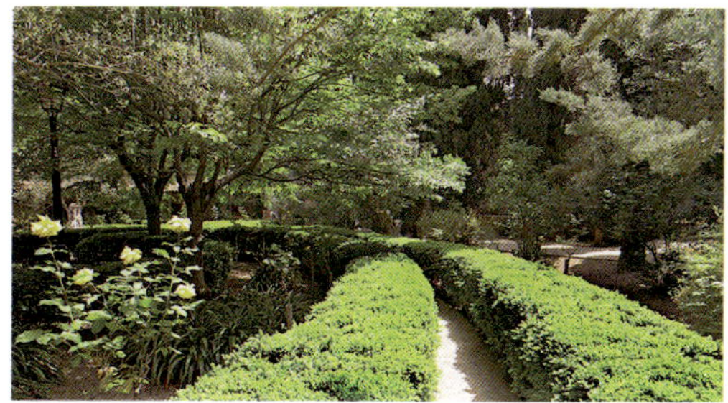

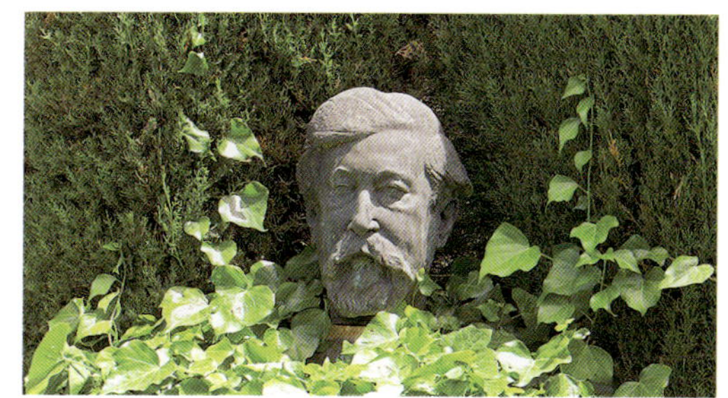

The Carthusian monastery of Valldemossa.

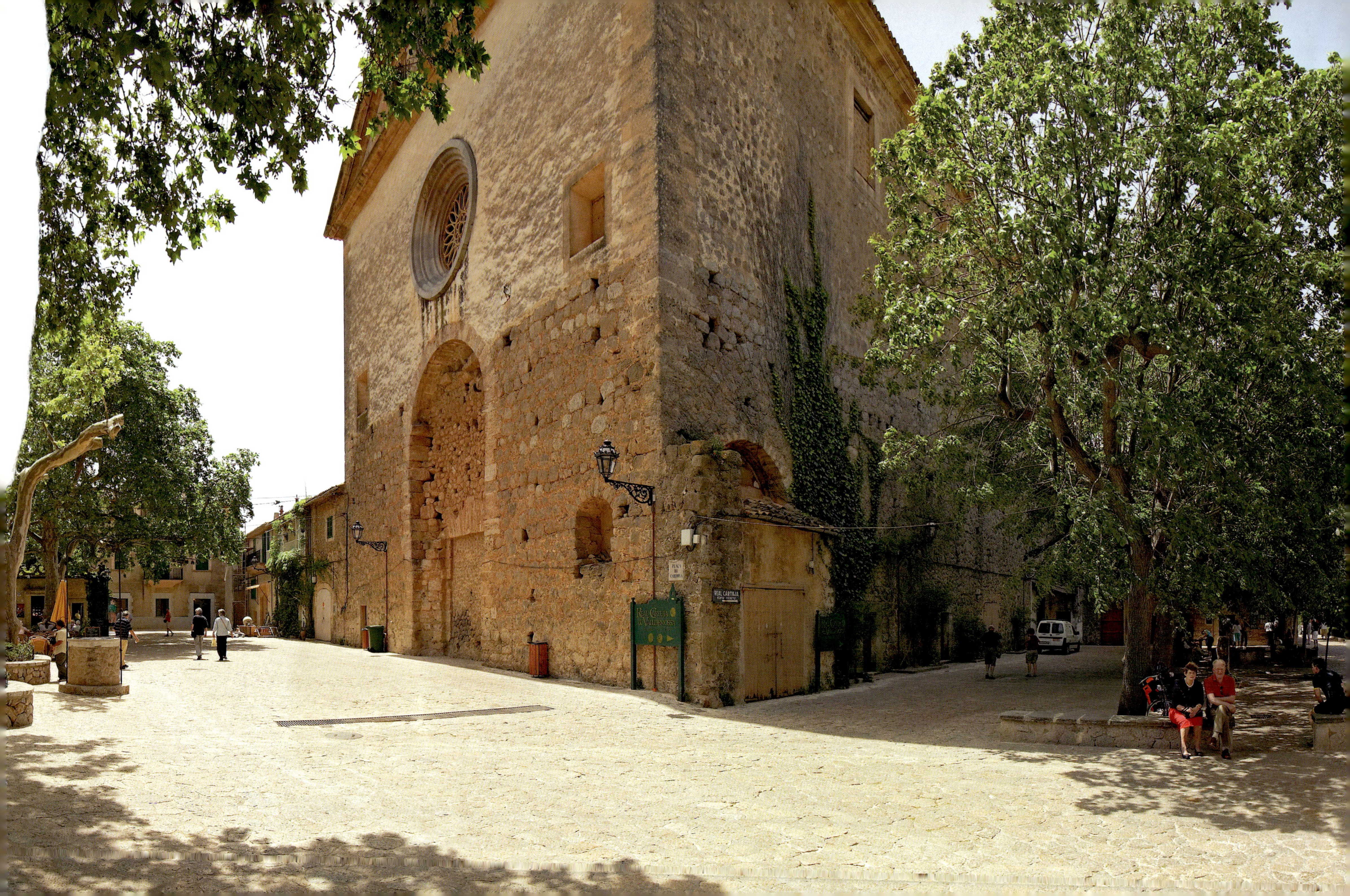

Real Cartuja
REAL CARTUJA

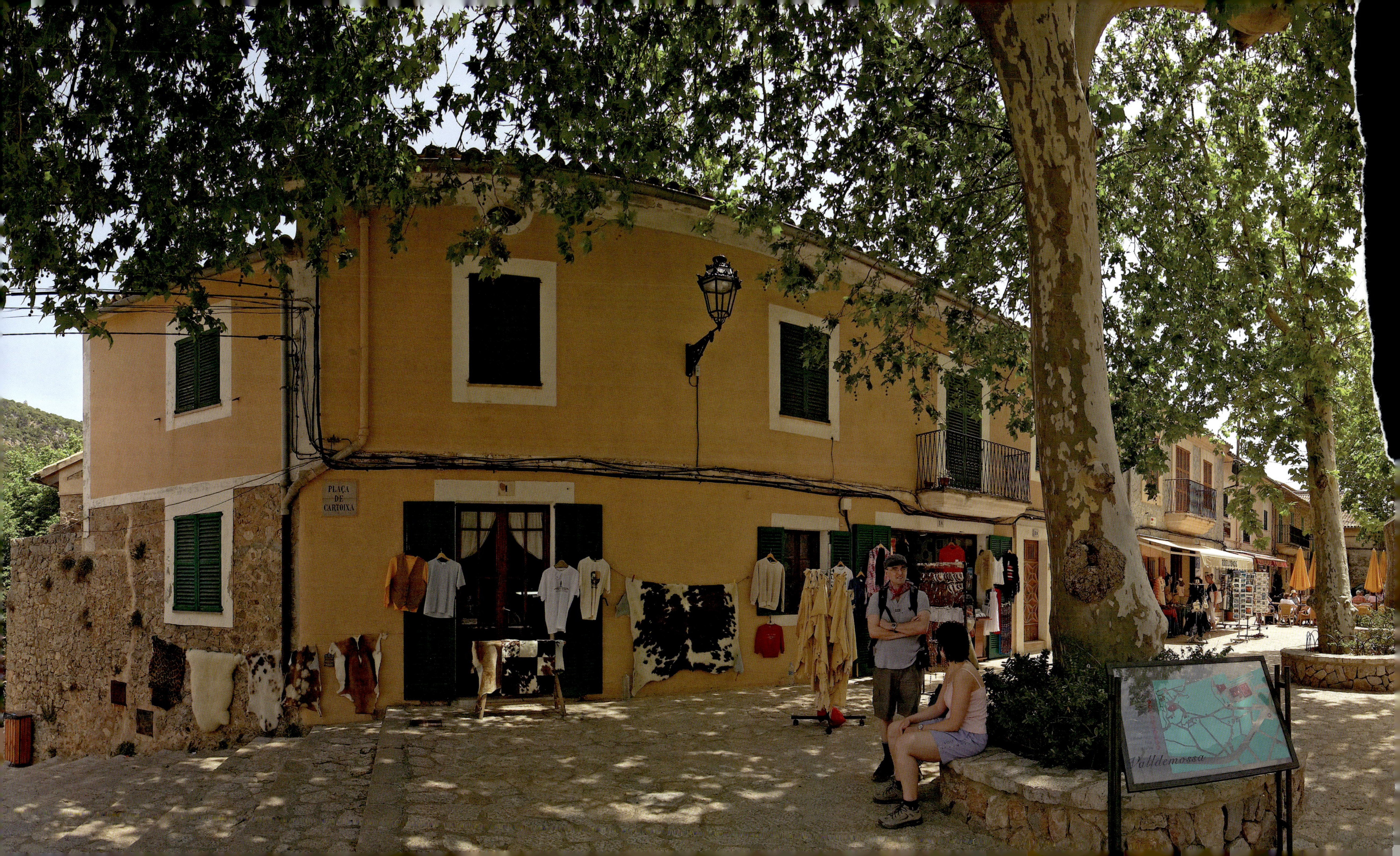
PLAÇA
DE
CARTOIXA
Valldemossa

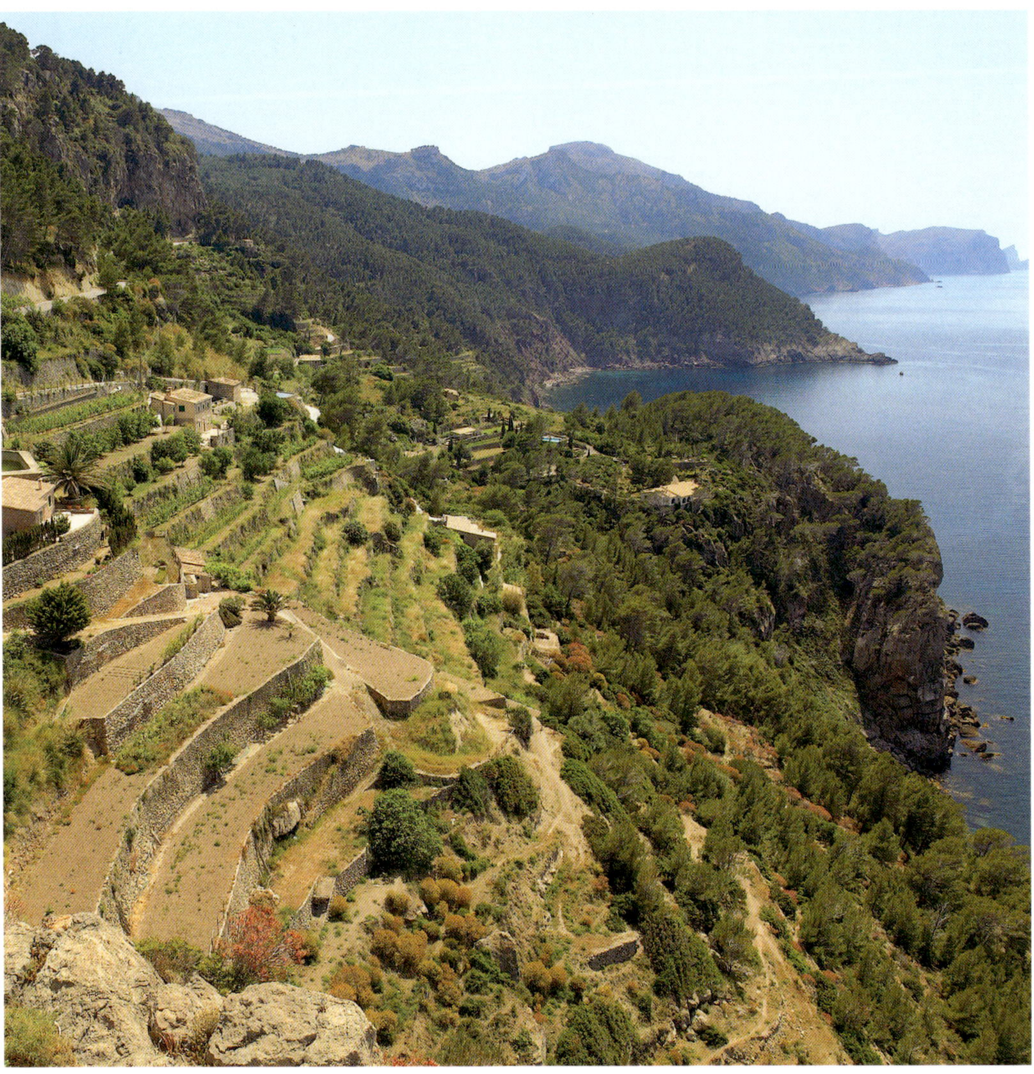

On the road between Estellencs and Banyalbufar, you can find the "Mirador de Ses Animes", one of Majorca's former 85 watchtowers. An iron ladder leads up to the top, from where you have a spectacular view of the blue-green sea and the terraces of Banyalbufar. The grapes growing on the steep slopes of Banyalbufar are turned into fine wines.

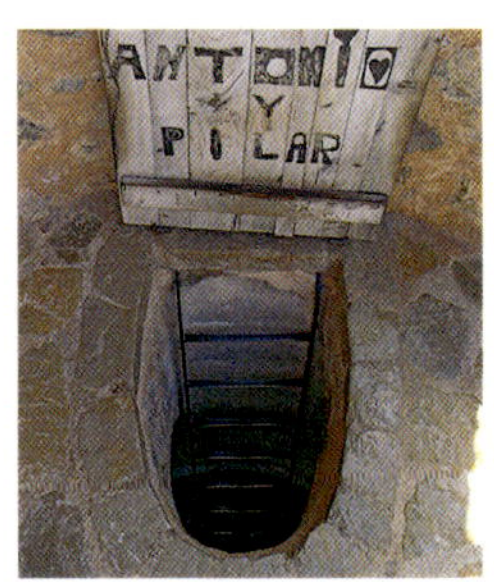

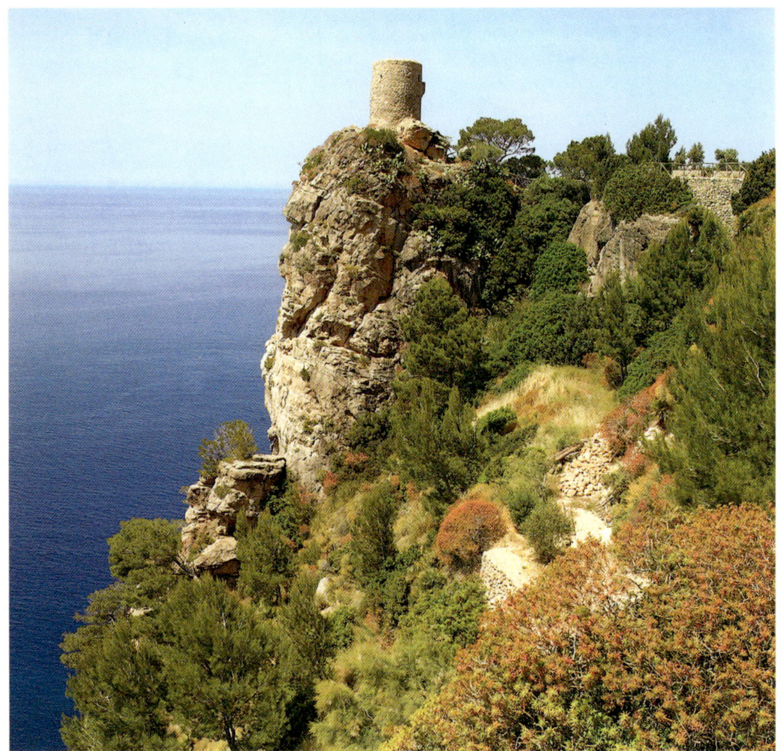

Terraces between Estellencs and Banyalbufar; the „Mirador de Ses Animes"

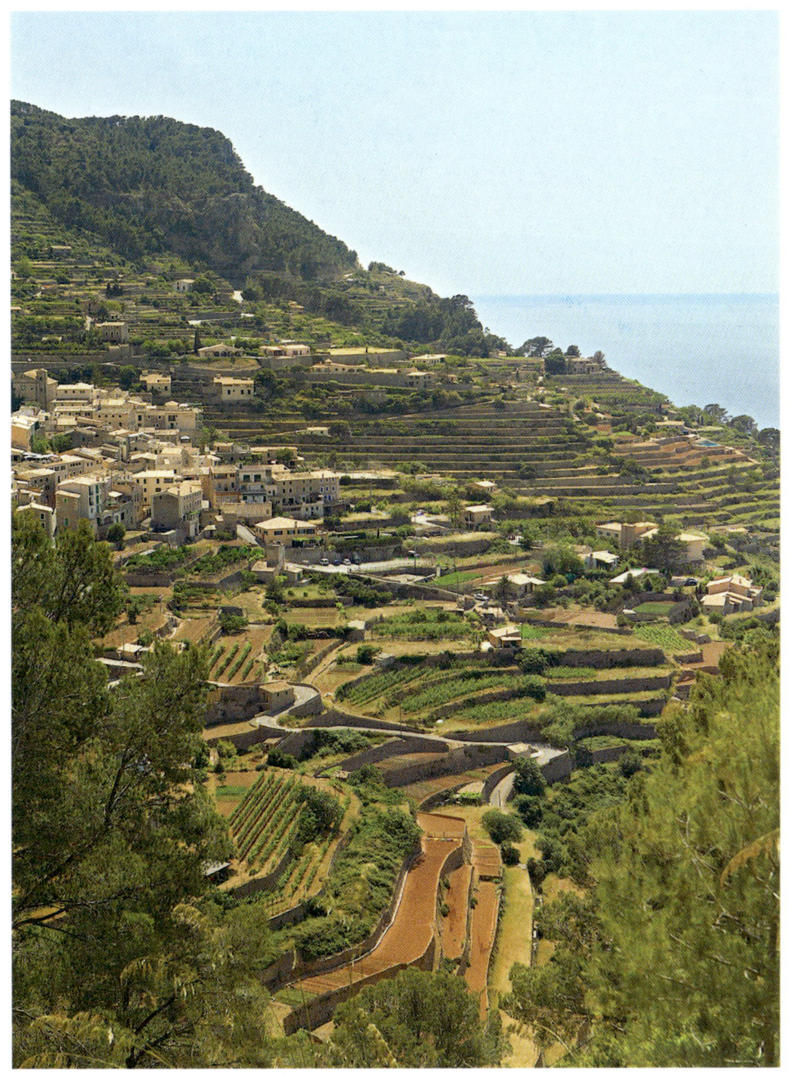

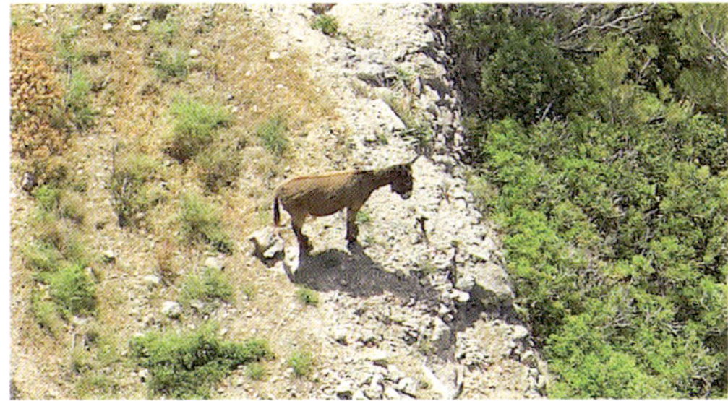

On the slopes of the Tramuntana Mountains lies the tiny village of Banyalbufar, surrounded by citrus orchards and vineyards. On a spectacular hike, you reach Port des Canonge, a quiet fishing bay with narrow pebble beaches. The route leads through a shady pine forest, past bizarre rock formations, almost unnoticeably downhill to reveal ever changing beautiful views.

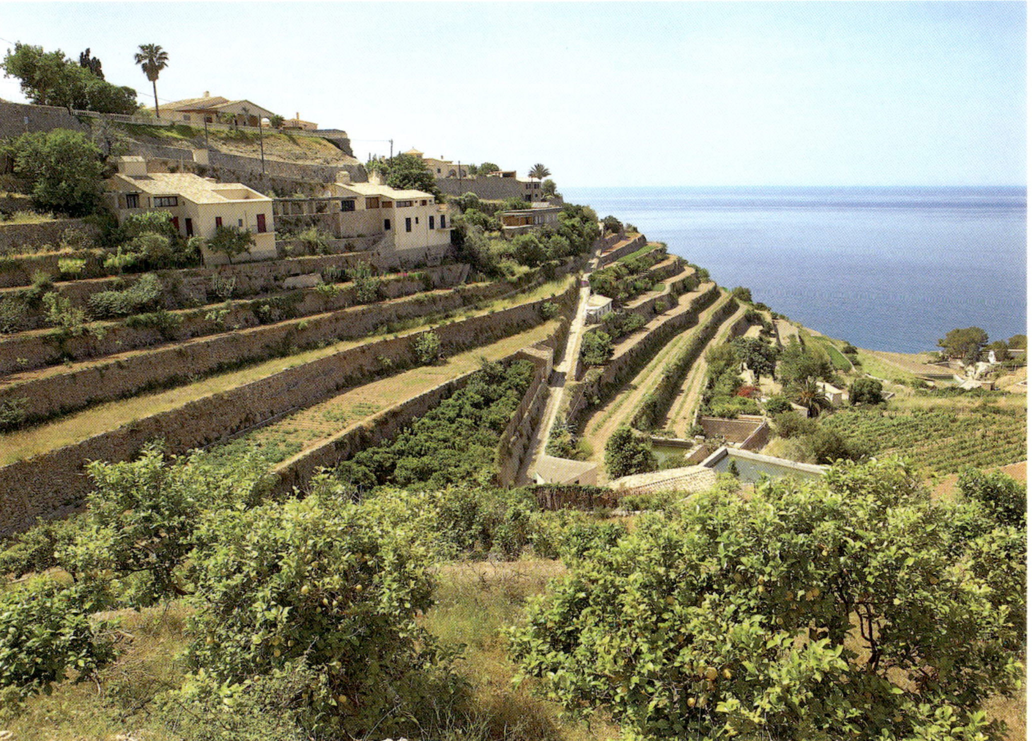

The grapes growing on the steep slopes of Banyalbufar are turned into fine wines.

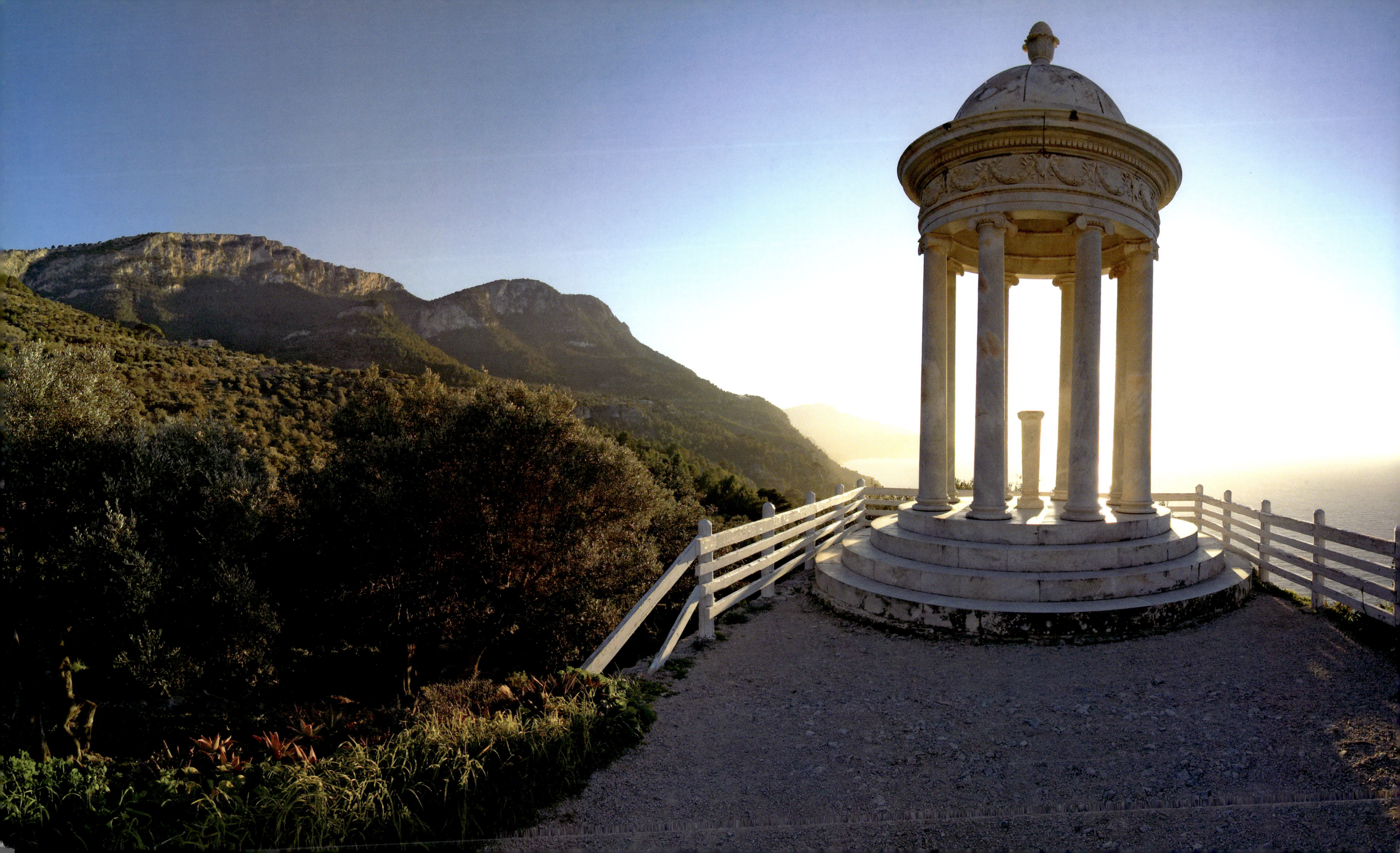

SON MARROIG

Son Moragues

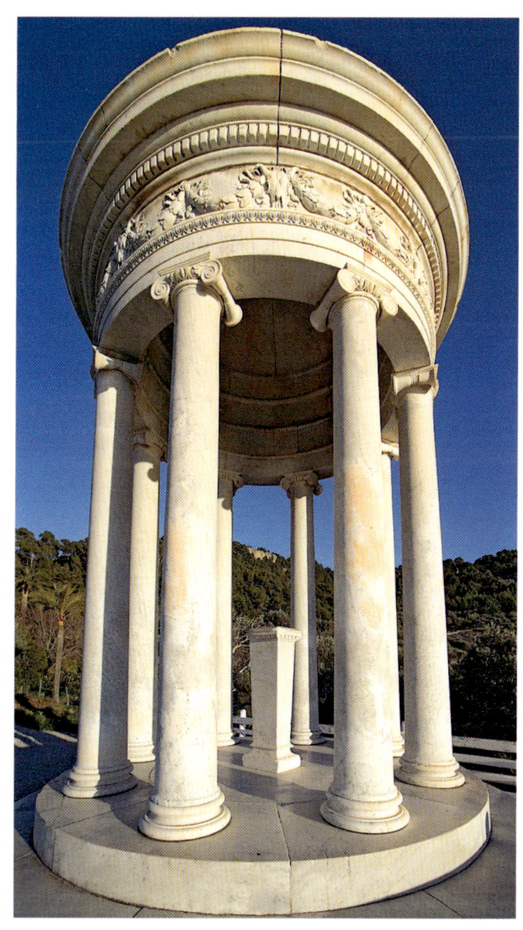

Austrian archduke Ludwig Salvator bought several Majorcan estates and chose the palace-like mansion "Son Marroig" (previous 360° panoramic photo, on the right) as his retirement residence in 1872. Ludwig Salvator, author of more than 60 books, is said to be the founder of Majorcan tourism. He built a pavilion made from Italian marble that offers a spectacular view of the peninsula Sa Foradada. At the tip of the peninsula, there is a hole of 18 m in the middle of the rock, resembling an eye the colour of the shimmering blue sea. Right next to the mansion lies the natural park "Son Moragues", one of Majorca's last authentic vegetation zones and the home of many bird species. Today, "Son Marroig" is used for exhibitions and musical performances.

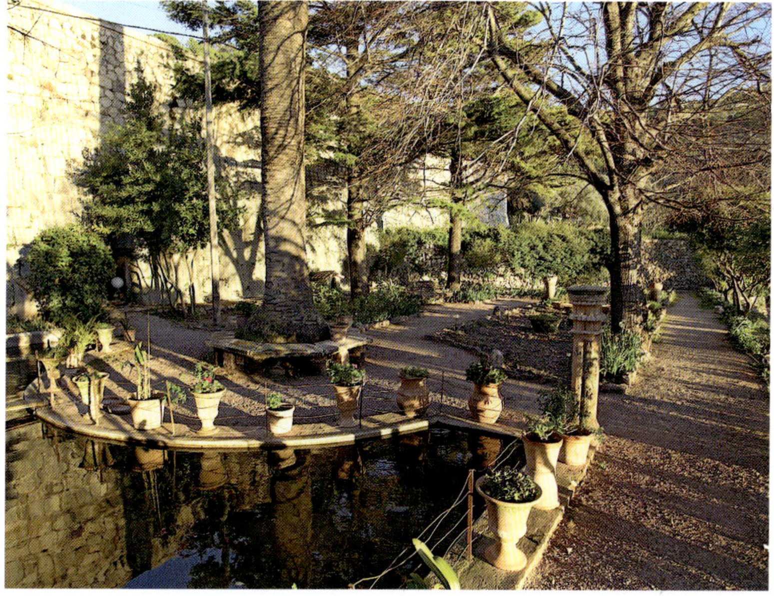

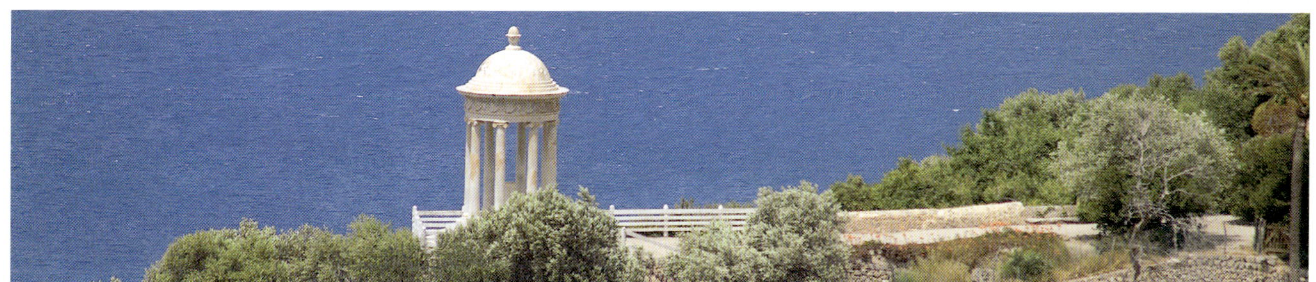

Son Marroig

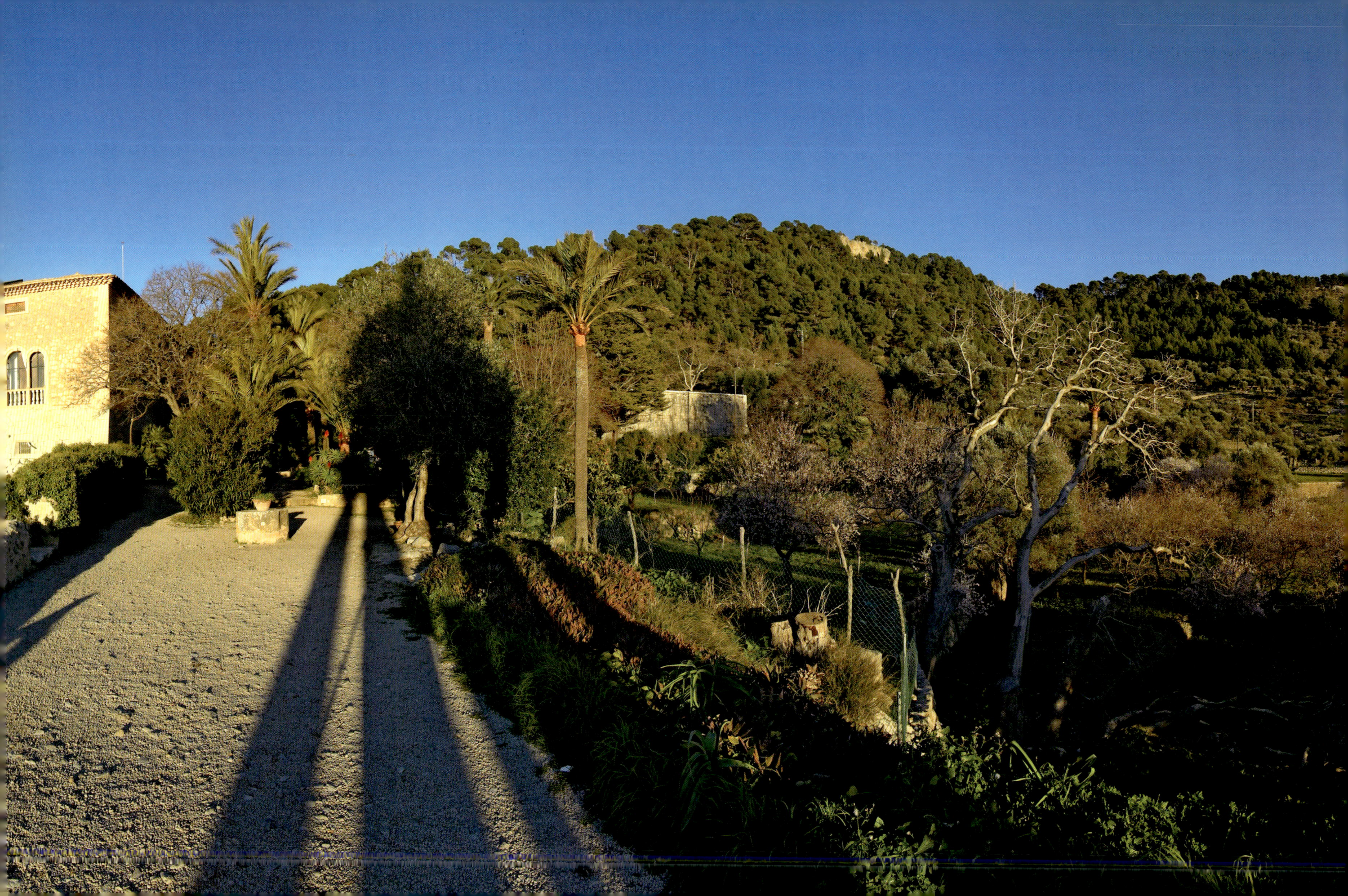

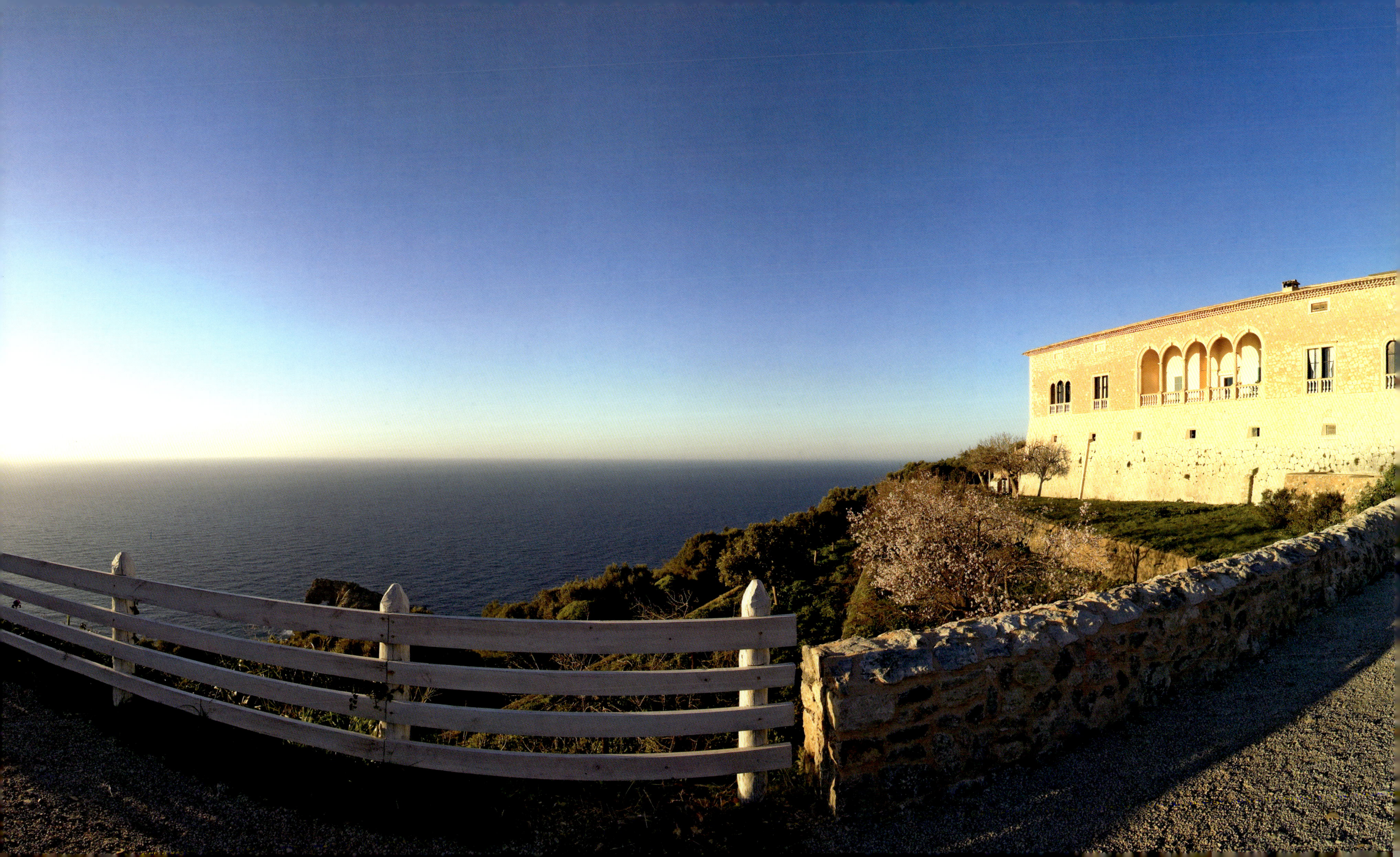

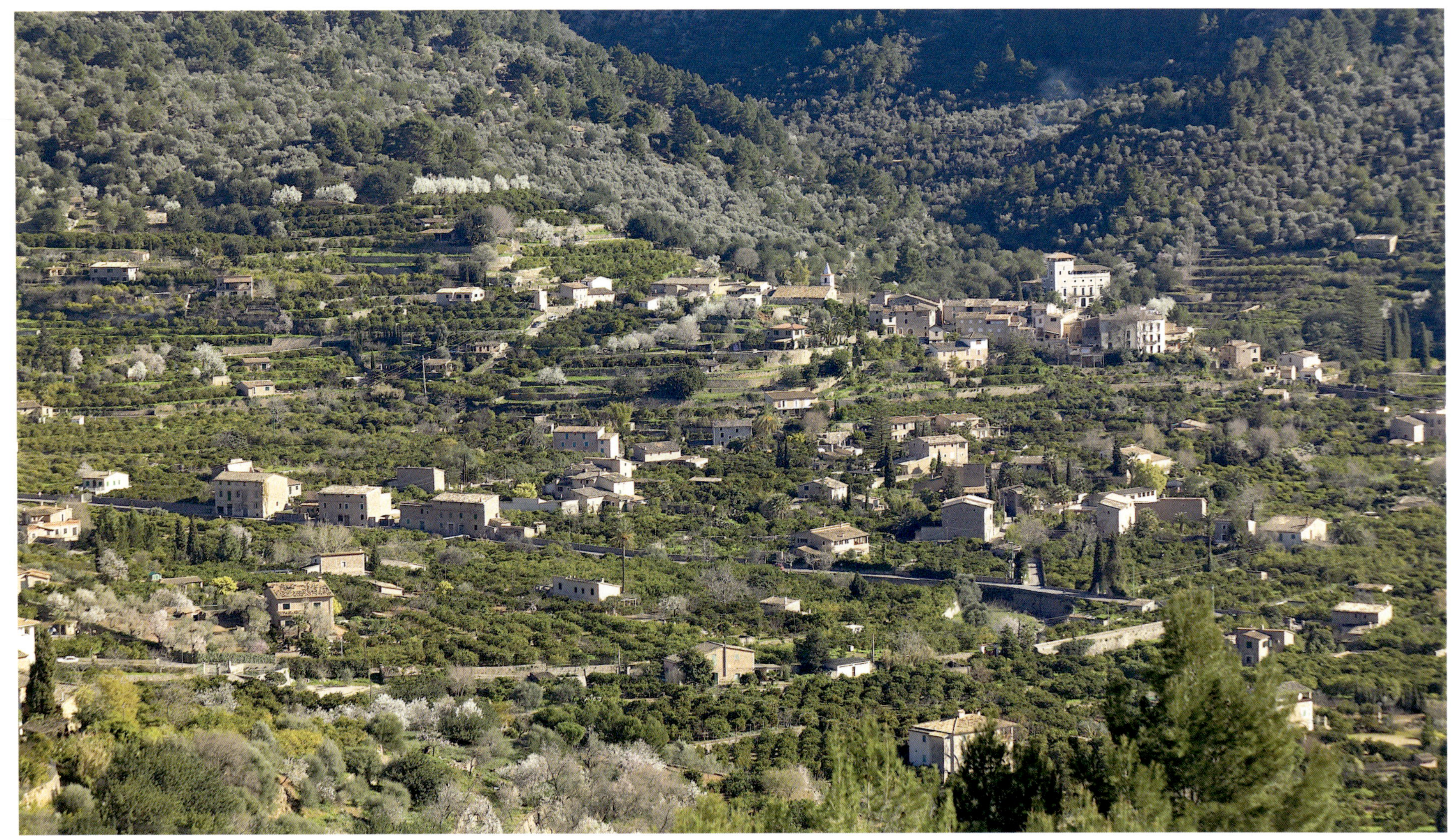

lThe area of Sóller.

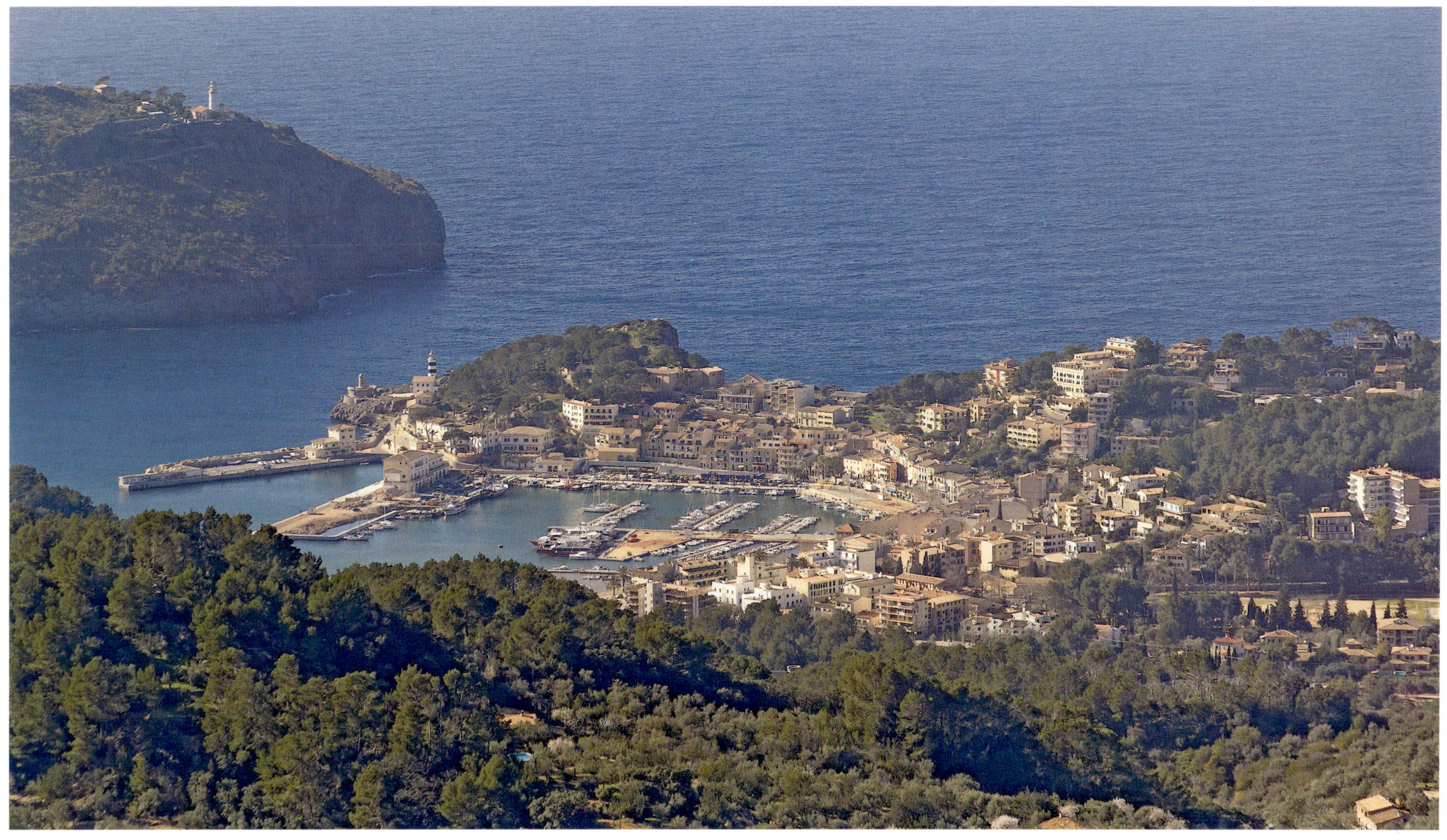

Sóller

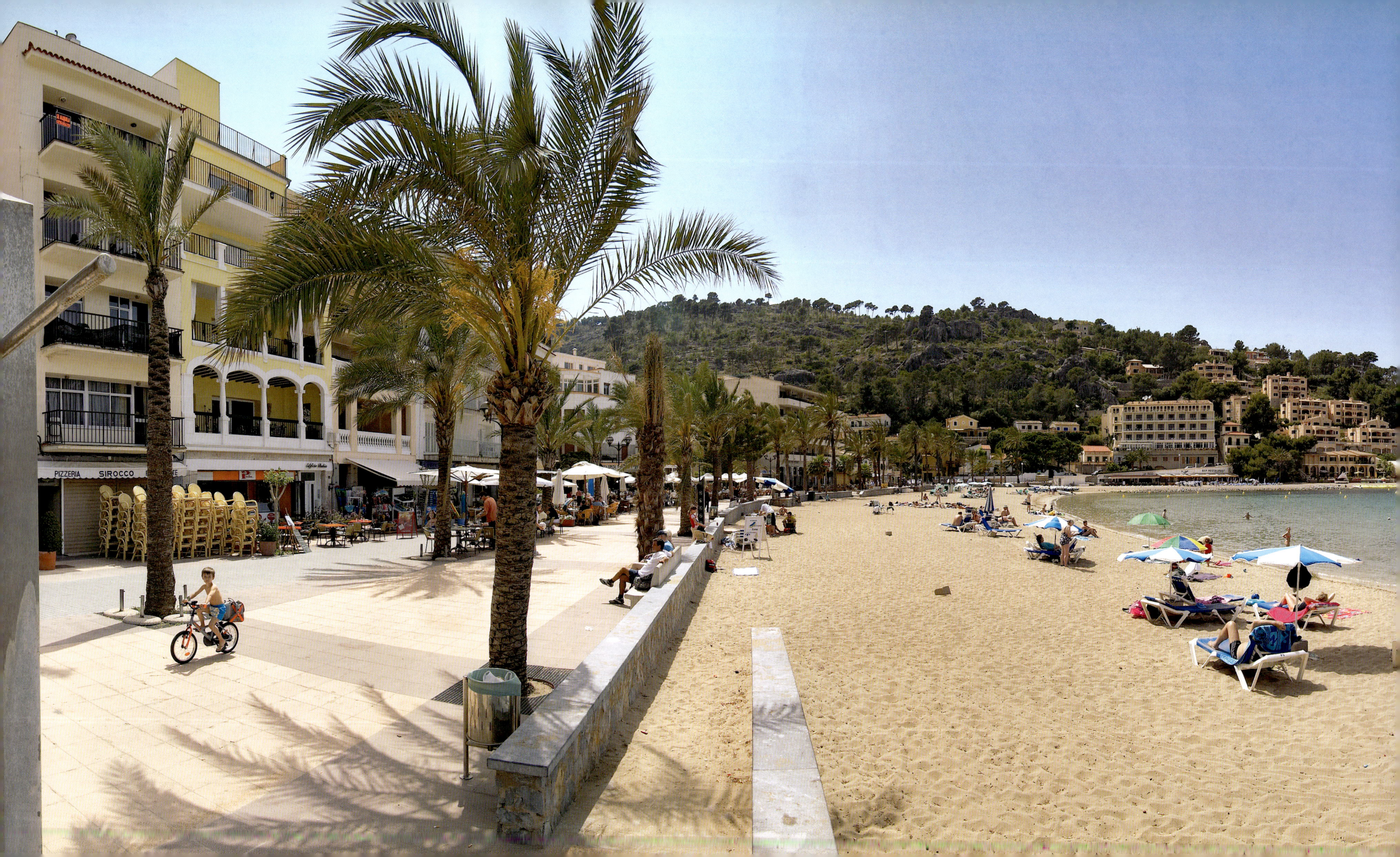
PIZZERIA SIROCCO

Port de Sóller

After the port of Sóller was burned down by pirates in 1561, the citizens built lighthouses and fortifications on both ends of the bay. The town, surrounded by four peaks (about 1,000 m each) of the Tramutana mountain range, was built by French fugitives in the late 18th century with a layout similar to a seashell on the shore. The fertility of the valley secured the wealth of its inhabitants, reflected in the magnificent facades of some historic buildings. At "Camp d'En Prohom", the island's only botanic garden, the seeds of 1,700 autochthonous plants are shock-frozen and conserved.

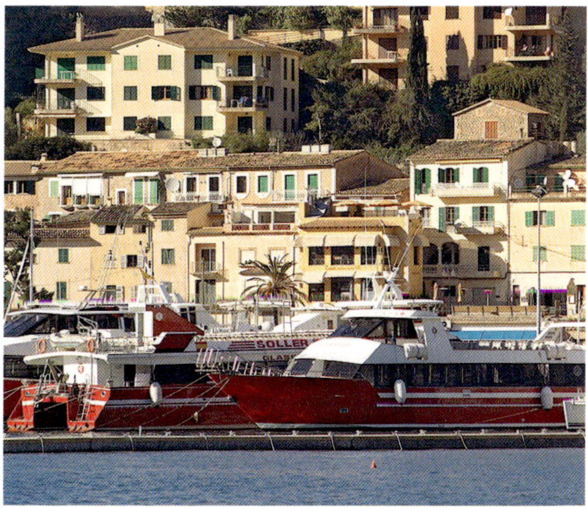

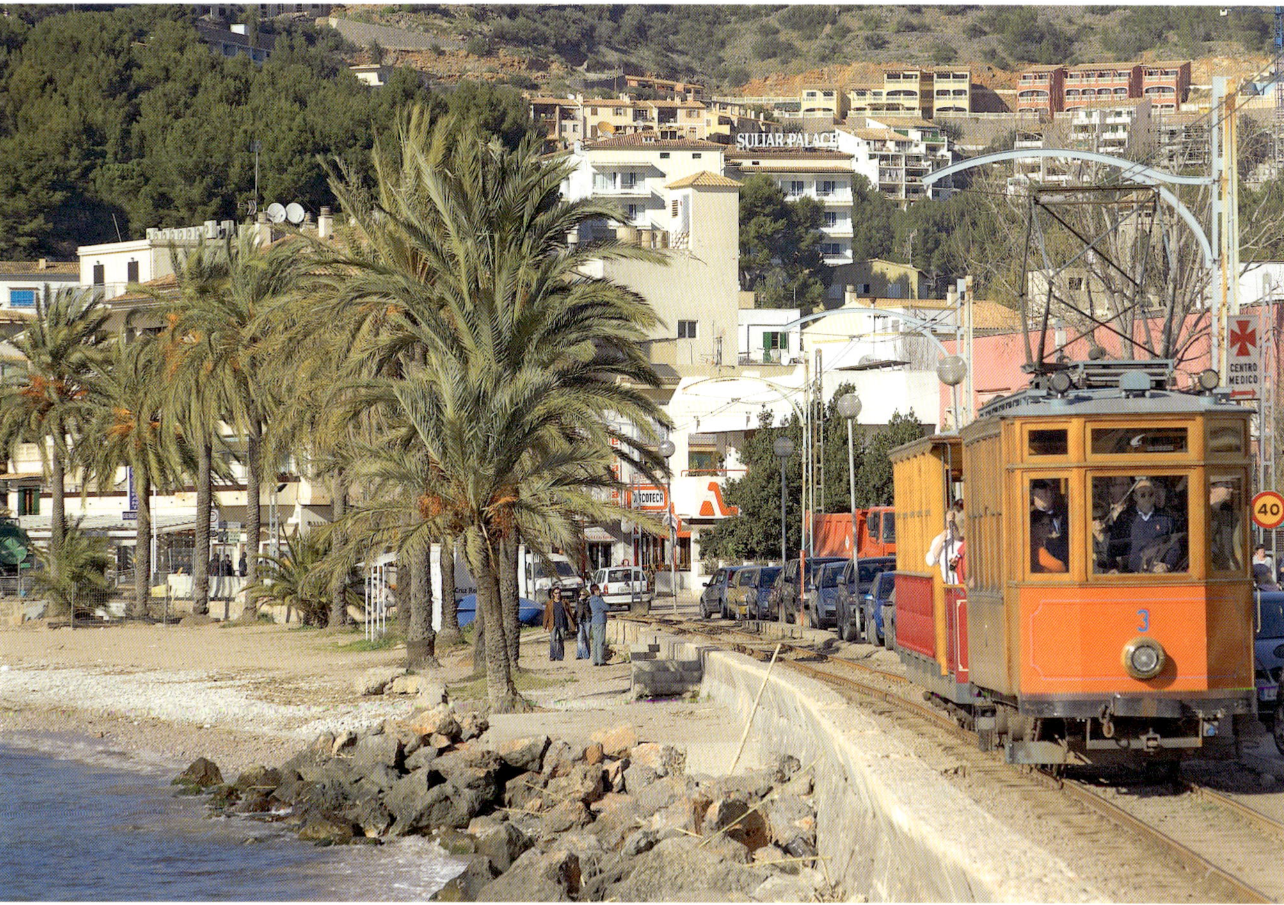

Sóller and the „Red Lightning".

360° panoramic photo: The beach of Sóller 12

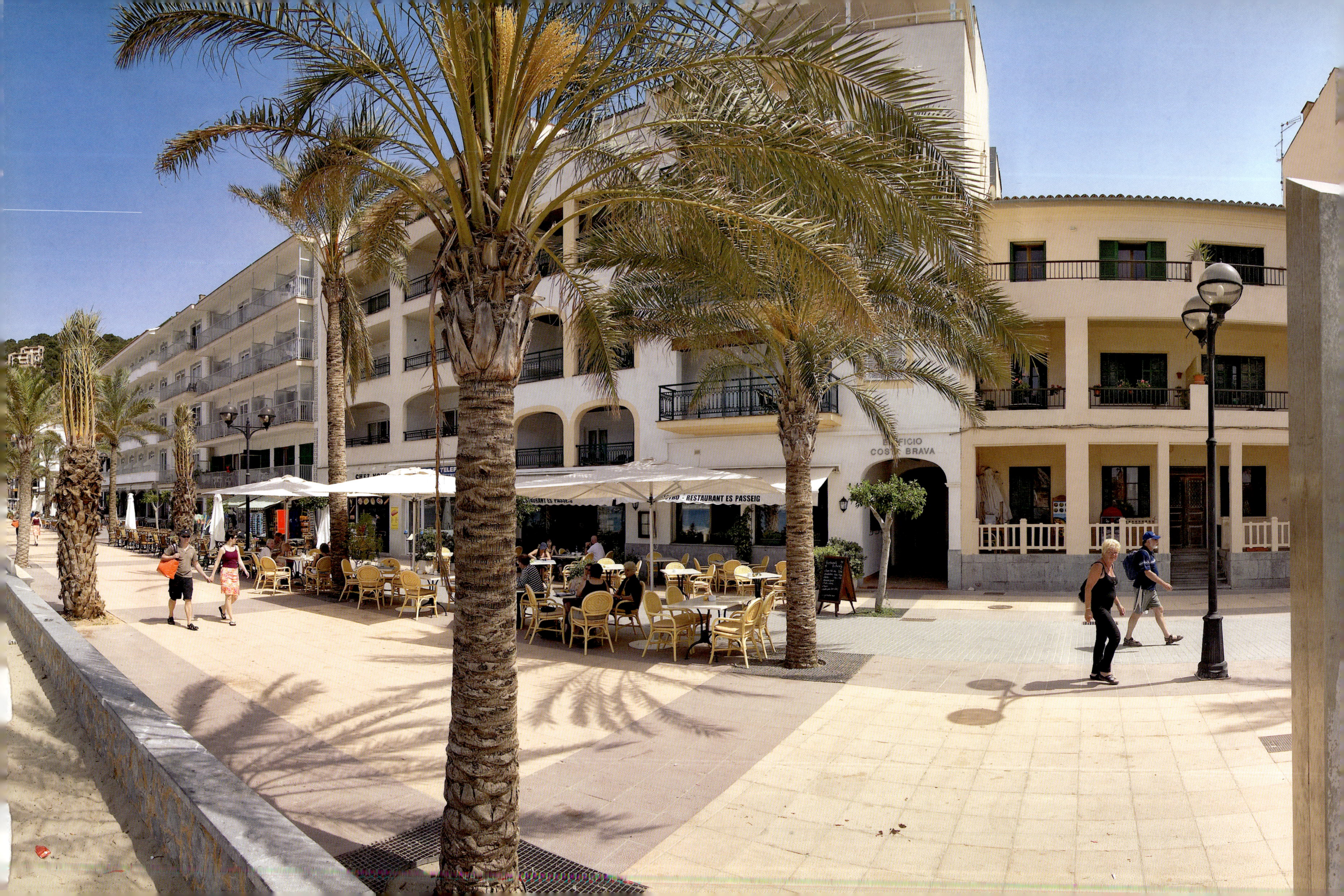
RESTAURANT ES PASSEIG
BRAVA

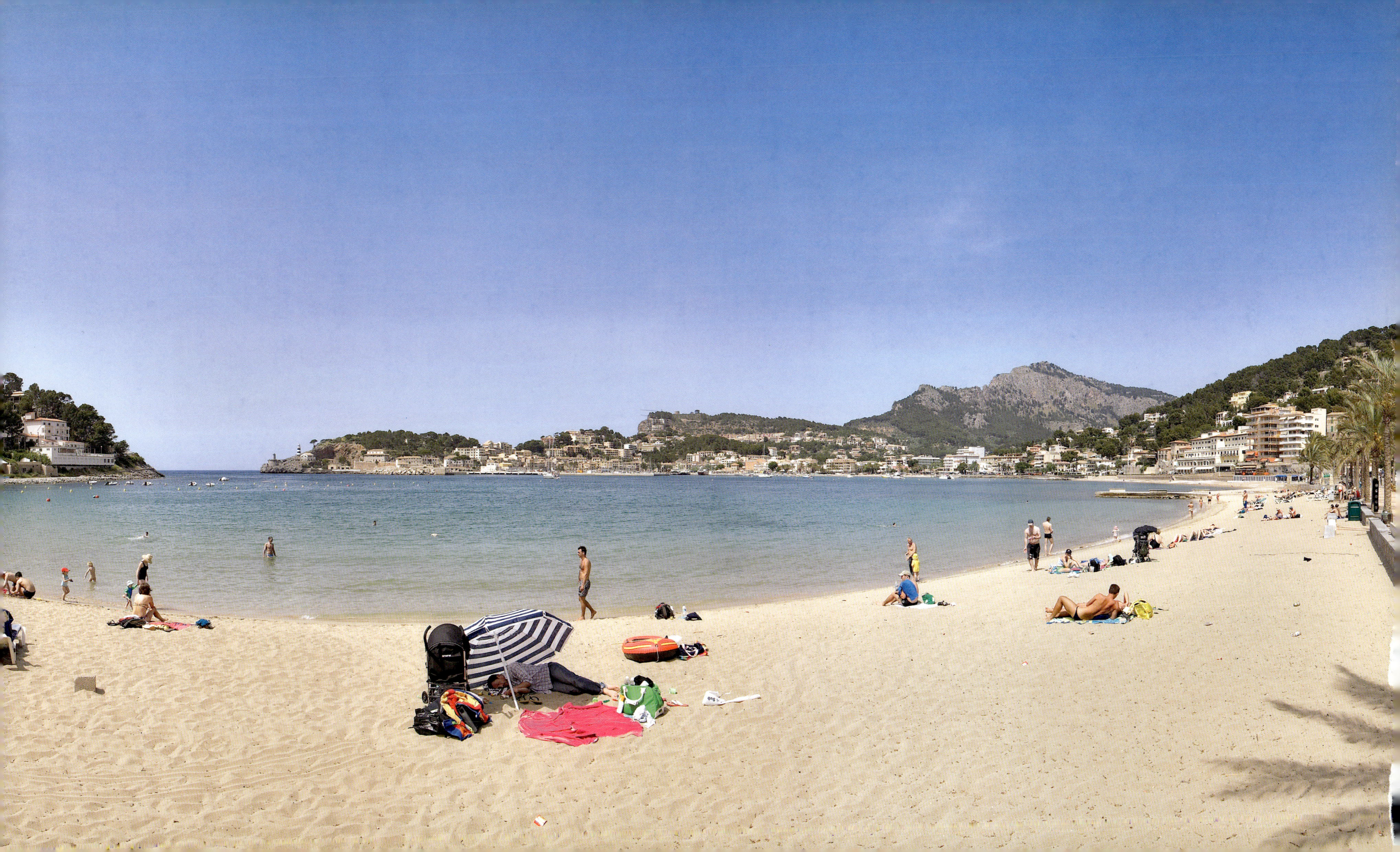

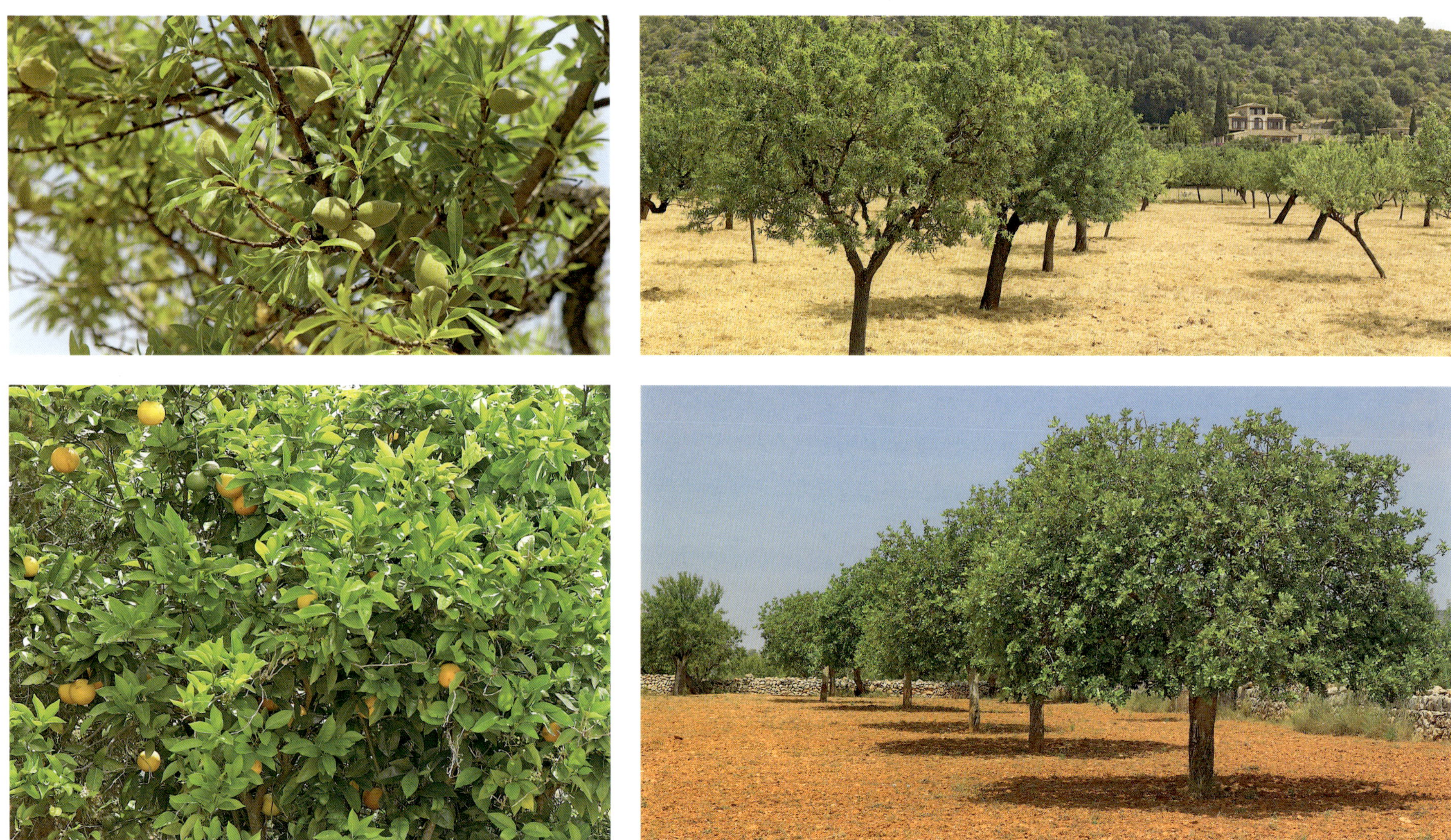

Almond and orange trees in the Sóller region.

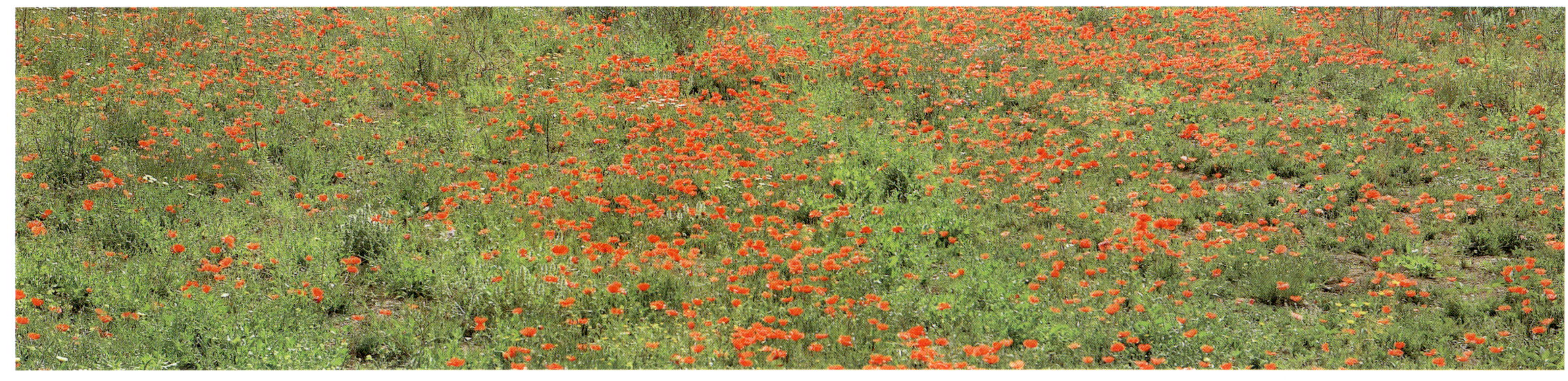

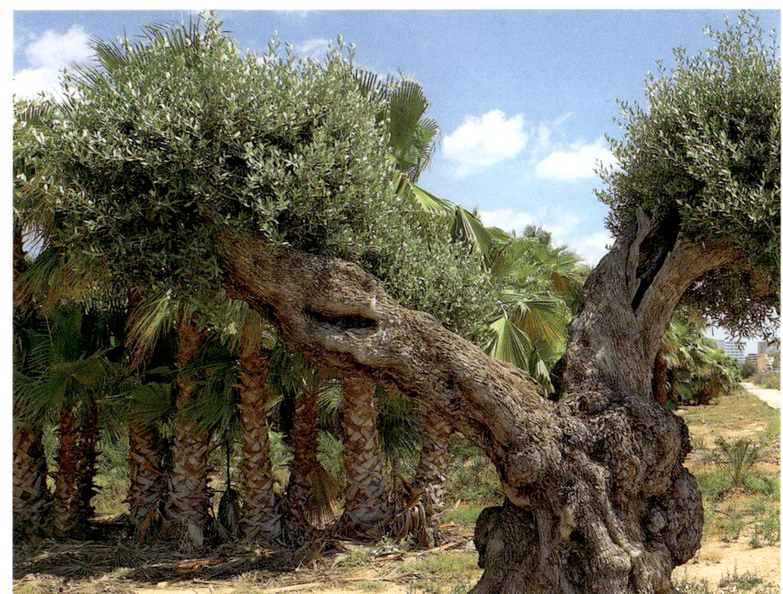

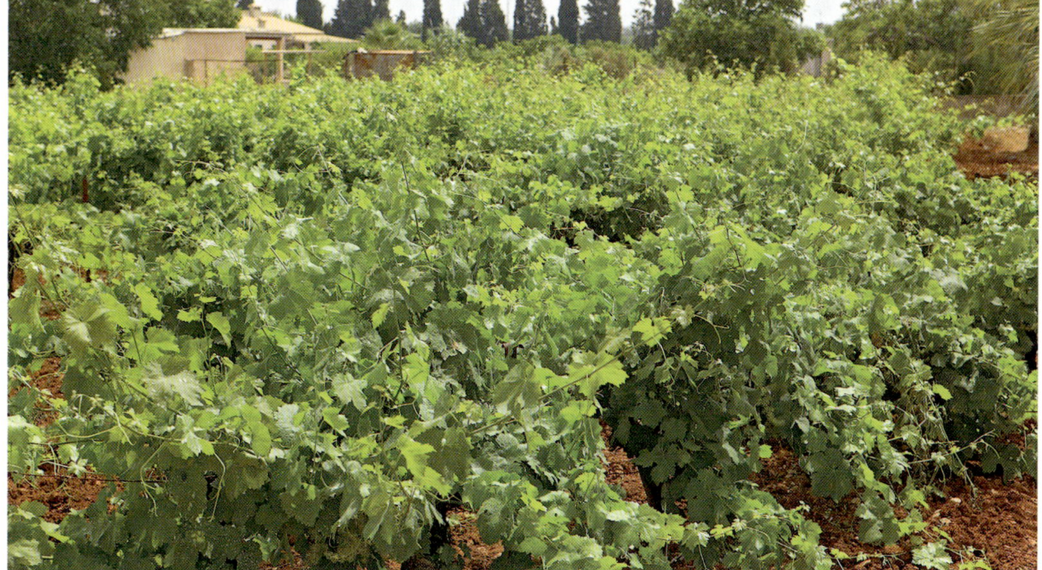

Poppy blossoms, olive trees and wine.

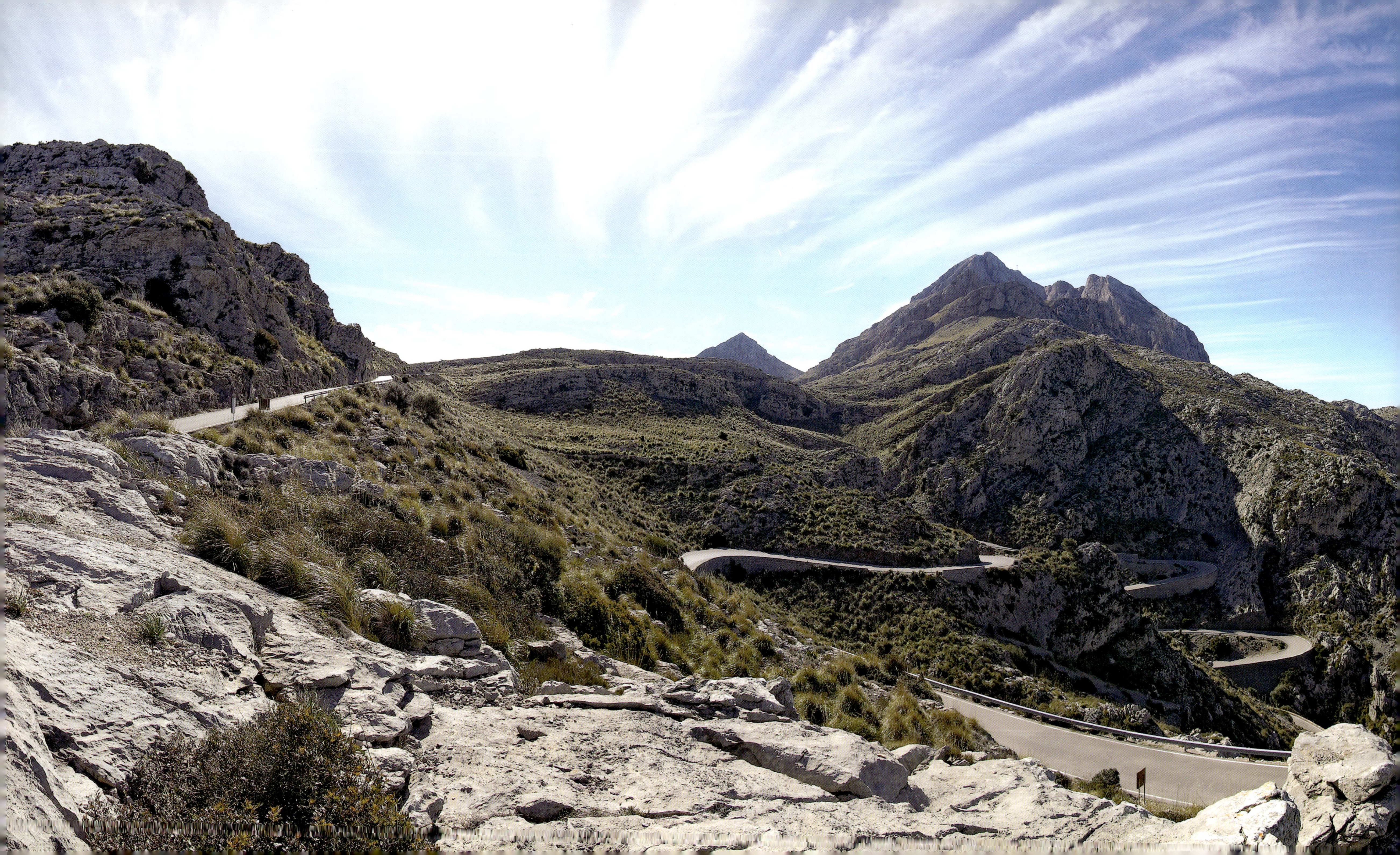

Mirador – Nus de sa Corbata

In earlier days, the tiny village of Sa Calobra could only be reached by see or on a very difficult round through the Torrent de Pareis. In 1932, the Italian engineer Antonio Paretti planned a masterpiece of road construction and built the serpentine road PMV 2141 (previous 360° panoramic photo) through the mountain range of without the use of machines. On a stretch of 12 km, the road covers more than 800 m in height with 12 hairpin curves. The two ends of the road are only 4 km apart, if measured as the crow flies. By Sa Moleta, he built his famous "tie knot", the "Nus de sa Corbata". There, the road traverses a rock ledge of 8 m in a 270° curve by crossing under itself. 31,000 m³ of rock had to be moved to build this part of the road.

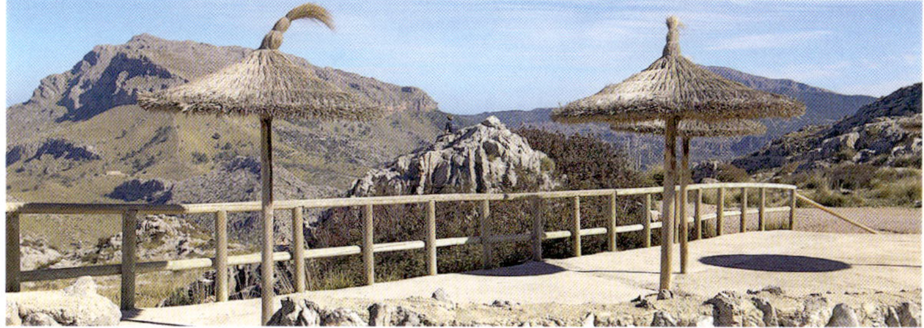

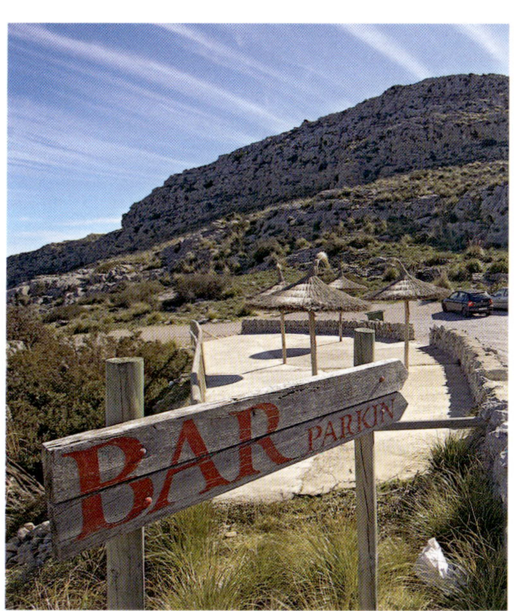

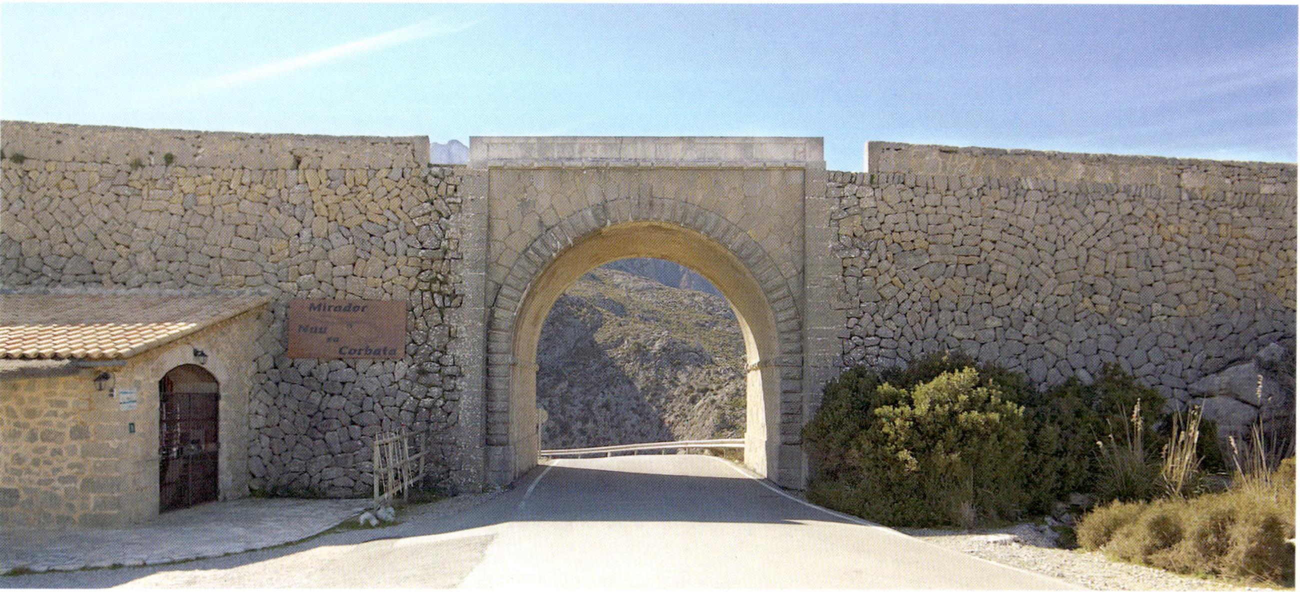

Alongside the serpentine road PMV 2141.

360° panoramic photo: Paretti's „tie knot", the „Nus de sa Corbata

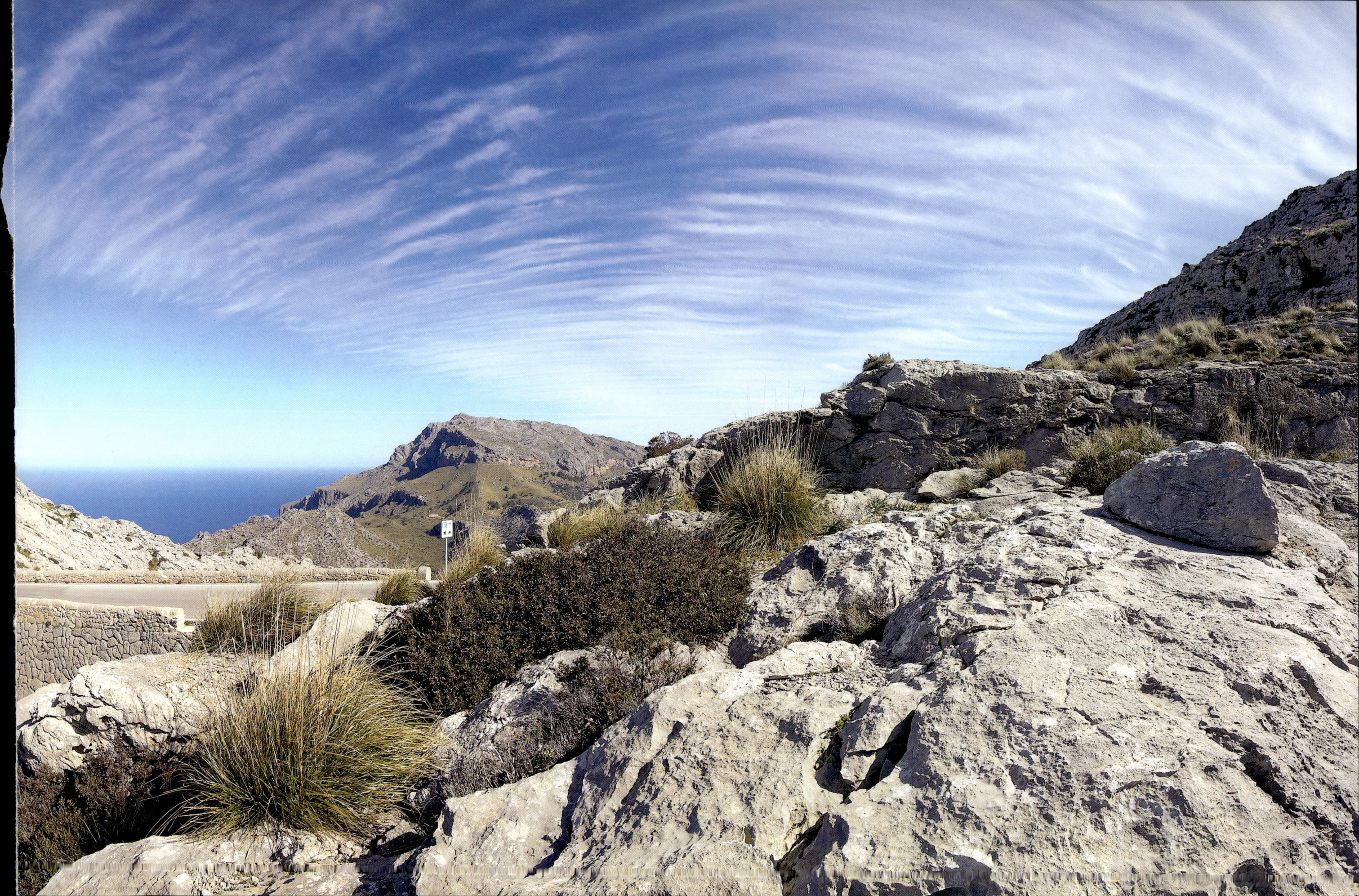

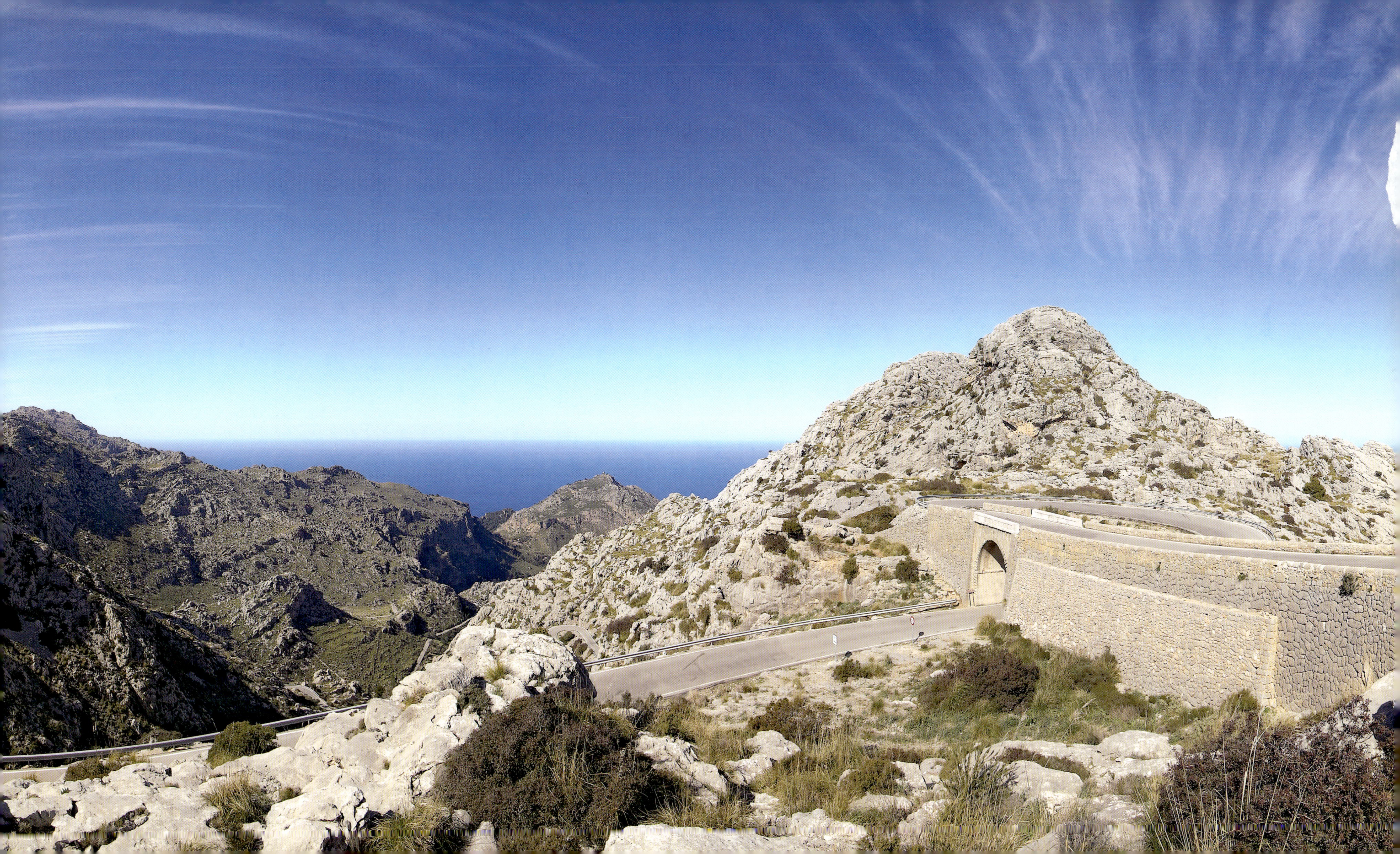

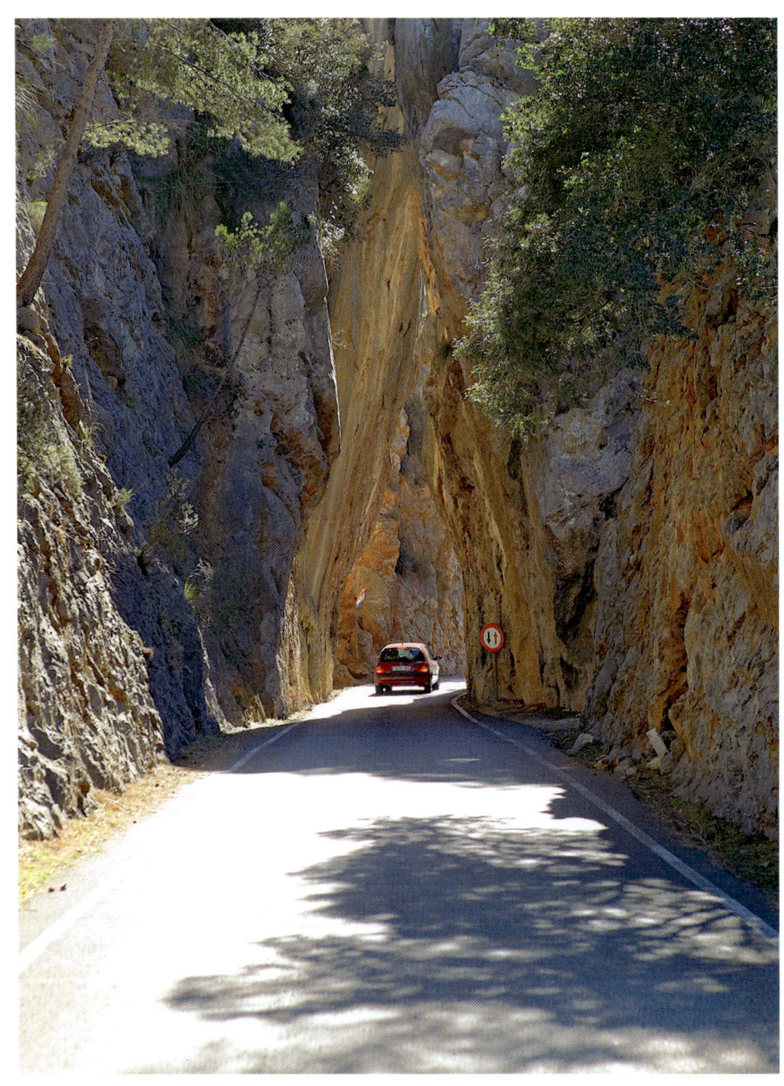

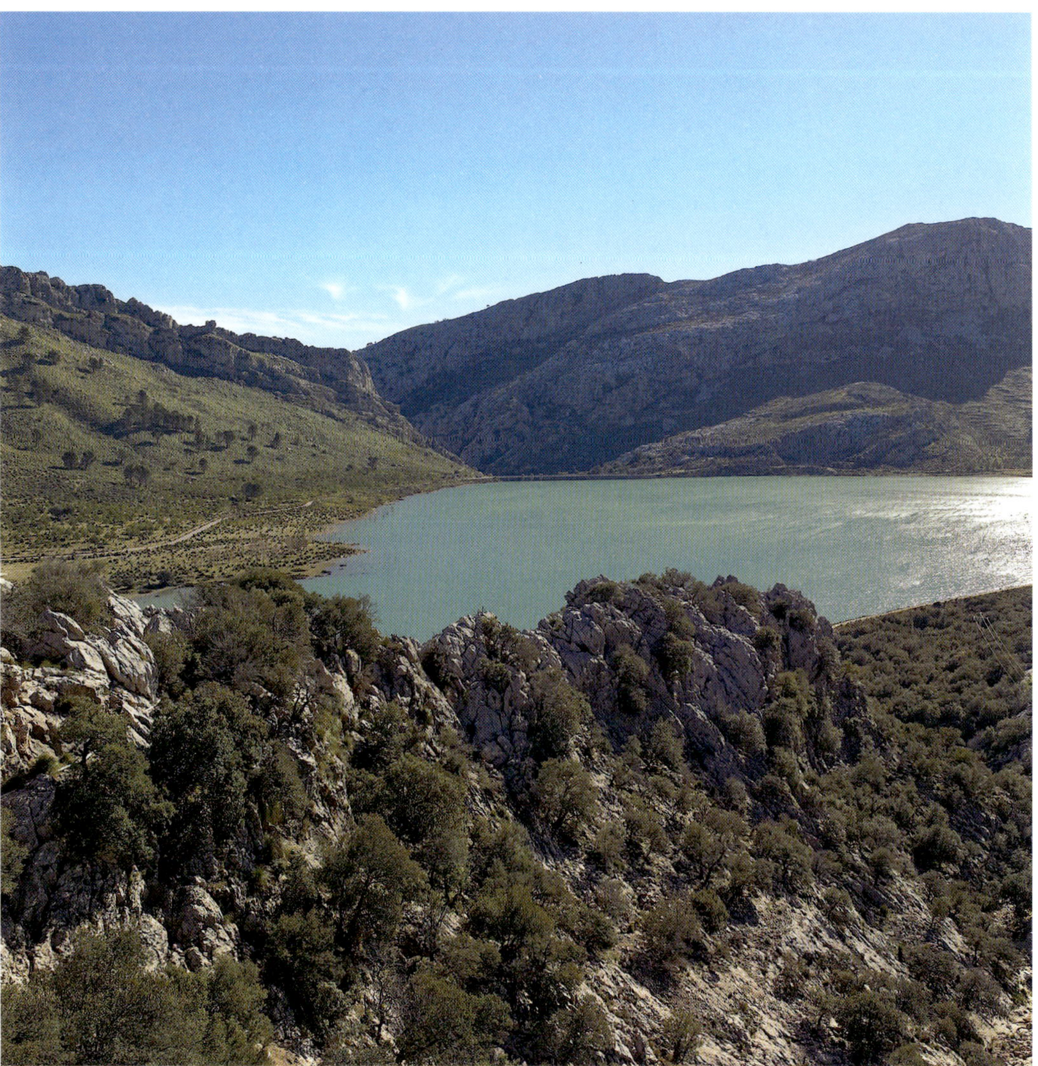

Road to Sa Calobra; Reservoir Embalse de Cuber

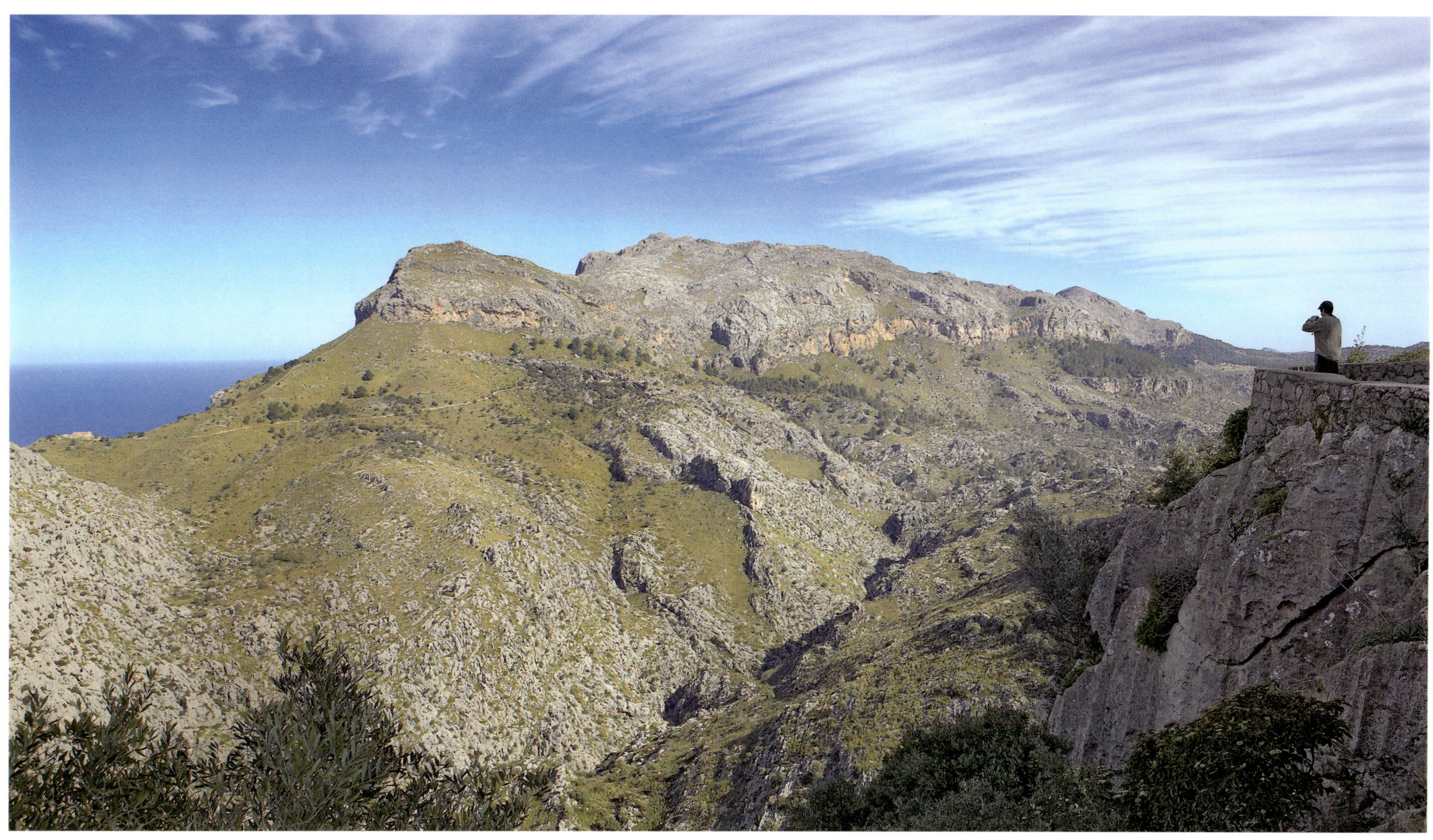

View of the mountains of the Serra Tramuntana

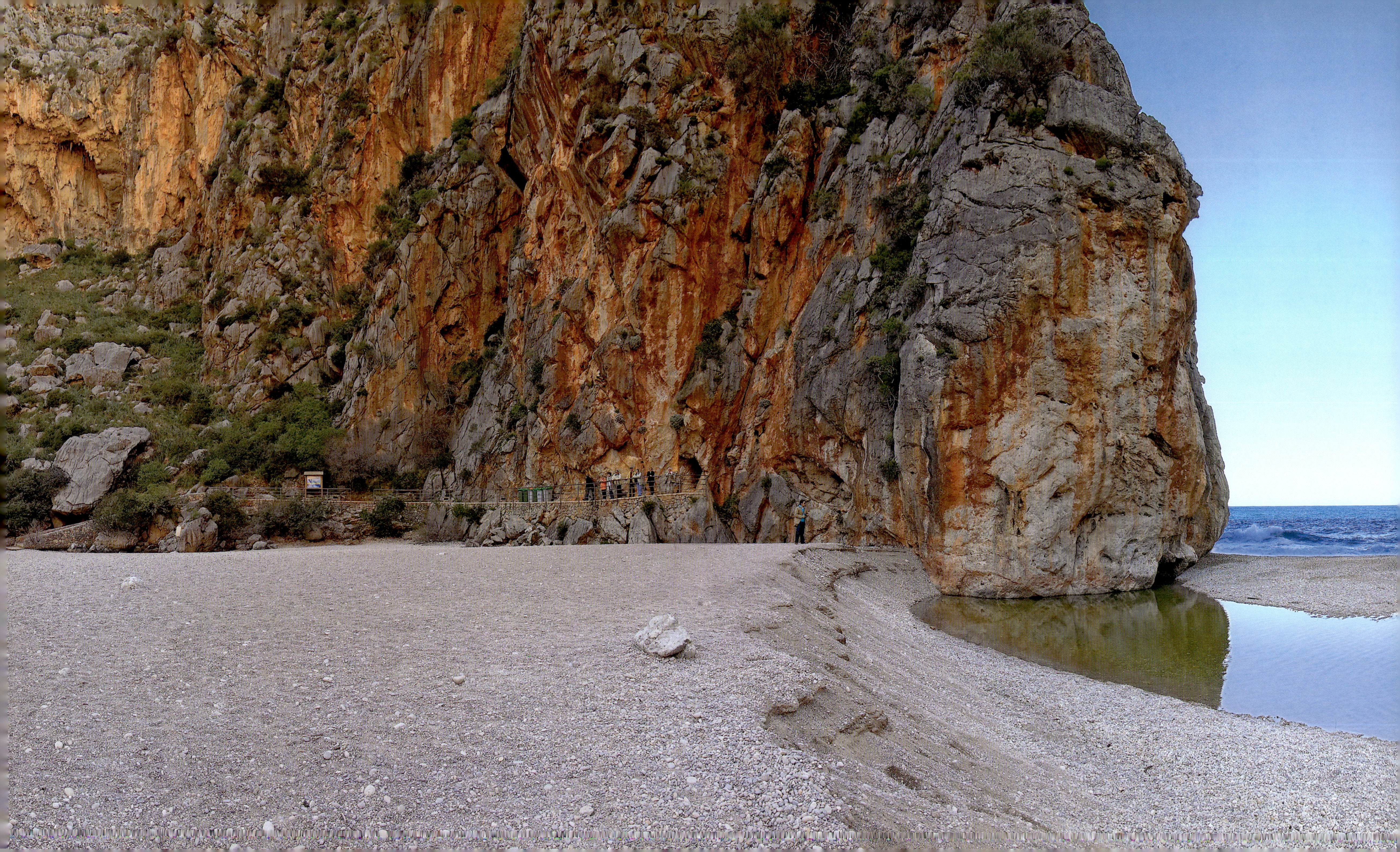

SA CALOBRA

Torrent de Pareis

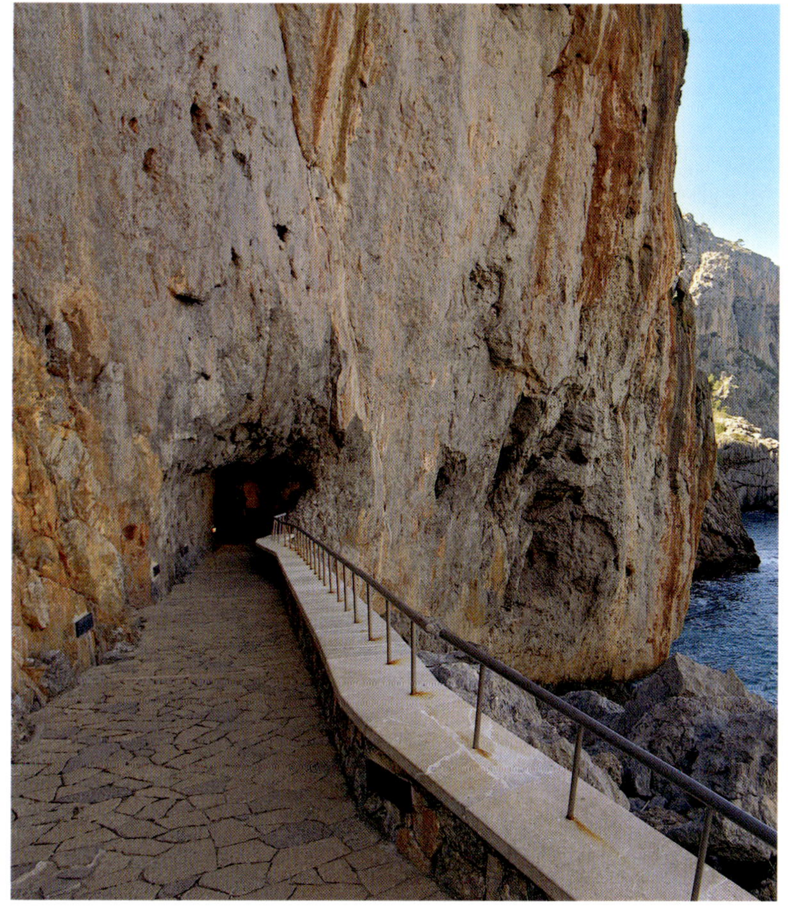

Majorca's most popular day trip destination is the bay of Sa Calobra, which can be reached on an idyllic drive through the ragged landscape of the Serra Tramuntana. Coming from the south, you pass the Puig Major (1,445 m) and two reservoirs, before reaching the pebble beach with a length of 50 km. From the bay, you can reach the 4 km long Torrent de Pareis, cut into the rock by the streams of the Serra from the Lucc monastery towards the sea. The "paradise canyon", whose jagged rock walls rise up to a height of 400 m, is one of the most famous canyons in the Mediterranean.

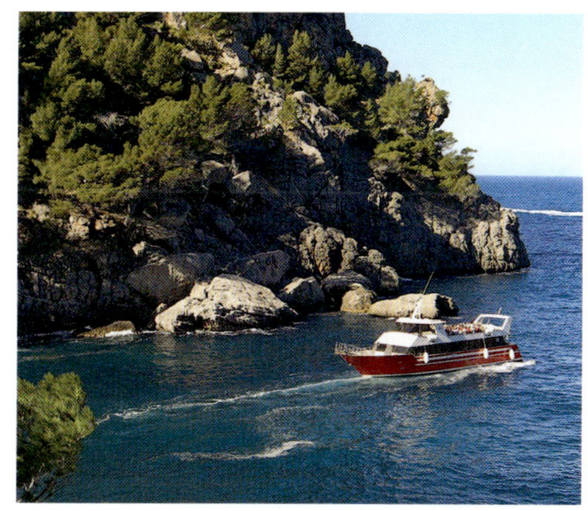

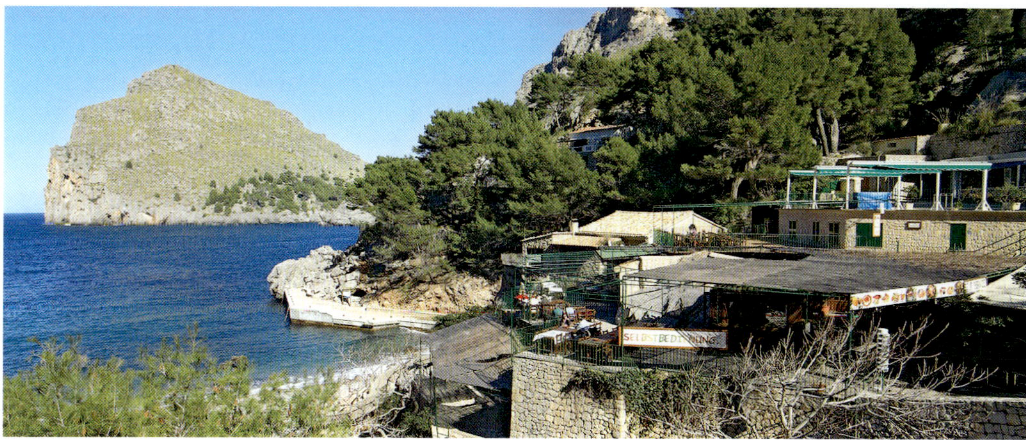

Cala de Sa Calobra

360° panoramic photo: Sa Calobra bay and the Torrent de Pareis

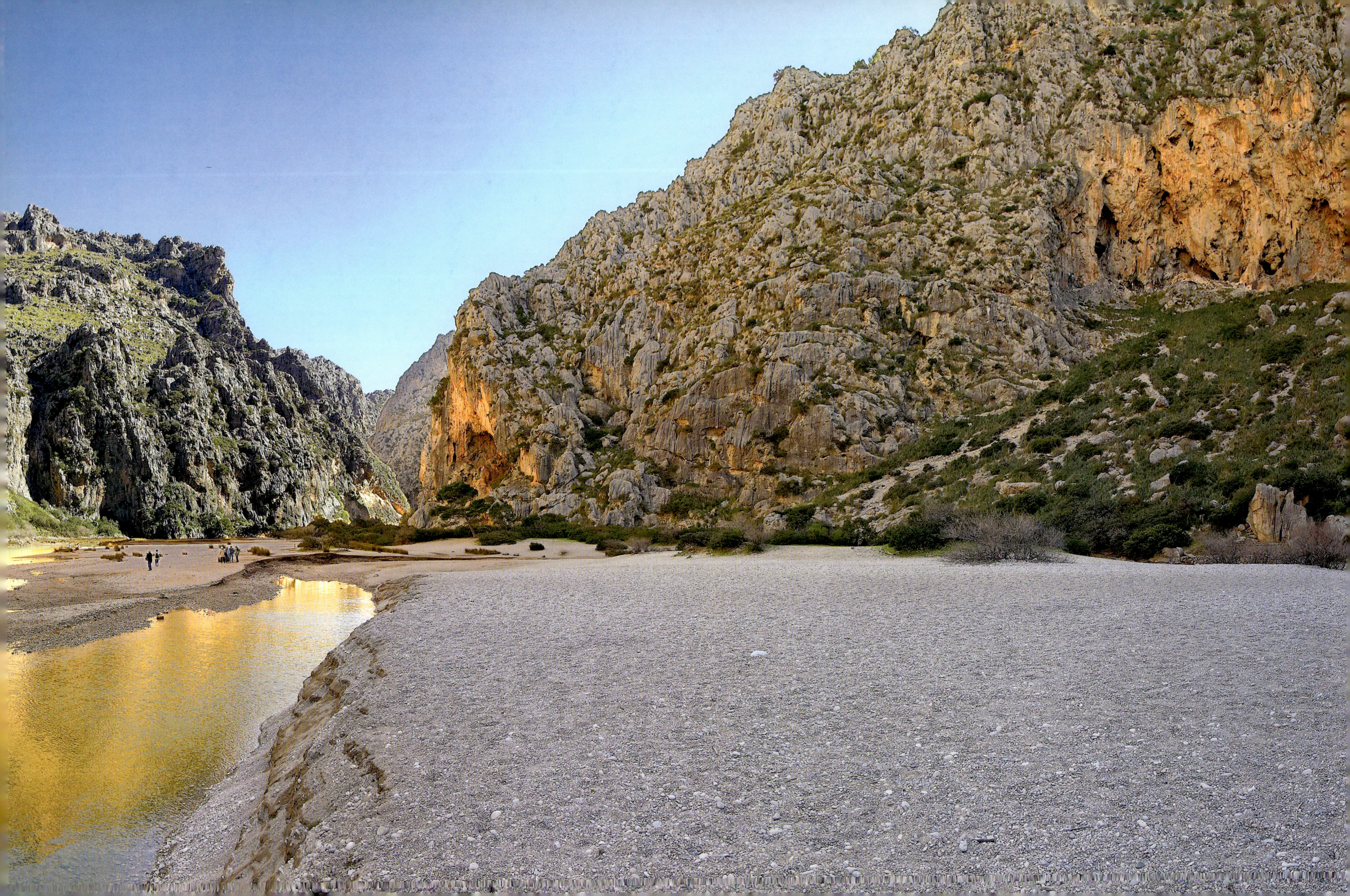

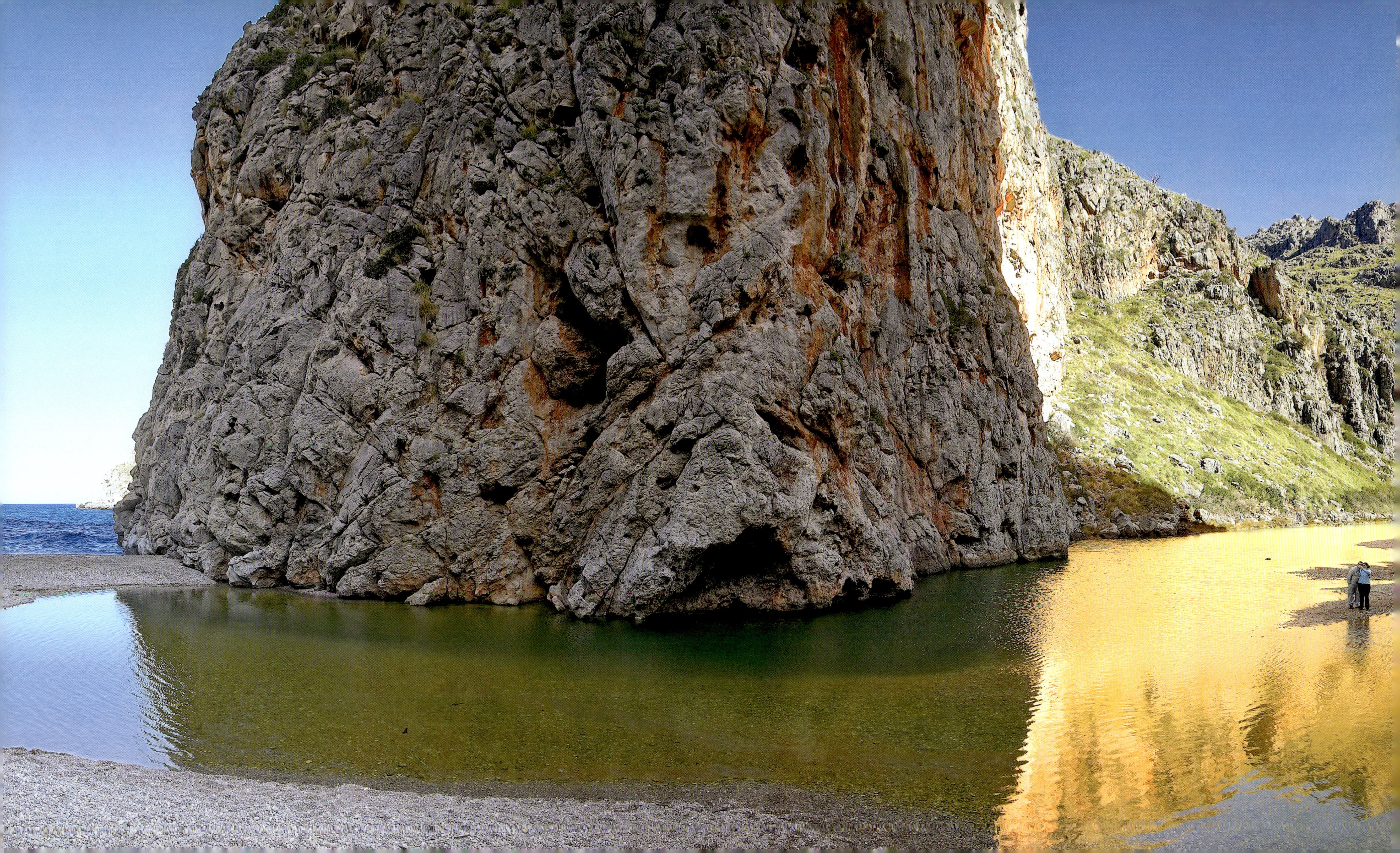

Manacor is Majorca's third-biggest town. It received its town charter from Jaime II. in 1300. The first traces of human settlement date back to pretalayotic times, evident in the prehistoric Talayot settlement "Hospitalet Vell". A few historic buildings from the days of the city's foundation still survive. One of the oldest landmarks is the church "Son Peretó" from the 5th and the tower "Torre dels Enagistes" from the 14th century. The city's development was influenced by the foundation of the monastery "Sant Vicenç Ferrer", which was taken over by the government in 1835. Many windmills once characterized the city, with the mill "Moli en Polit" from the 19th century still standing today. The Historicist church of "Nostra Senyora dels Dolors" was built in the late 19th century. Not far from there, you can find the caves "Coves del Drac".

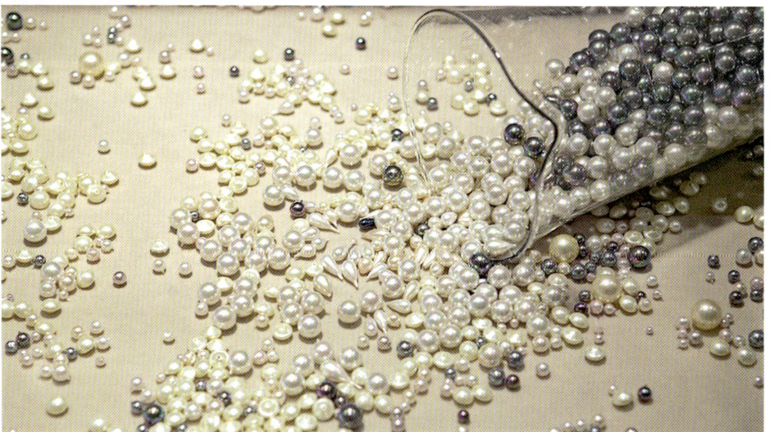

Pottery has a long tradition in Manacor, and since 1948, the famous "Majòrica" beads are produced here. They were developed in 1897 in Barcelona by the German Friedrich Hugo Heusch. The core of the beads is hardened at high pressure, then dipped up to 30 times into a mixture of fish scales and sea sand.

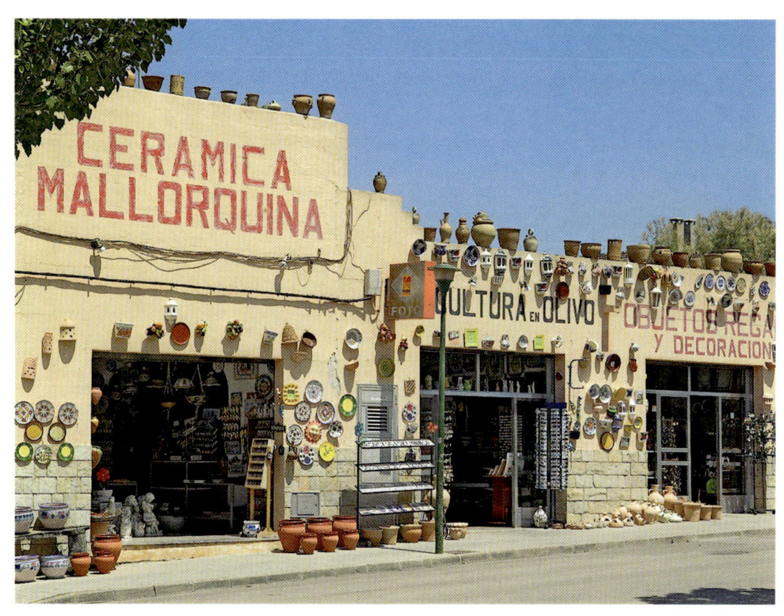

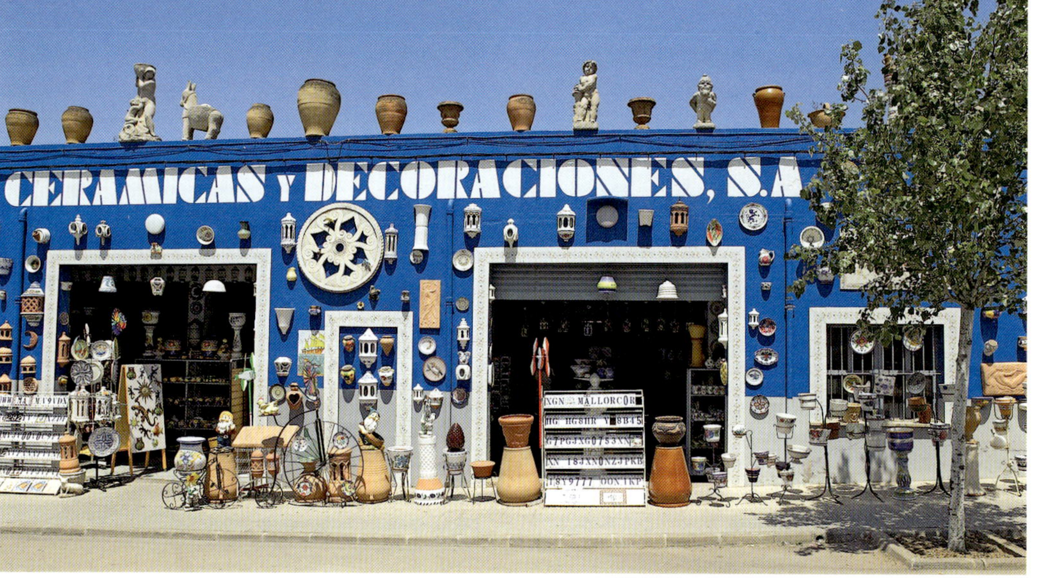

Potteries in Manacor

On the way from Manacor to Palma, you pass Algaida and Majorca's oldest glassworks. In the workshop of the Gordiola family, you can watch glass blowers produce beautiful, artistic pieces, which are offered for sale in the shop on the premises. Glass blowing is one of Majorca's old arts and crafts traditions. Since 1719, the Gordiola's company has been manufacturing figurines, vases, souvenirs and other glass objects. The workshop is located in a replicated castle. In 1975, a museum was added to display the family's collection of glass art from different eras in numerous showcases.

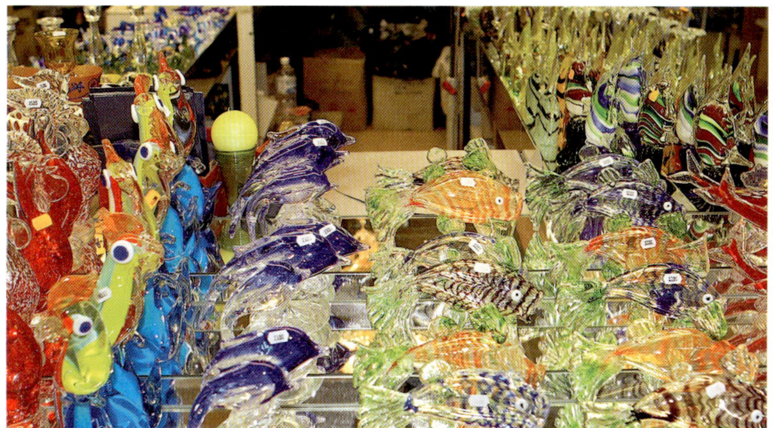

Algaida was first documented in 1232, famous for its table mountain Puig de Randa, the location of three monasteries. On the lower terrace stands the "Santuario de Nuestra Señora de Gracia" from the 15th century, the second has the "Santuario de Sant Honorat" from the 14th century, and on top of the mountain the "Santuario Nuestra Señora de Cura". The latter is a Franciscan hermitage and was the home of Ramon Llull (1232-1315), Majorca's great religious philosopher, scholar and logician who was the author of 260 works and the founder of Catalan literature.

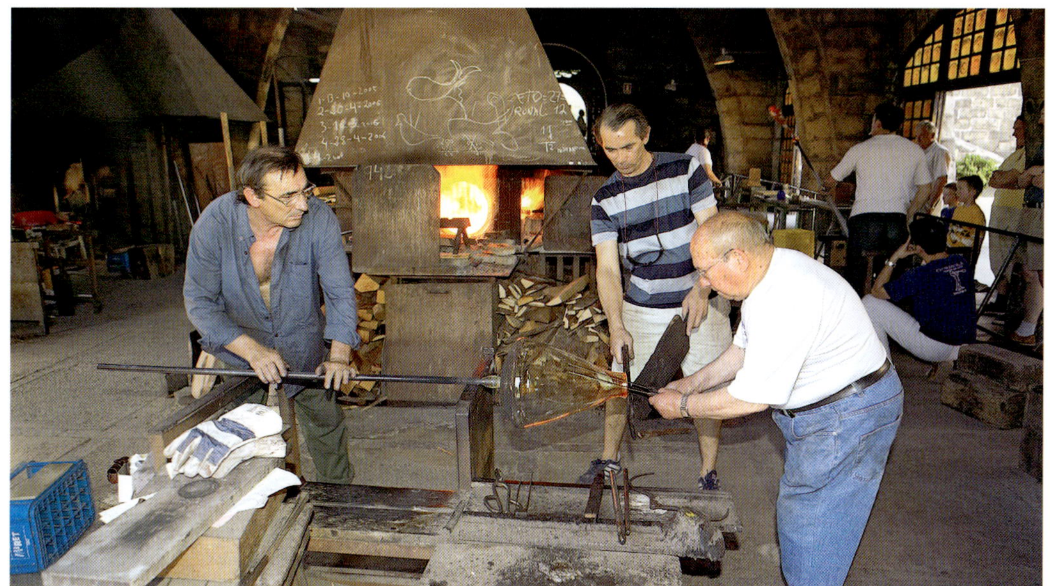

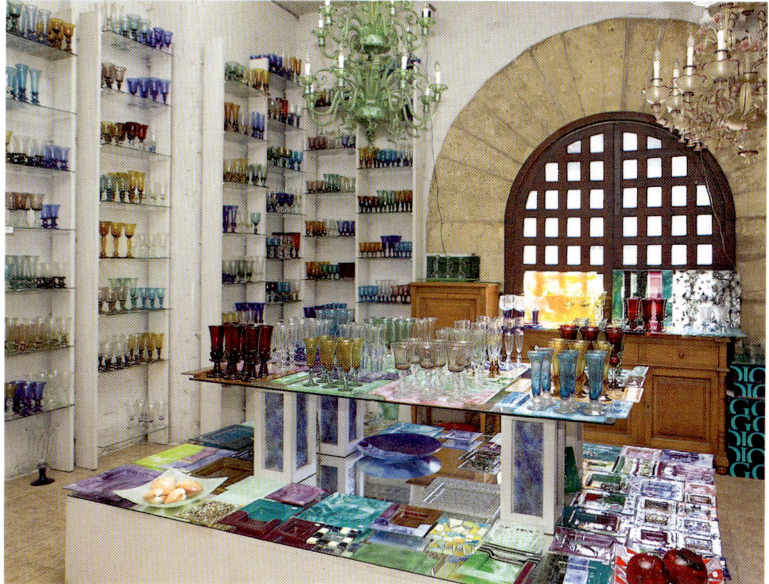

Majorca's oldest glassblower's workshop.

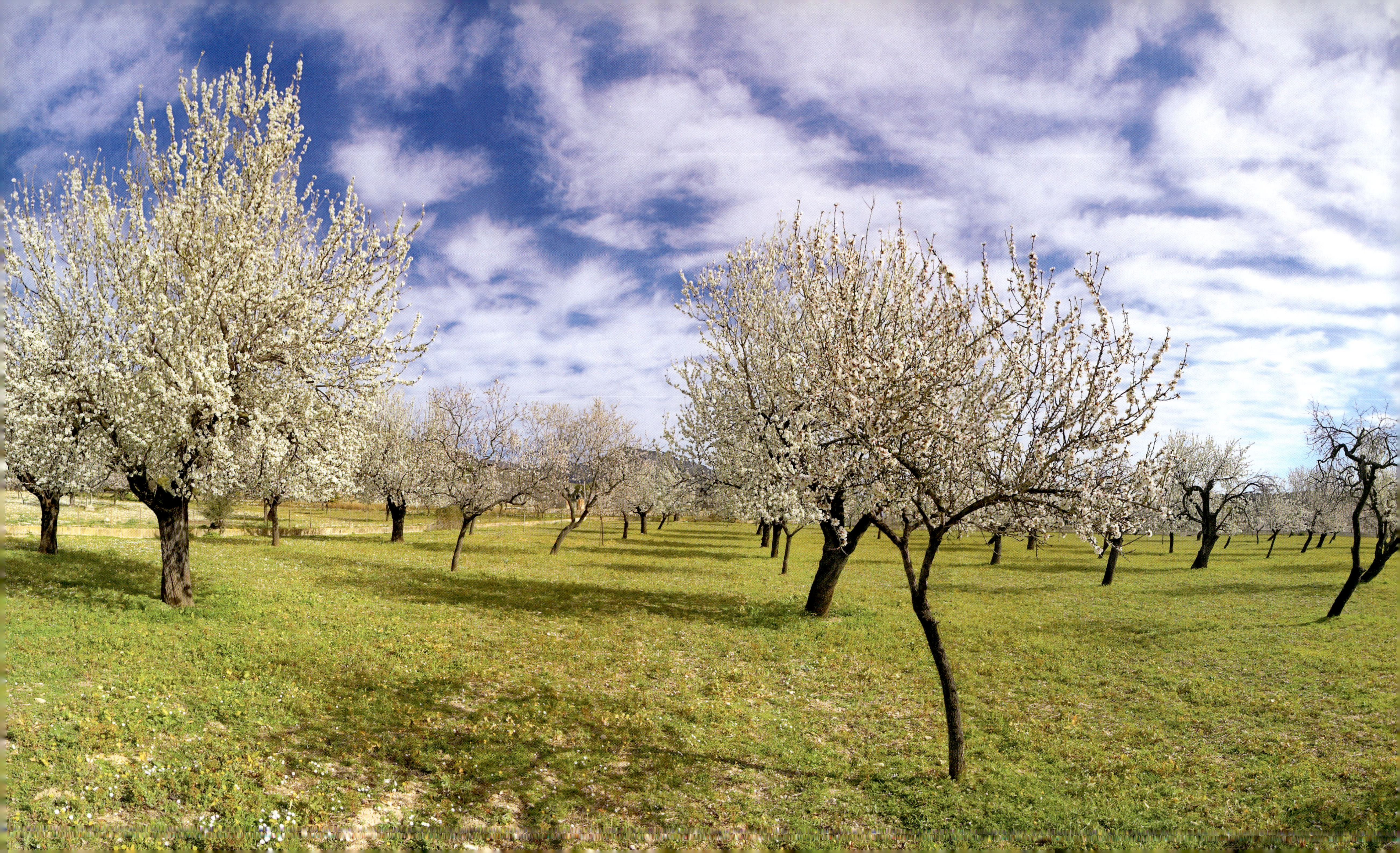

Almond bloom

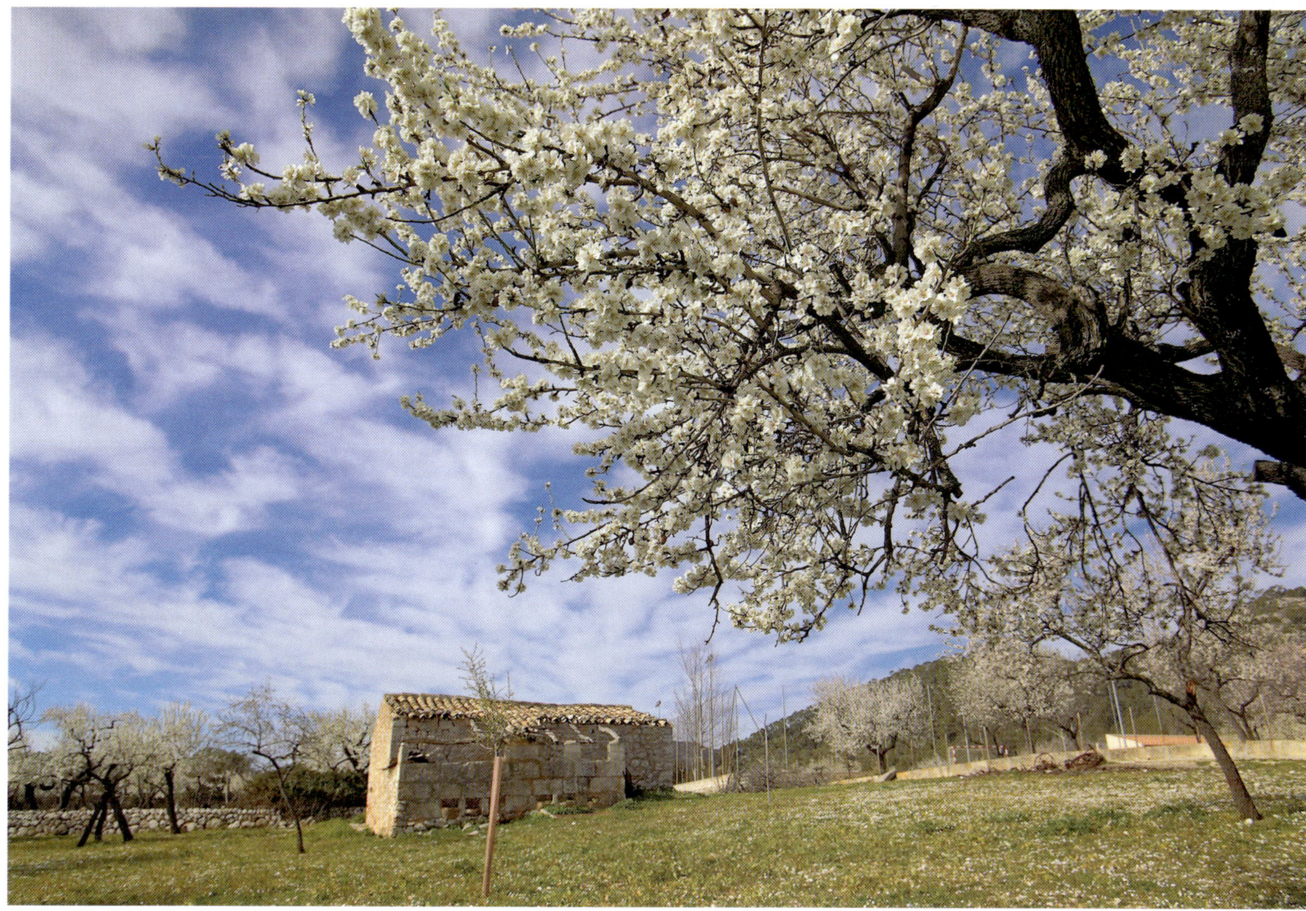

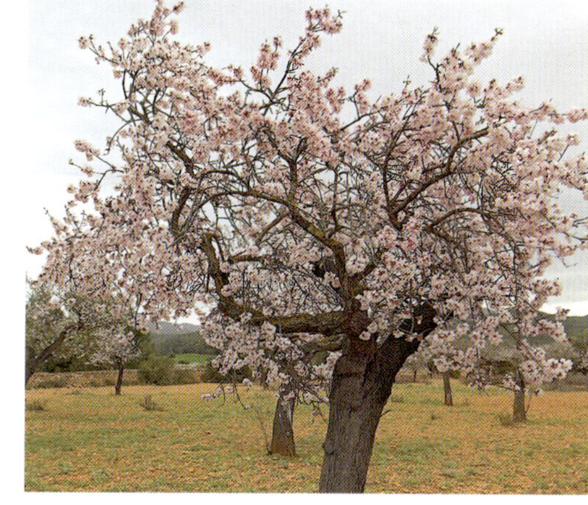

Between January and late February, about seven million blooming almond trees transform the island's landscape into something magical. The white or pink blossoms with their sweet fragrance attract countless tourists, thus being an important part of the local economy with more than their fruit. Almonds with the seal of "Ametla de Majorca" are characterized by their unique taste and soft kernel. Almonds receiving this quality seal are subjected to rigorous quality controls and exported in great quantities all over the world. The "Gato de Almendra" is one of the island's most famous specialties.

Almond bloom

360° panoramic photo: Almond bloom

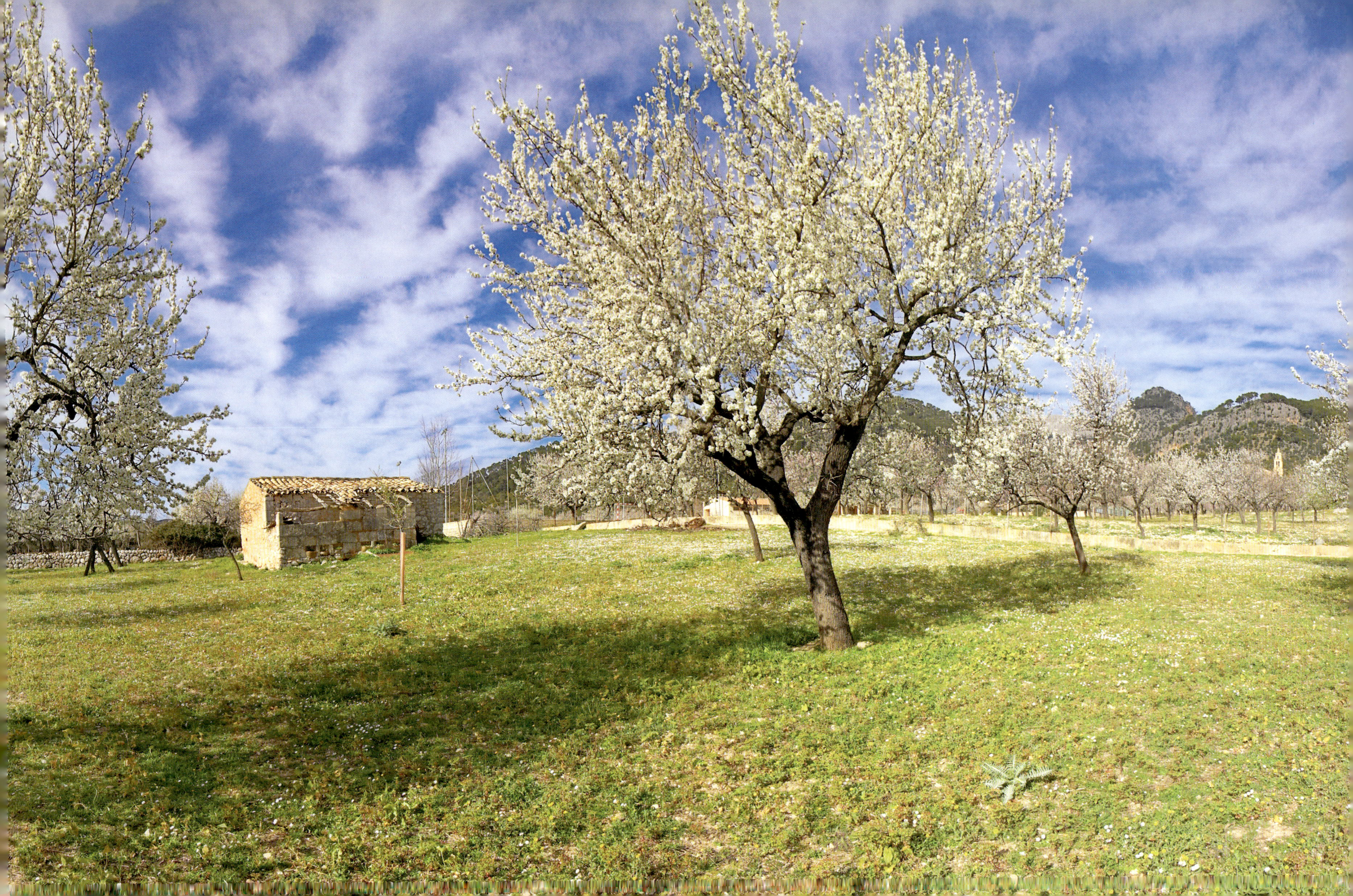

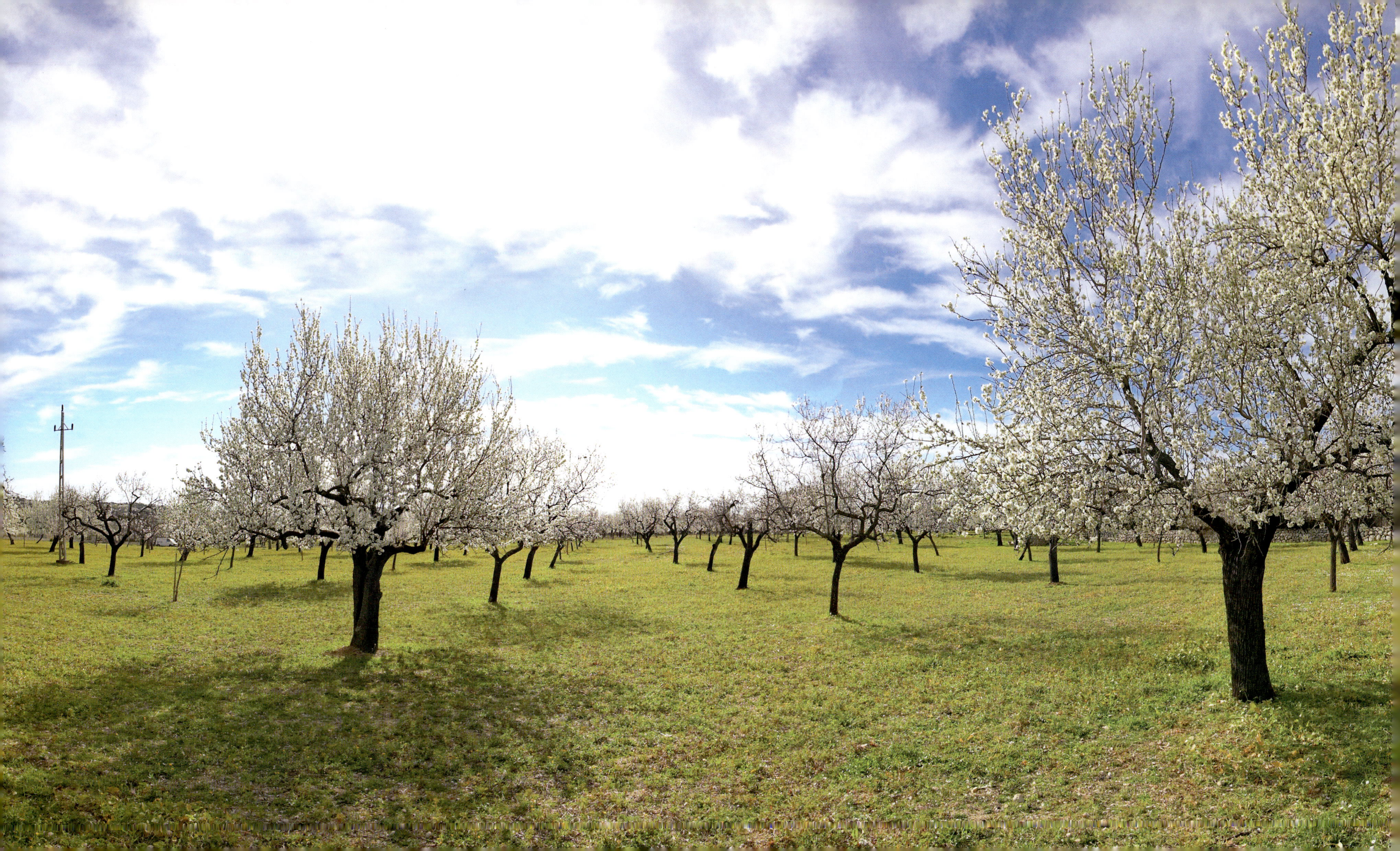

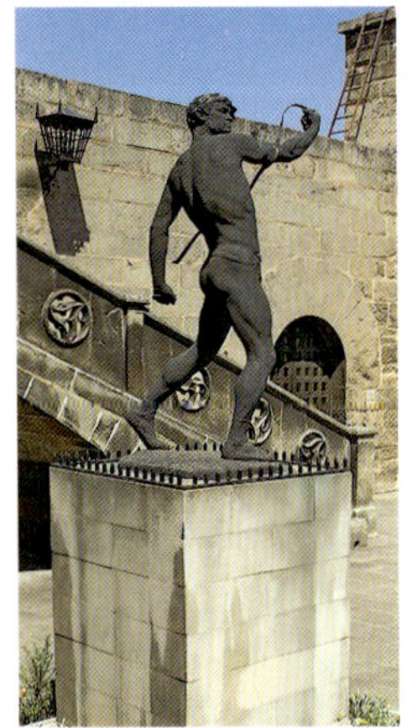
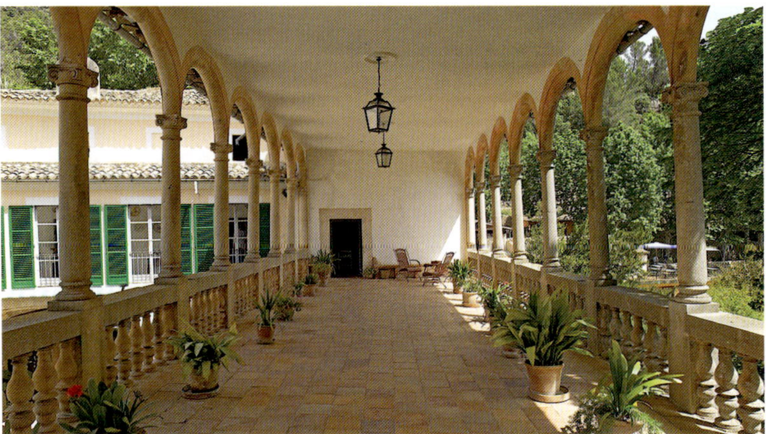
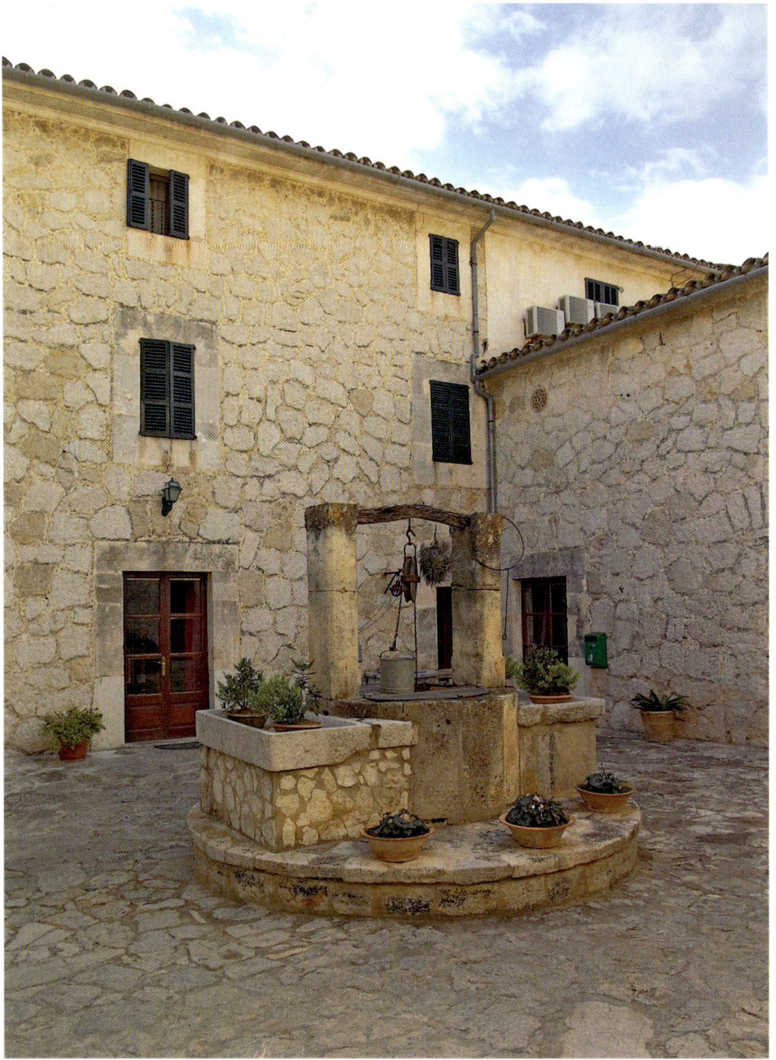
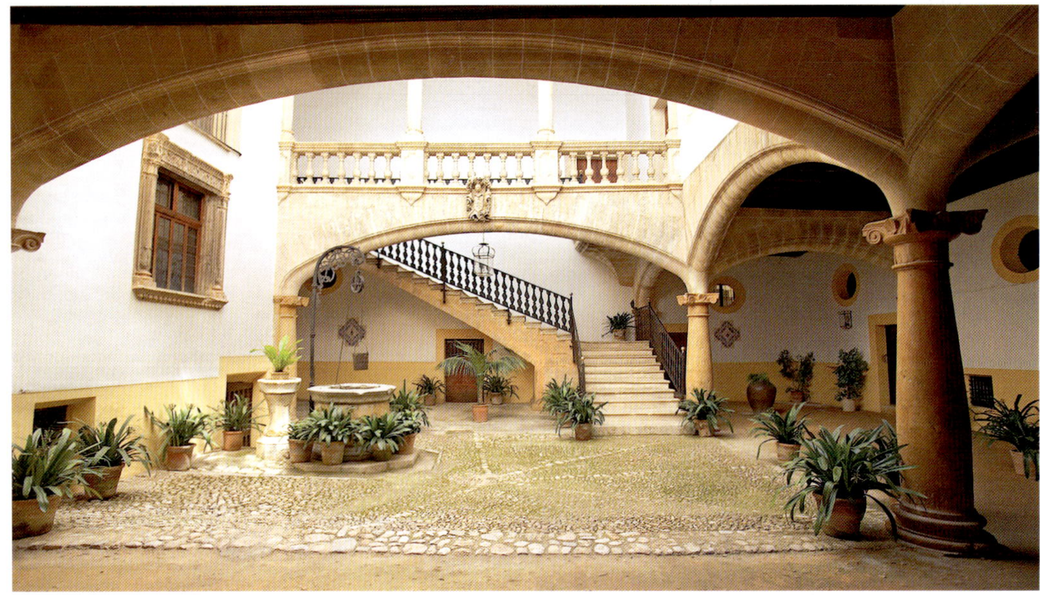

Majorcan fincas

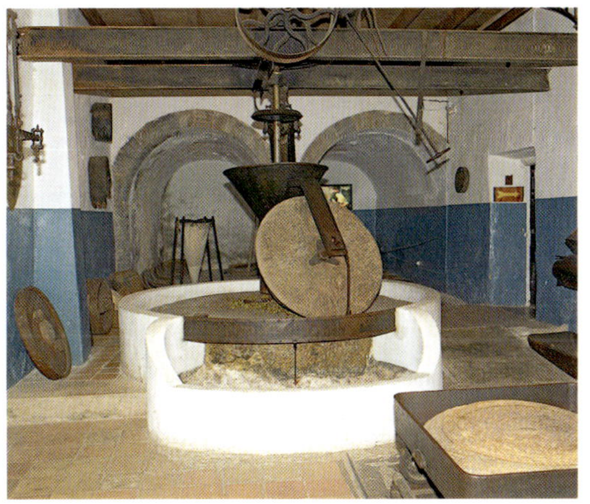

The original fincas look back on a long history, often dating back 300 years and more. Especially on Majorca, new buildings are being constructed that draw from the original style of the historic buildings.
Usually, a finca is an agricultural property with a house and farm land. But in tourism, the term often describes a rustic holiday home.
Apart from the Balearics, fincas can be found on the Canary Islands as well. The buildings often feature arcades and colonnades, rooms are designed to be rustic but very comfortable.

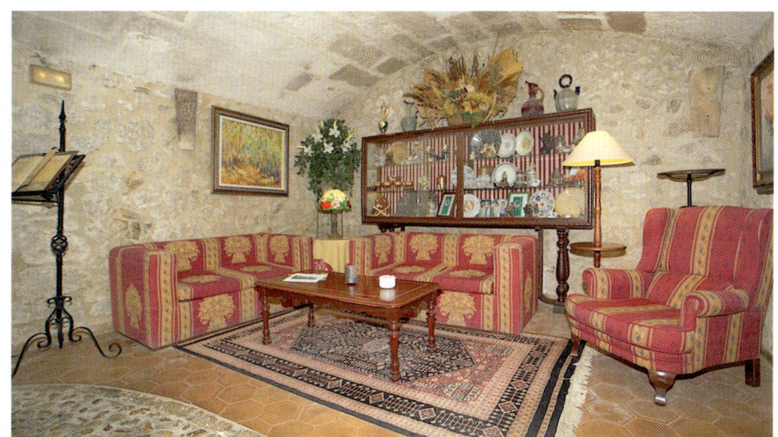

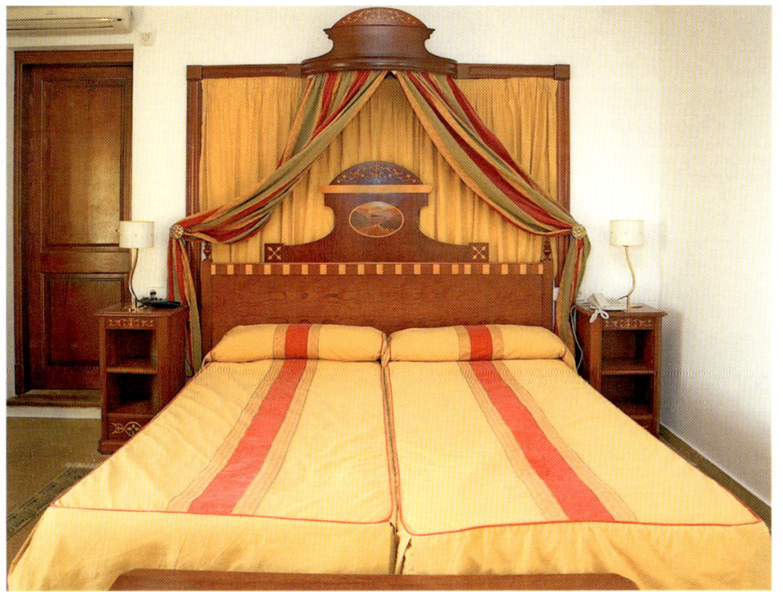

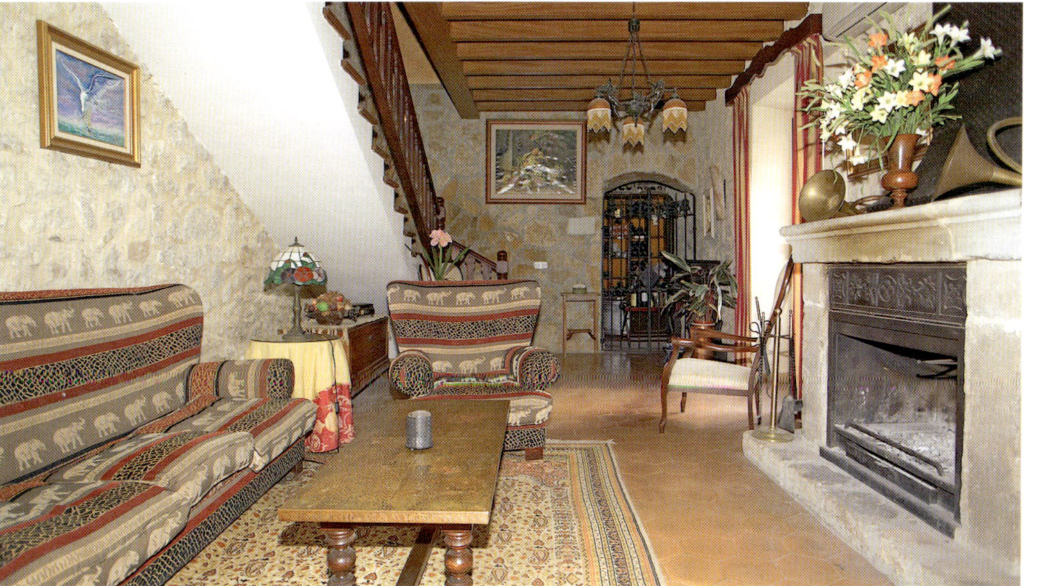

Majorcan fincas (interior).

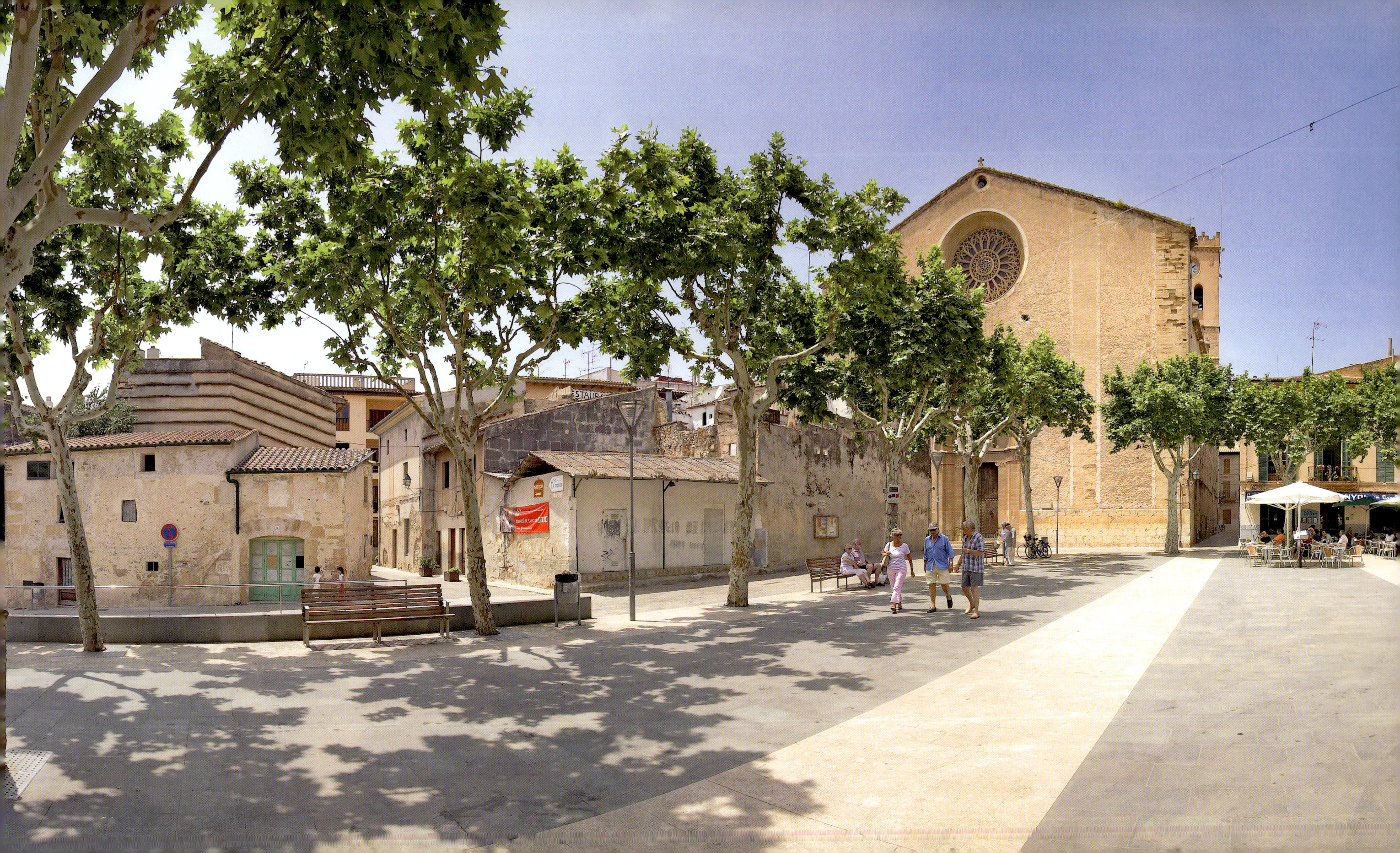

Plaça Major

The artists' village was founded by the Romans and is among Majorca's oldest settlements. One relic from those times can be found on the way out – the double arch bridge "Pont Romá" crossing the Torrent de Sant Jordi. The old part of the village is characterized by many narrow alleys. The shady, traffic-free Plaça Major is one of the town's most beautiful squares. On the square stands the parish church "Nuestra Señora de los Angeles", built in 1236 (previous 360° panoramic photo, centre). Many small shops sell crafts and other choice products, giving the town an air of prosperity. 365 steps lead up to a Baroque chapel, built in 1795 on the 170 m high Calvary Hill (photos this page), where you can also find a stone cross dating back to the 13th century. The hill offers a wonderful view of the city, the surrounding mountains and plains and the bay. Another interesting sight is the "Ermita de Nostra Senyora de Pruig" on the road to Palma.
Just a few kilometres outside of the town lies the marina Port de Pollença, a place that has kept its charm despite mass tourism, and a beautiful long, wide beach. The bay is bounded by the peninsulas Formentor and Victoria.

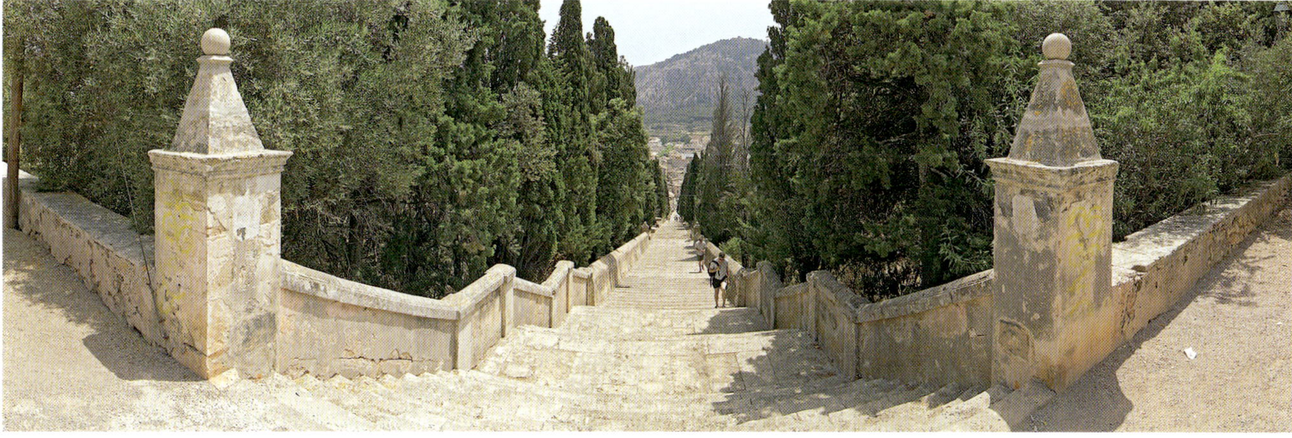

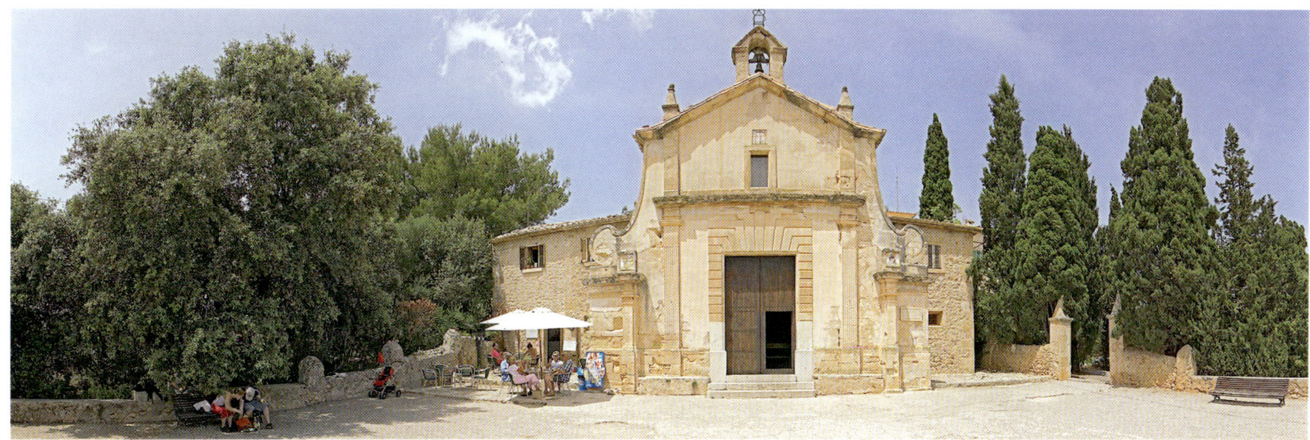

365 steps lead up Pollença's 170 m high Calvary Hill.

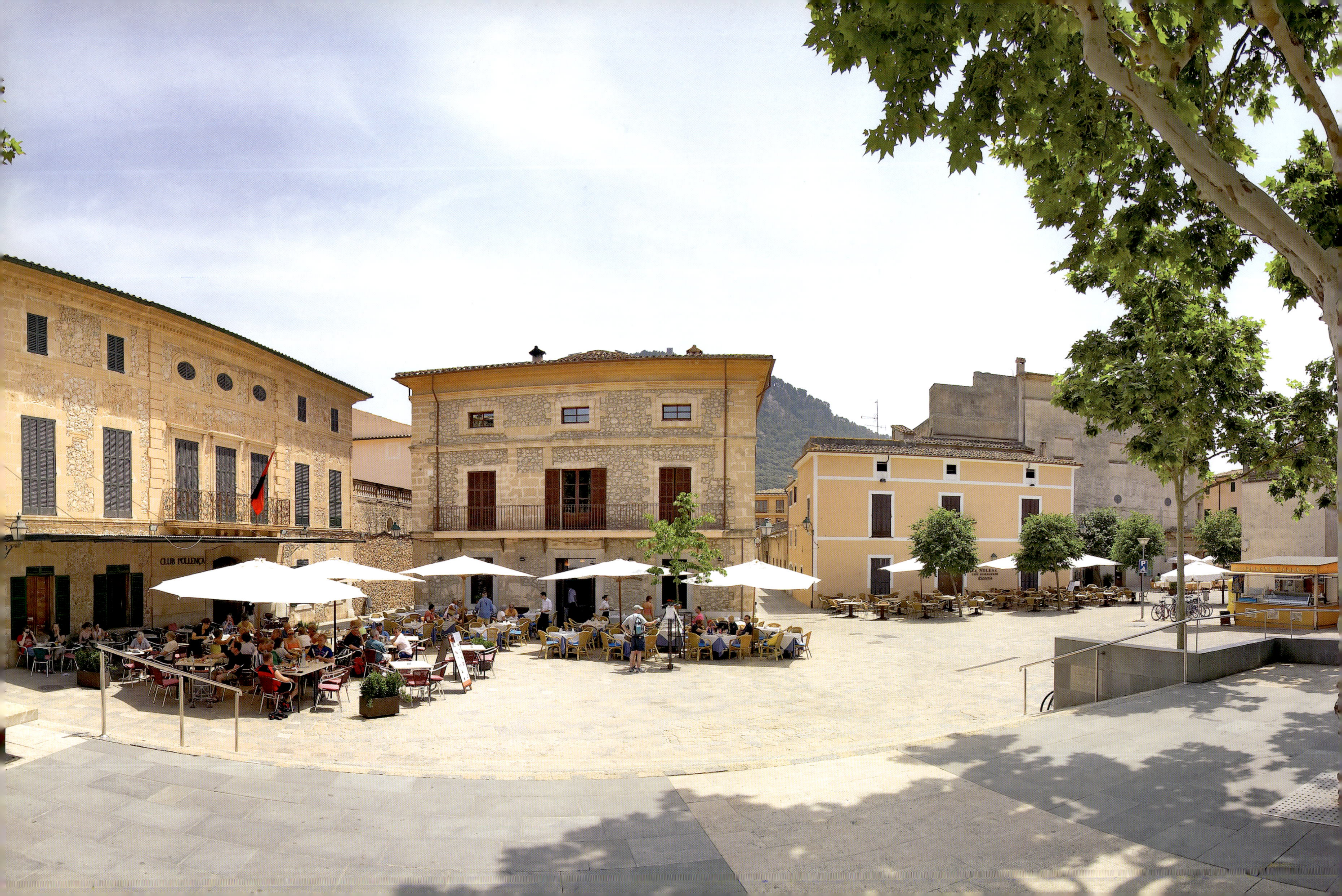
CLUB POLLENÇA

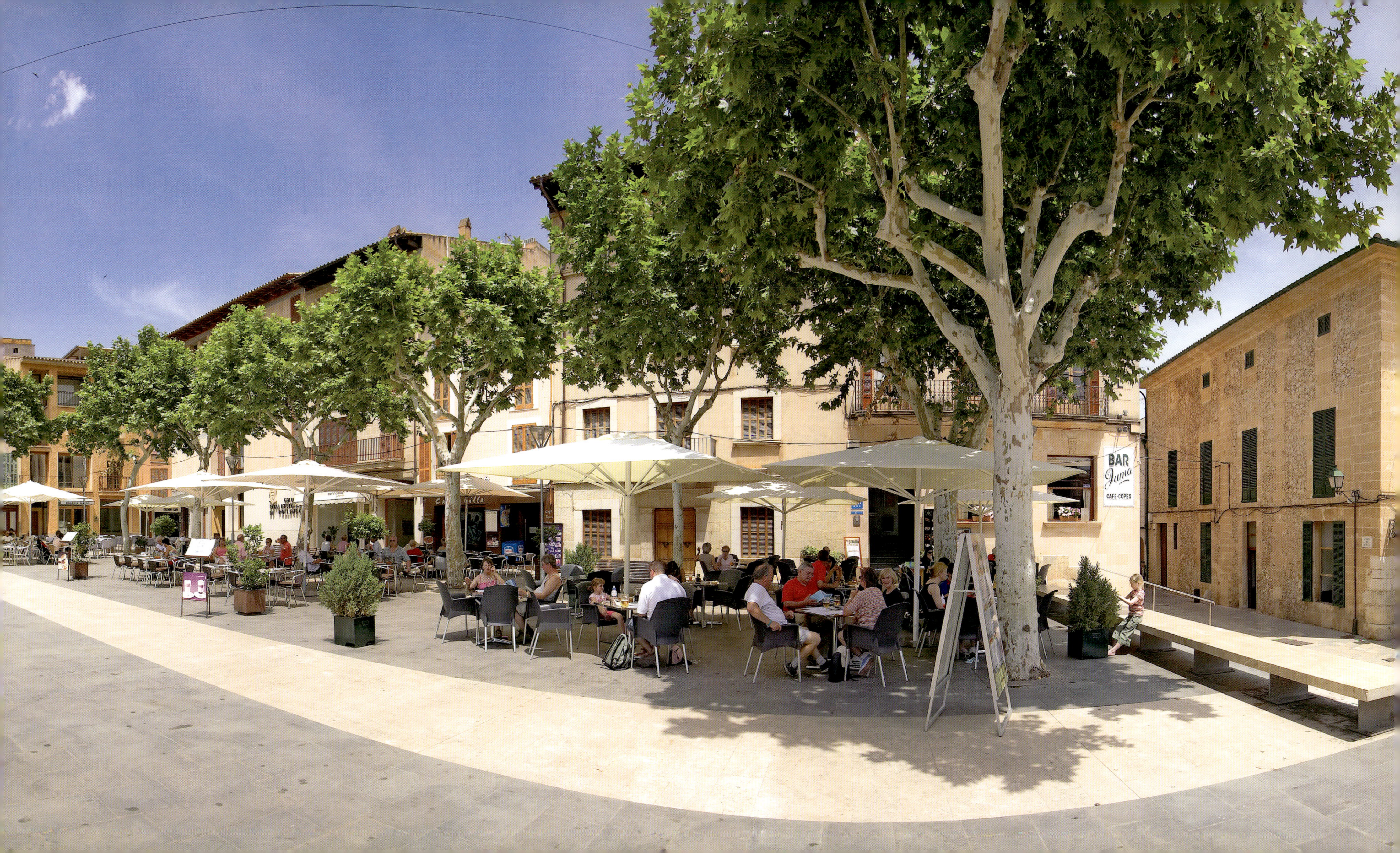
BAR
Juma
CAFE·COPES

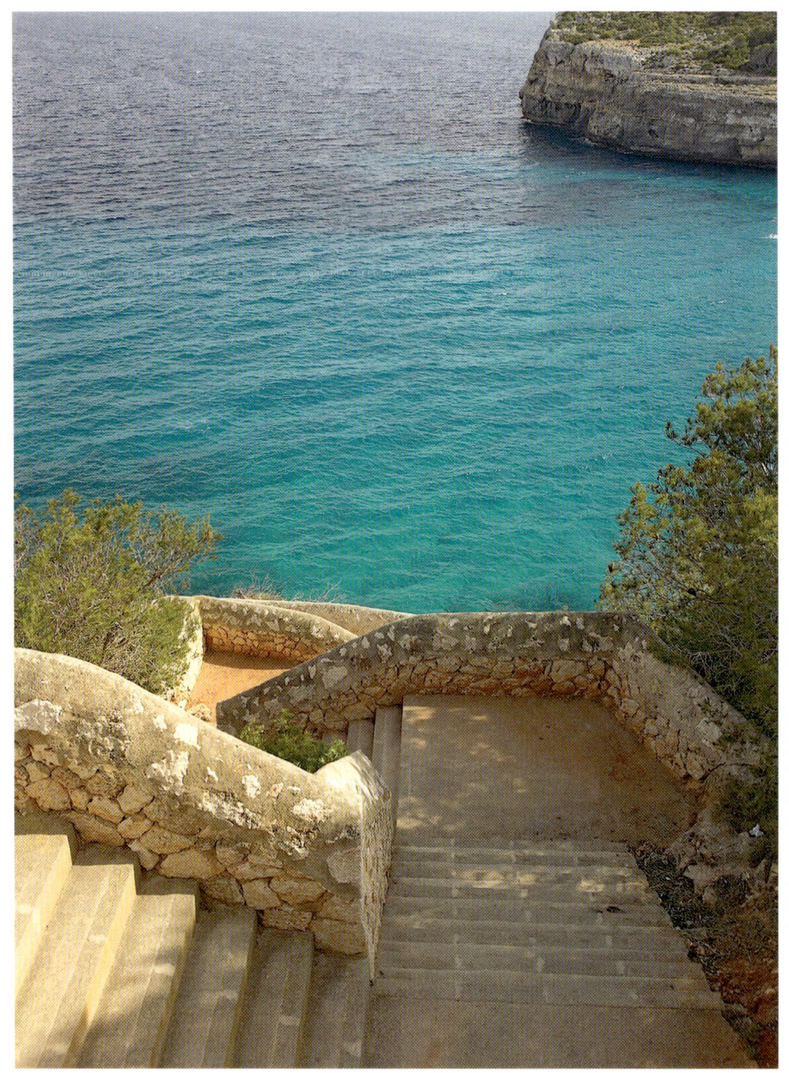

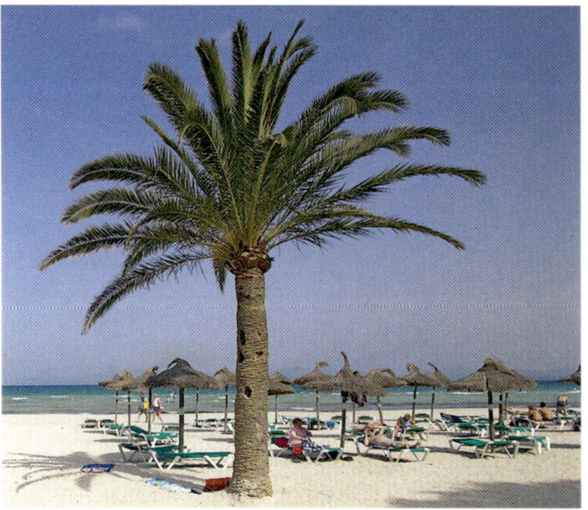

Majorca possesses countless beautiful beaches. On the east coast, located on a picturesque bay, lies the village of Cala Estany. Stone steps lead down to the ocean. Cala Mesquida is a natural beach in the north-east of the Balearic island. The bay of Cala Agulla, located in a part of Cala Rajada, is one of Majorca's most beautiful beaches. The beach of Alcúdia is especially suited for families. The coast of Es Trenc is surrounded by pine forests and dunes, offering perfect conditions for surfers. The beach with a length of 9 km today it is sometimes used as a movie location.

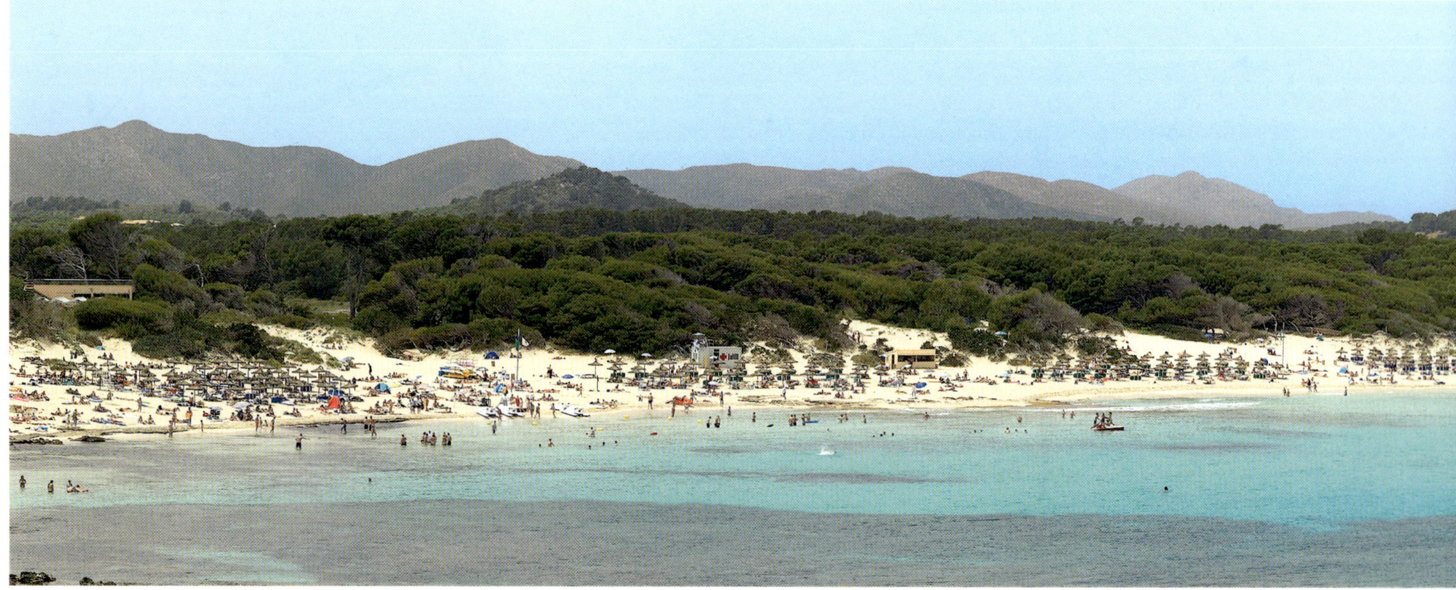

Cala Estany, Alcúdia beach; Cala Agulla

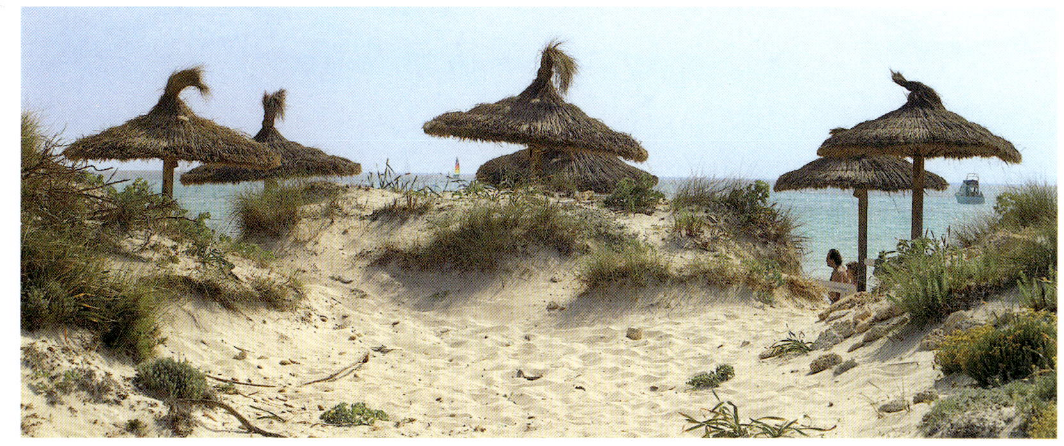

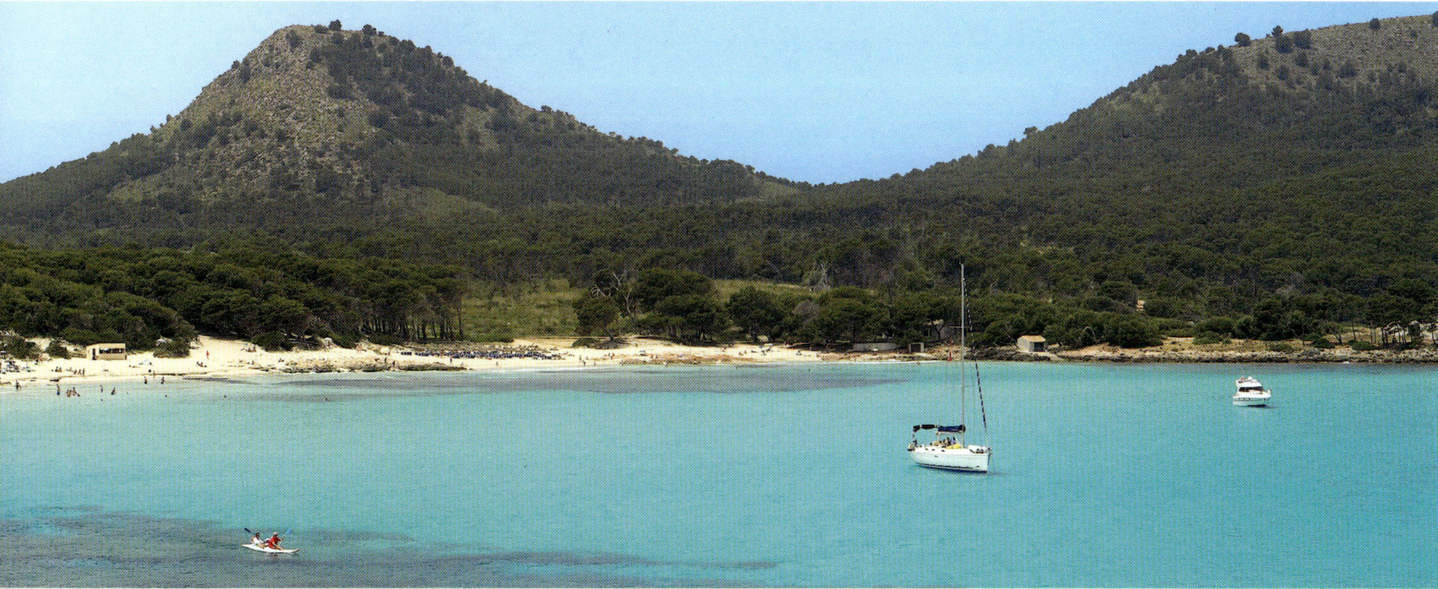

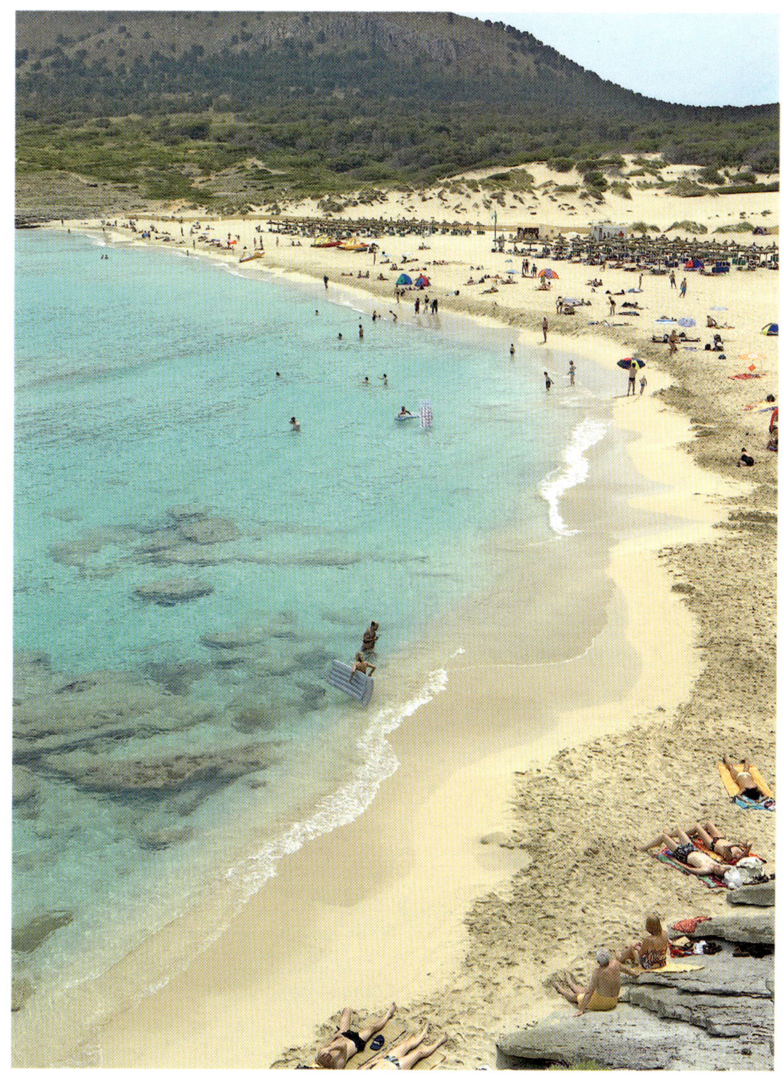

Es Trenc (top); Cala Mesquida (right).

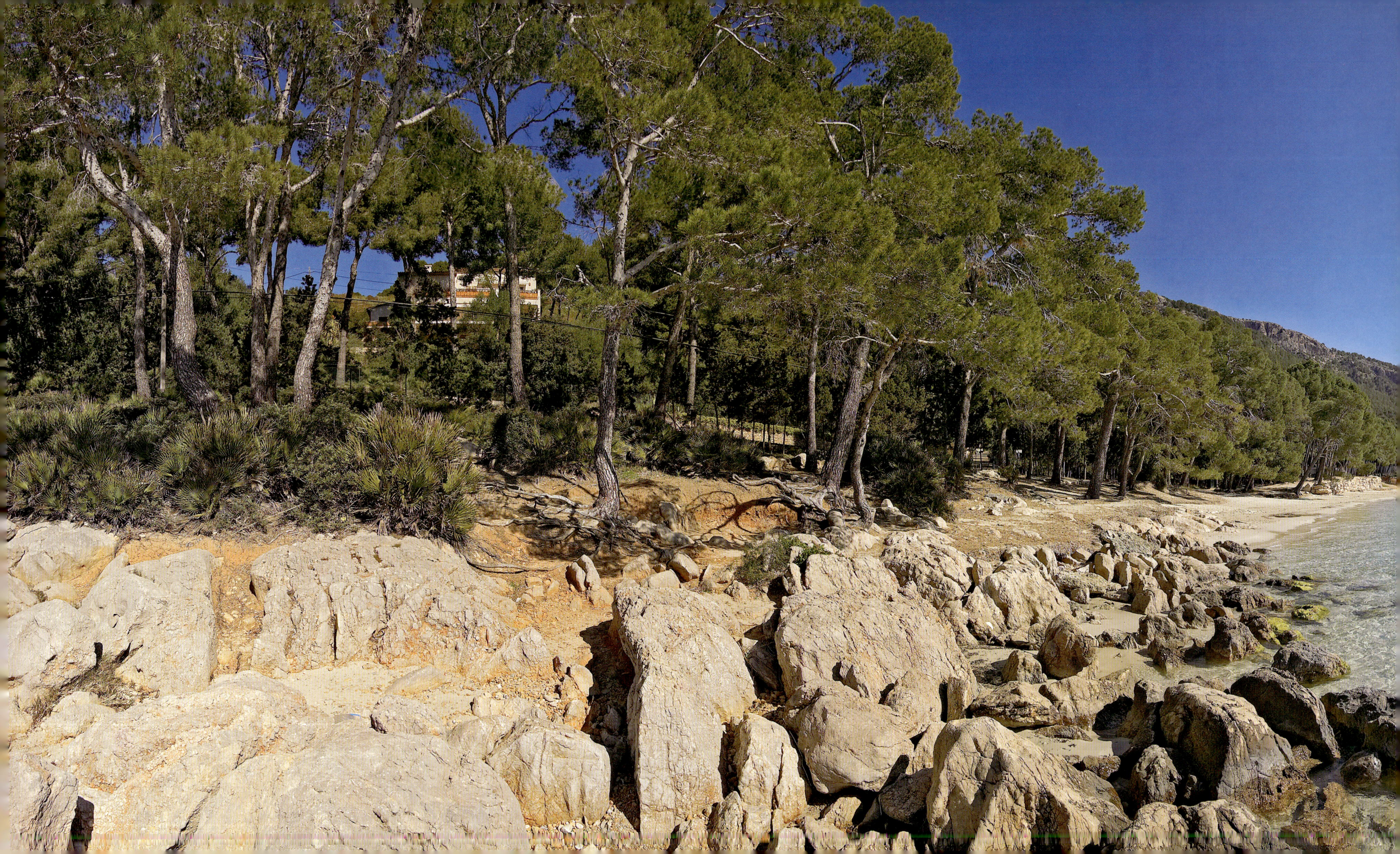

CAP FORMENTOR

Cala Pi de la Posada

The peninsula Formentor, also called "rendezvous of the winds" by the locals, is located on the north-east tip of Majorca. The outer edge of the peninsula is Cape Formentor with the Fumart (384 m), surrounded by the wonderful bays of Cala Figuera, Cala Murta and Cala Pi de la Posada (previous 360° panoramic photo).

The native Majorcans called the winds meeting at this point Tramuntana, Ponenet, Migjorn, Llevant, Gregal, Mestral, Llebetx and Xaloc. Many landscapes and mountain ranges derive their names from these winds, and they were very important for the simple life of the peninsula's inhabitants, because they planned the entire year around the winds.

The promontory offers a few lookout points with spectacular views. In 1892, people built stairs, walls and paths, as well as a lighthouse which is surrounded by rare protected plants. The peninsula used to belong to the poet Miquel i Llobera. After his death, it was divided into plots and sold. In 1928, art lover Adán Diehl built the Hotel Formentor on the long beach Platja de Formentor, which is now a meeting place for international celebrities. He uses his profits to patronize the arts.

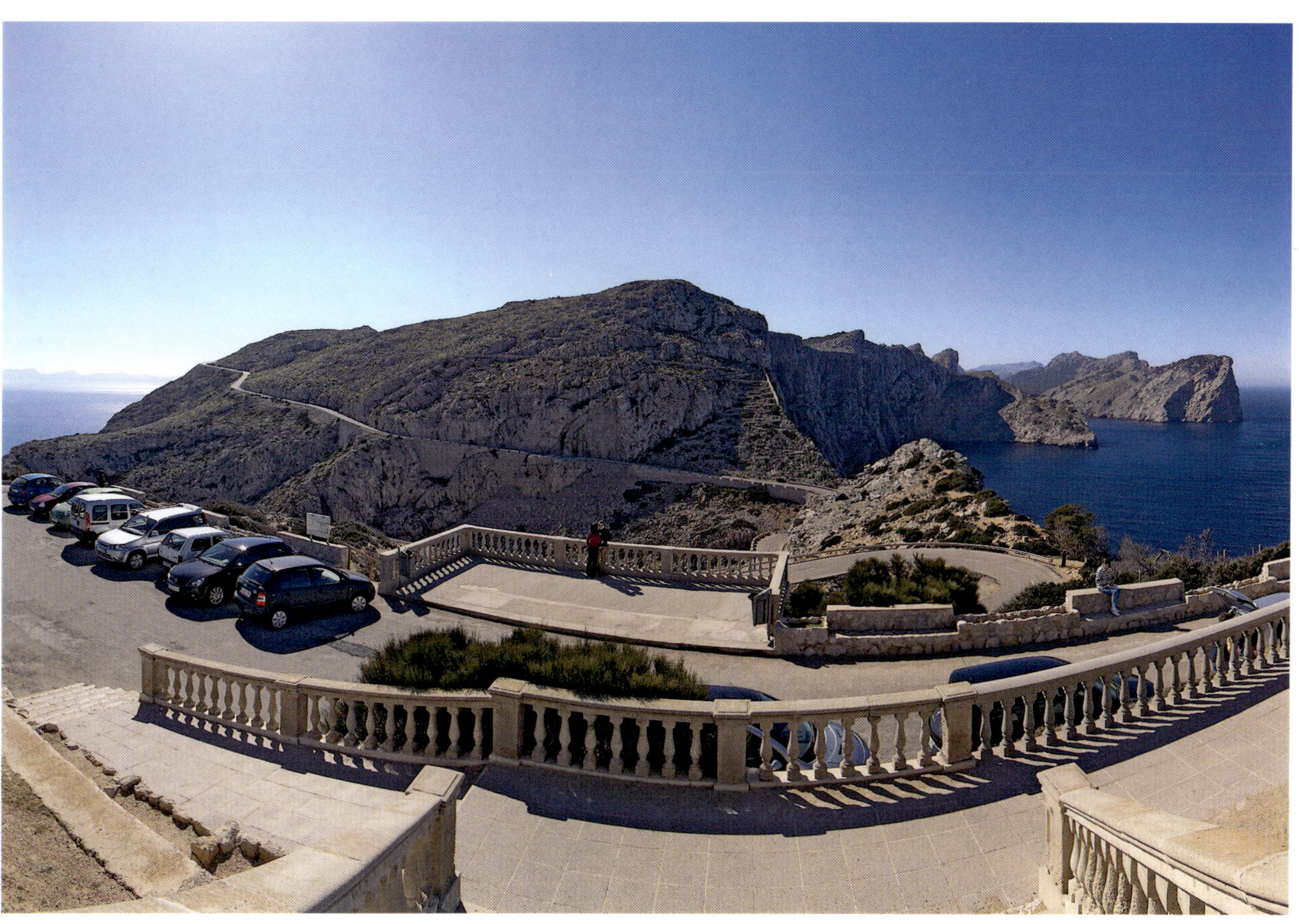

View from Punta de la Nao

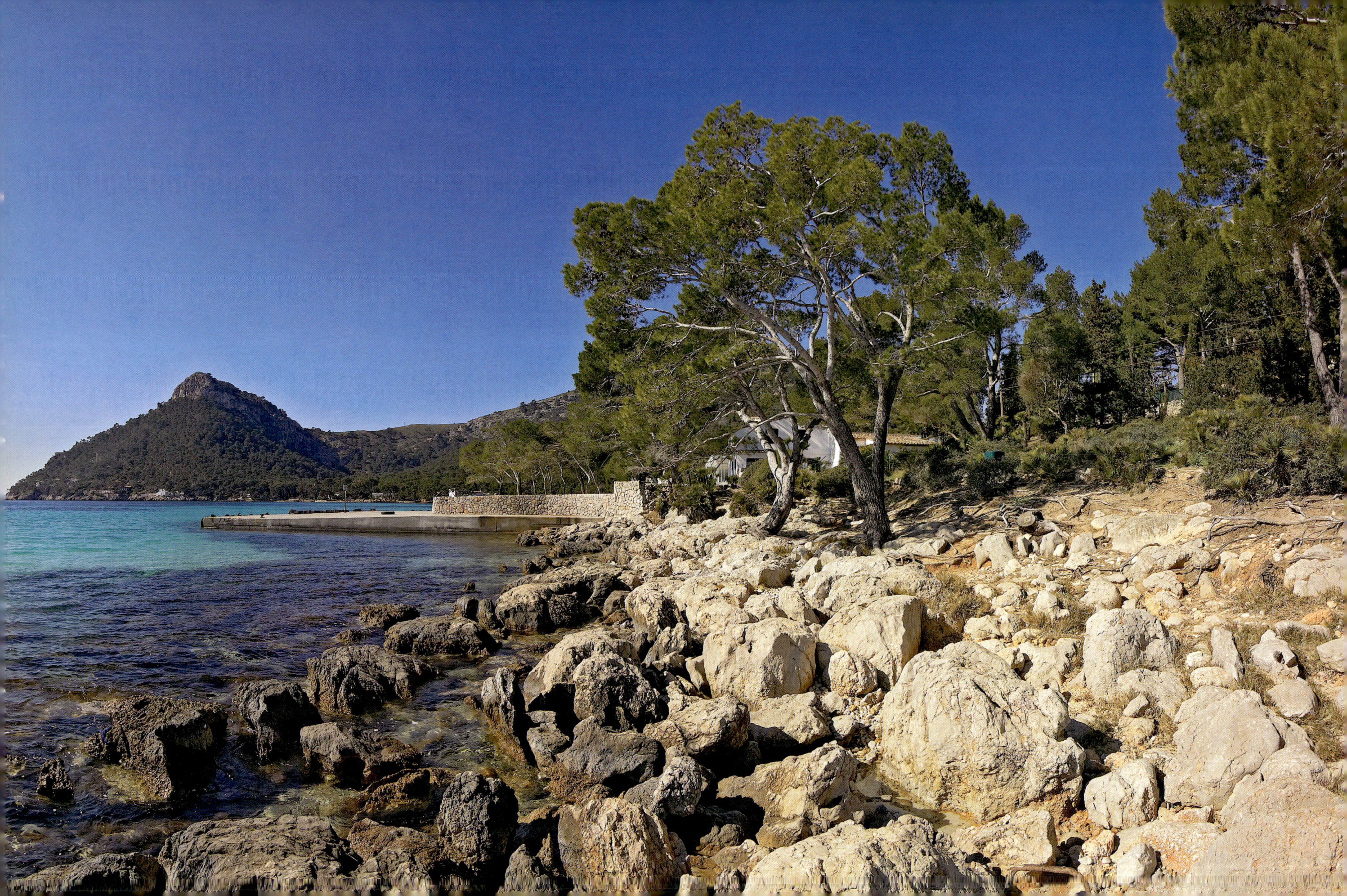

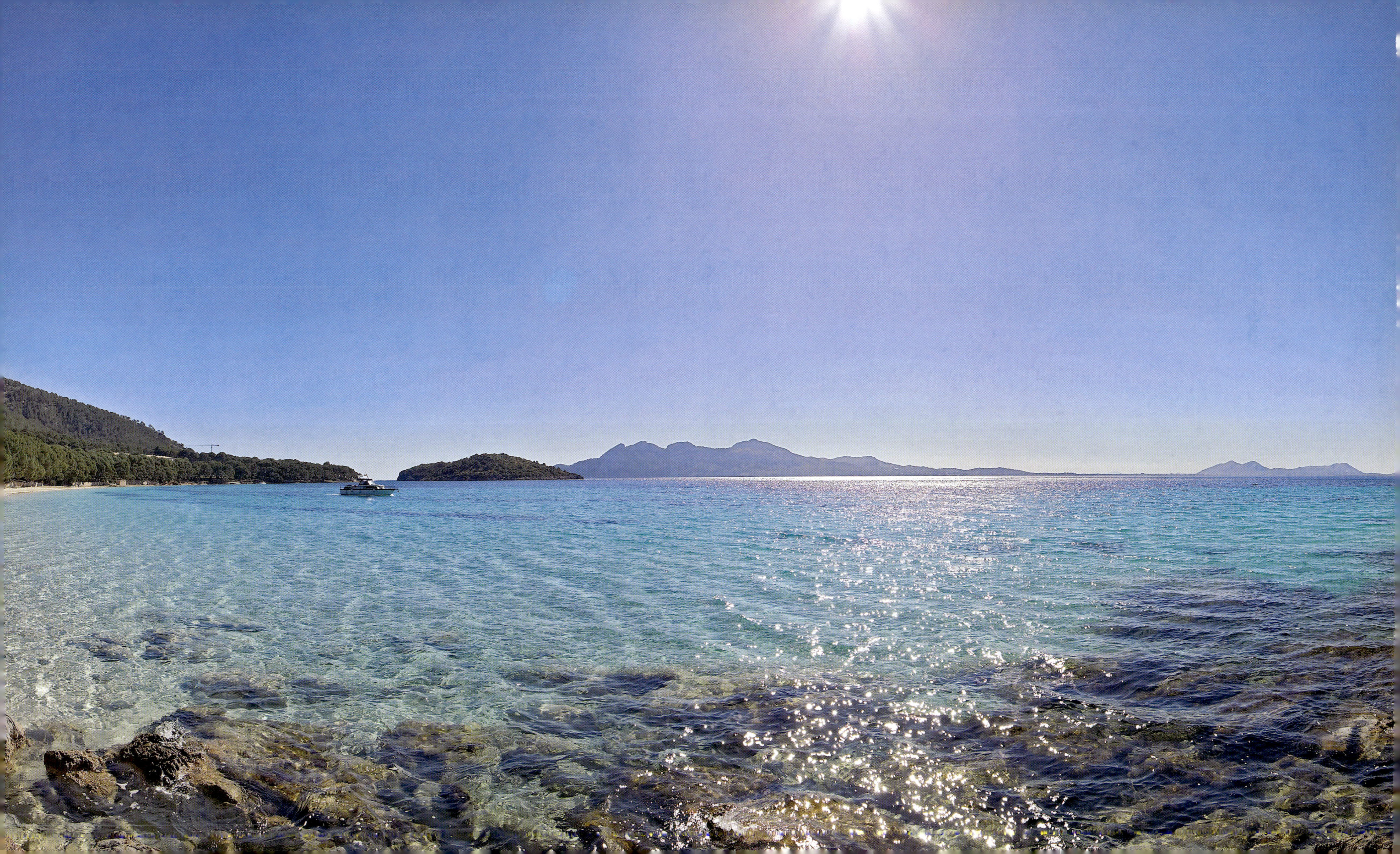

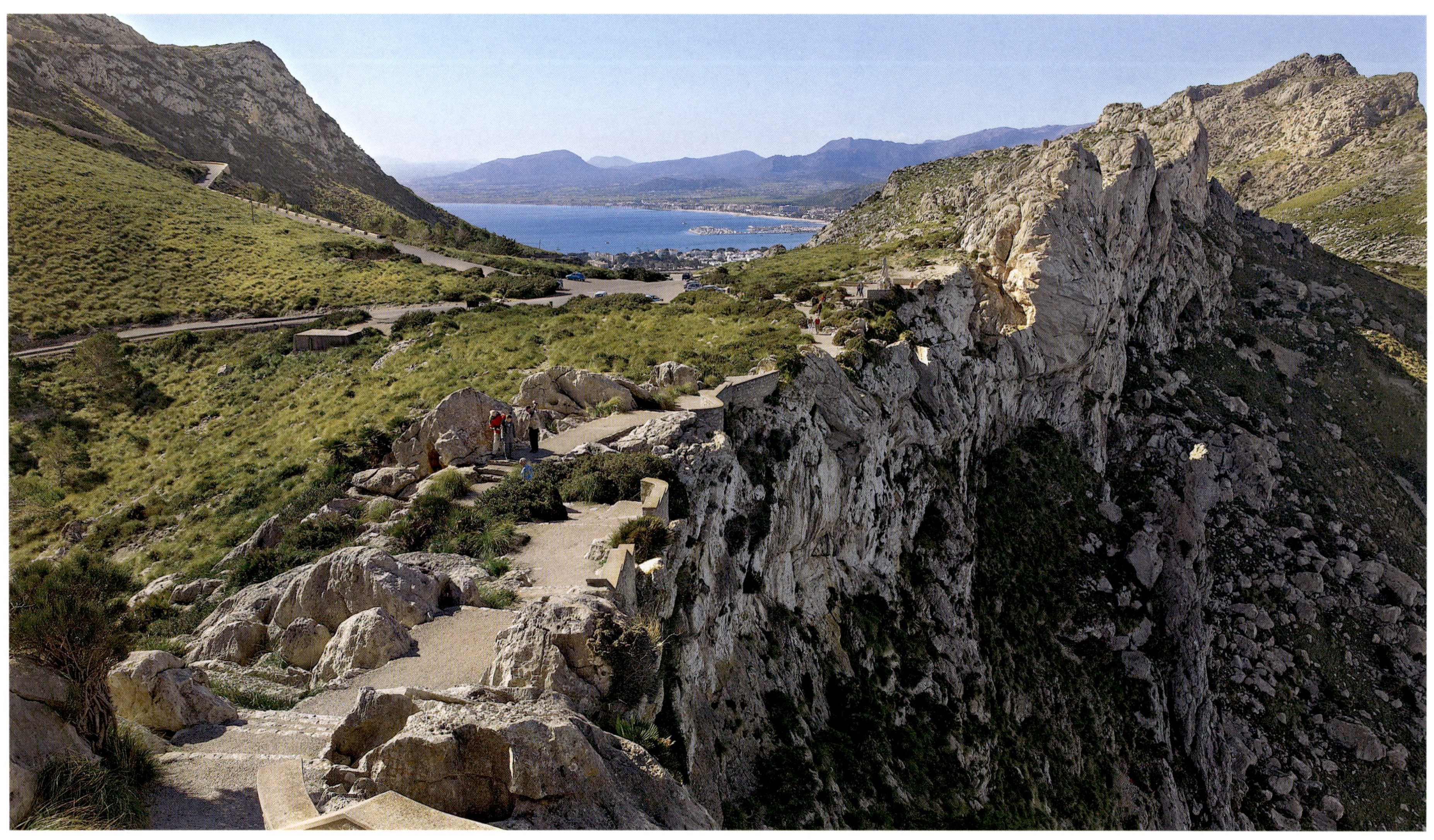

Formentor peninsula

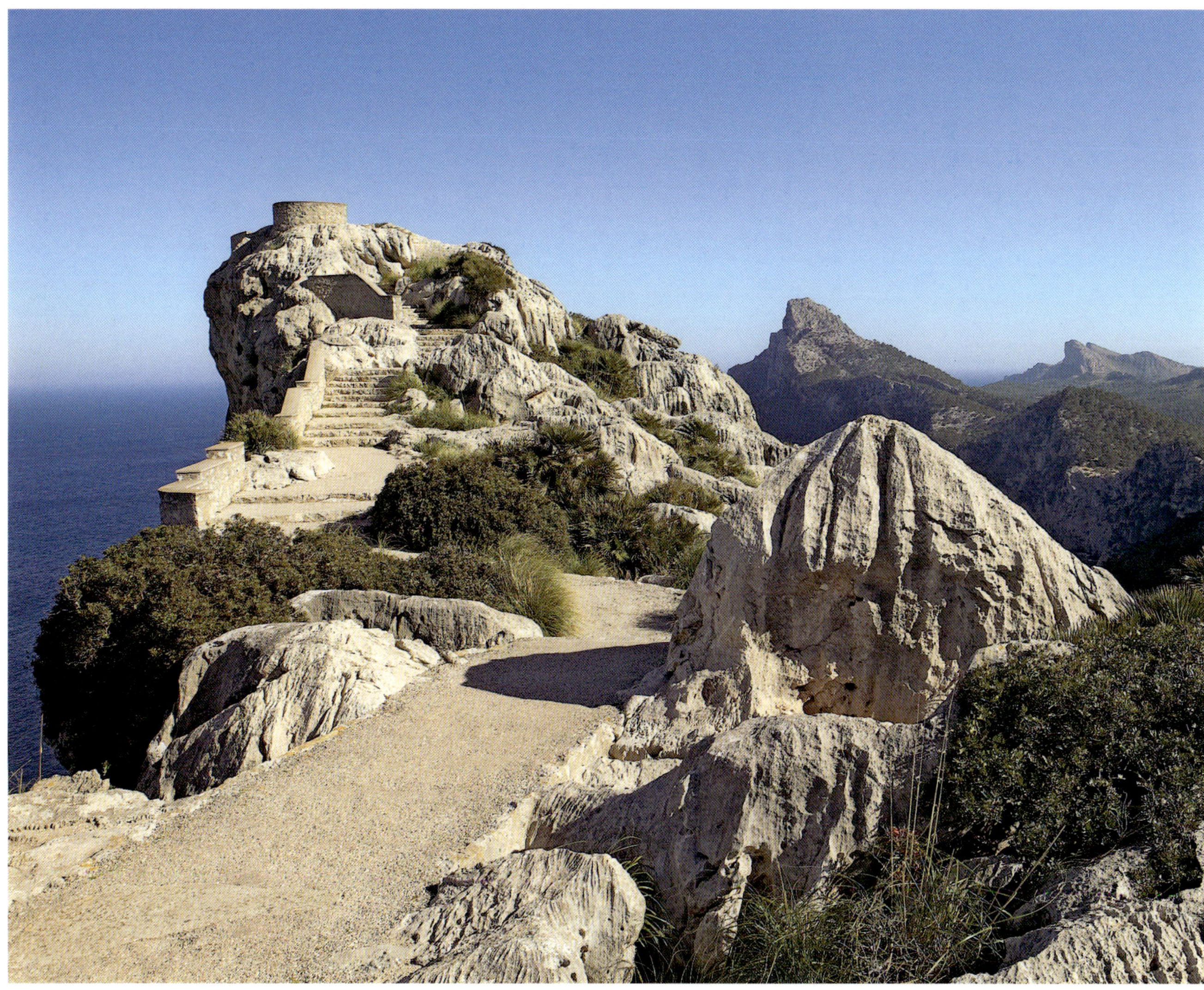

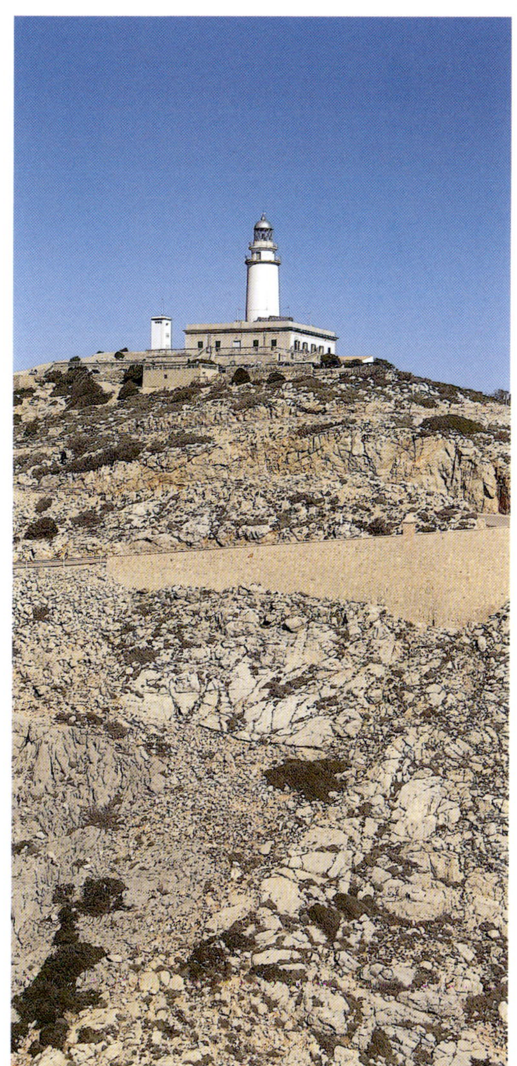

Bizarre rock landscape on the Formentor peninsula; Lighthouse at Cape Formentor.

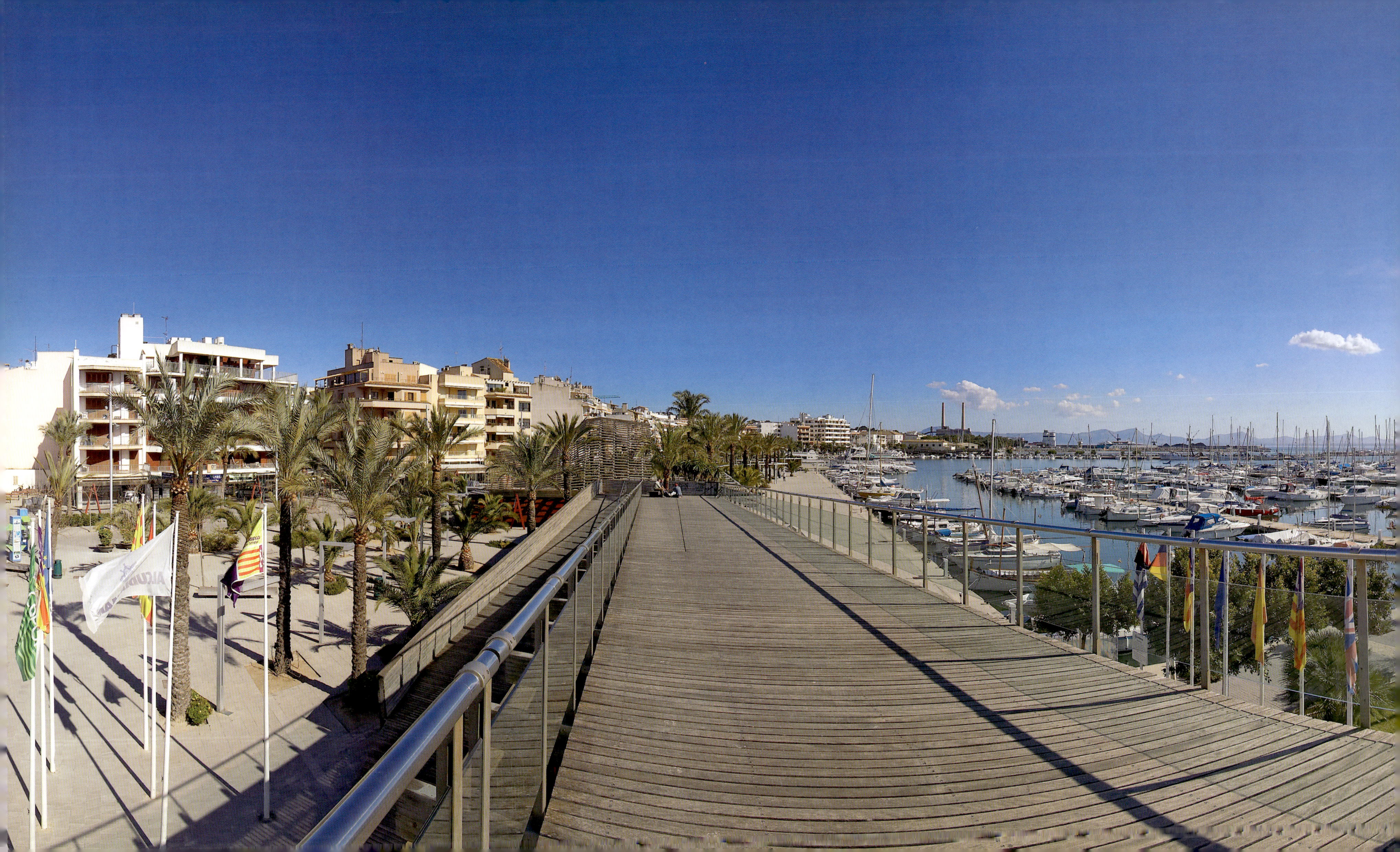

Port d'Alcúdia

The origin of the village, located on a mountain saddle, dates back to 2000 BC. In 123 BC, the Romans built the town of Pollentia. The archaeological excavations of the former town are among the great sights of Alcúdia. In 1298-1362, the town of today was developed, and for a few centuries it became a major seat of power in Majorca's north. In the 16th century, Alcúdia lost its economic importance. At this time, the city walls were expanded in the style of the Renaissance. It took until 1957 to improve the city's economy with the construction of a coal power station. Just as everywhere else on the island, tourism began in the 1960s. The beach with a length of 25 km and the surrounding mountains attract many visitors every year – a major source of income.

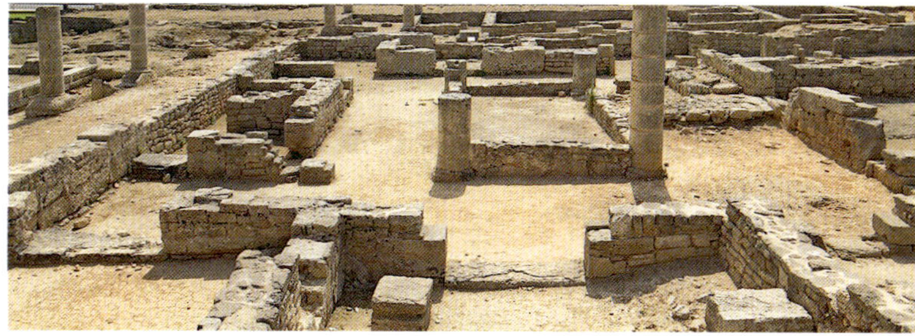

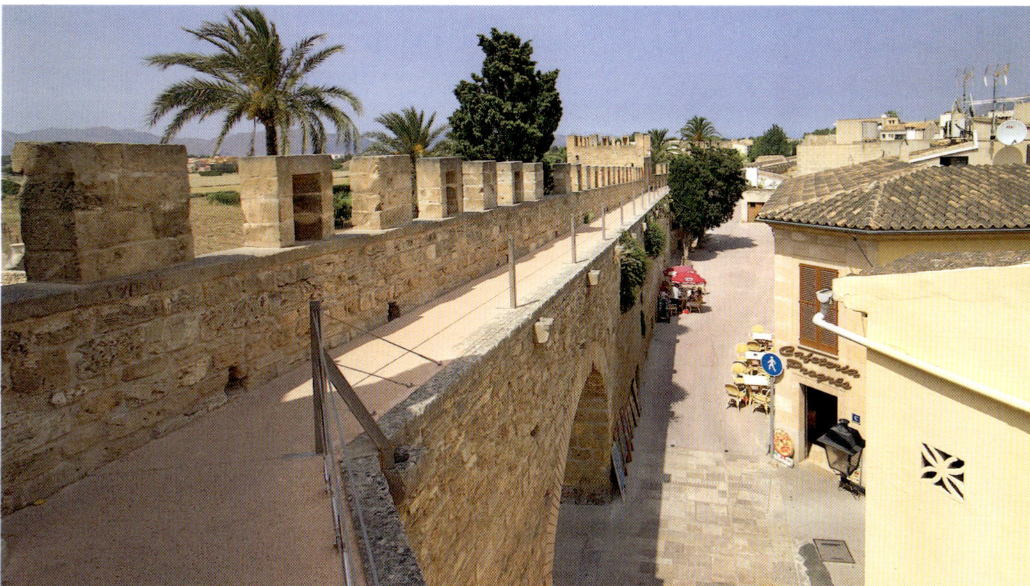

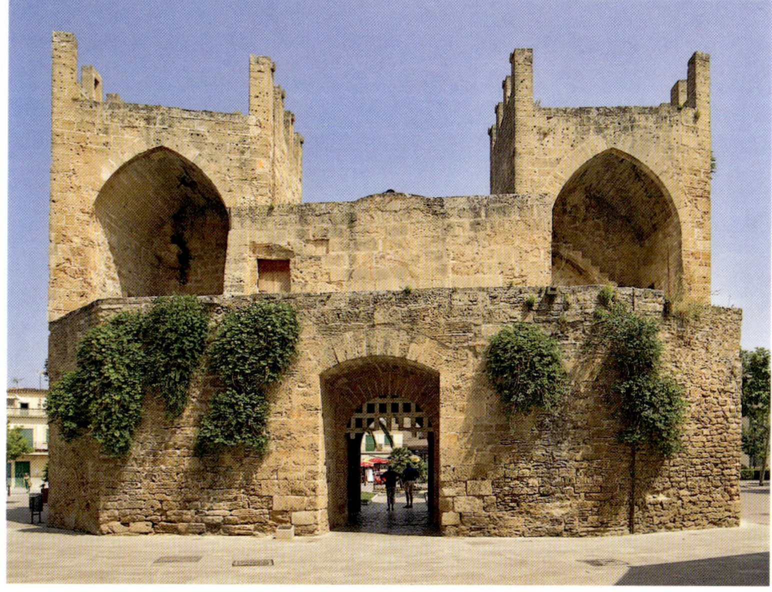

Alcúdia

360° panoramic photo: Marina and seaside promenade of Port d'Alcúdia 18

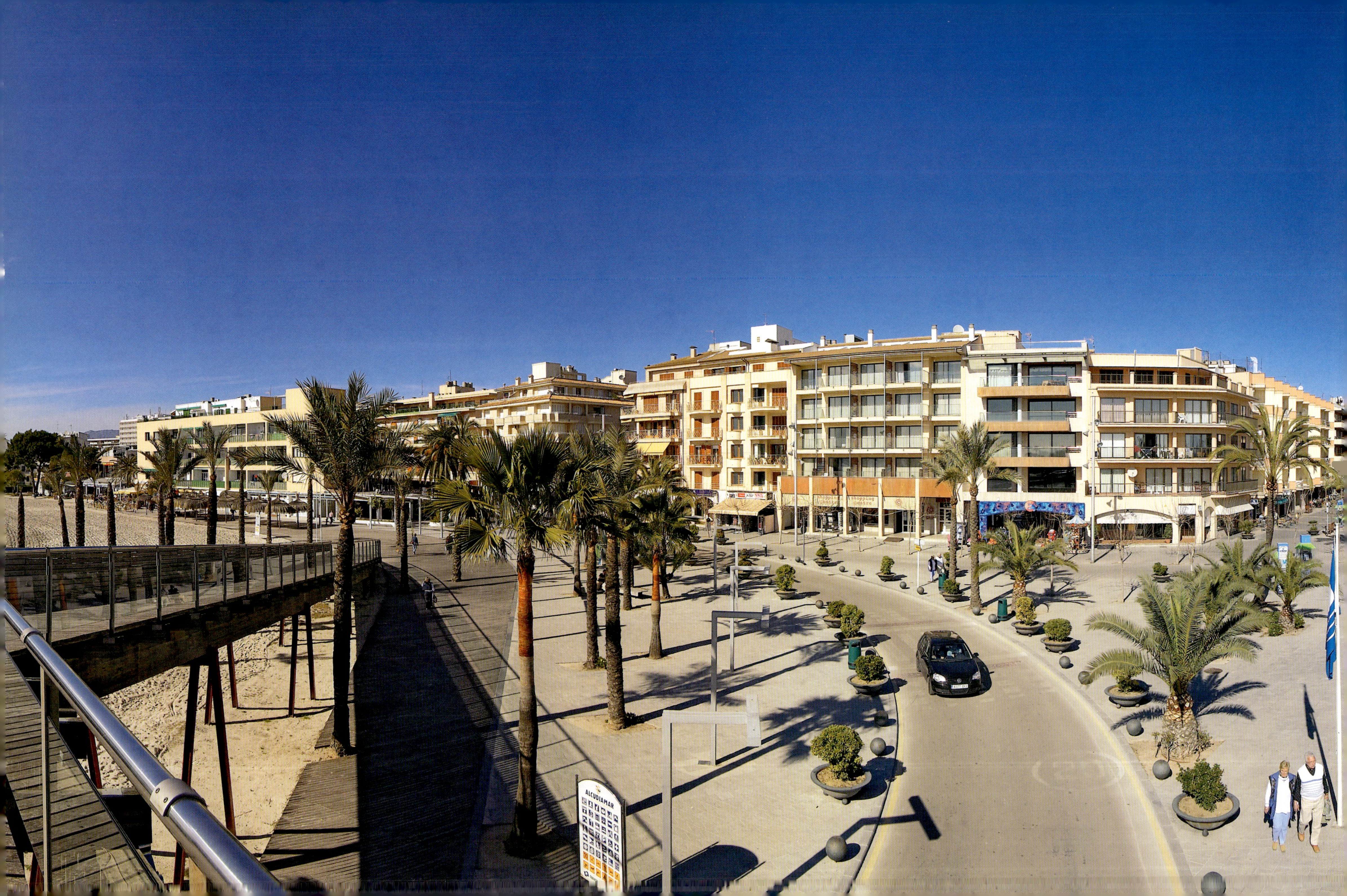
ALCUDIAMAR

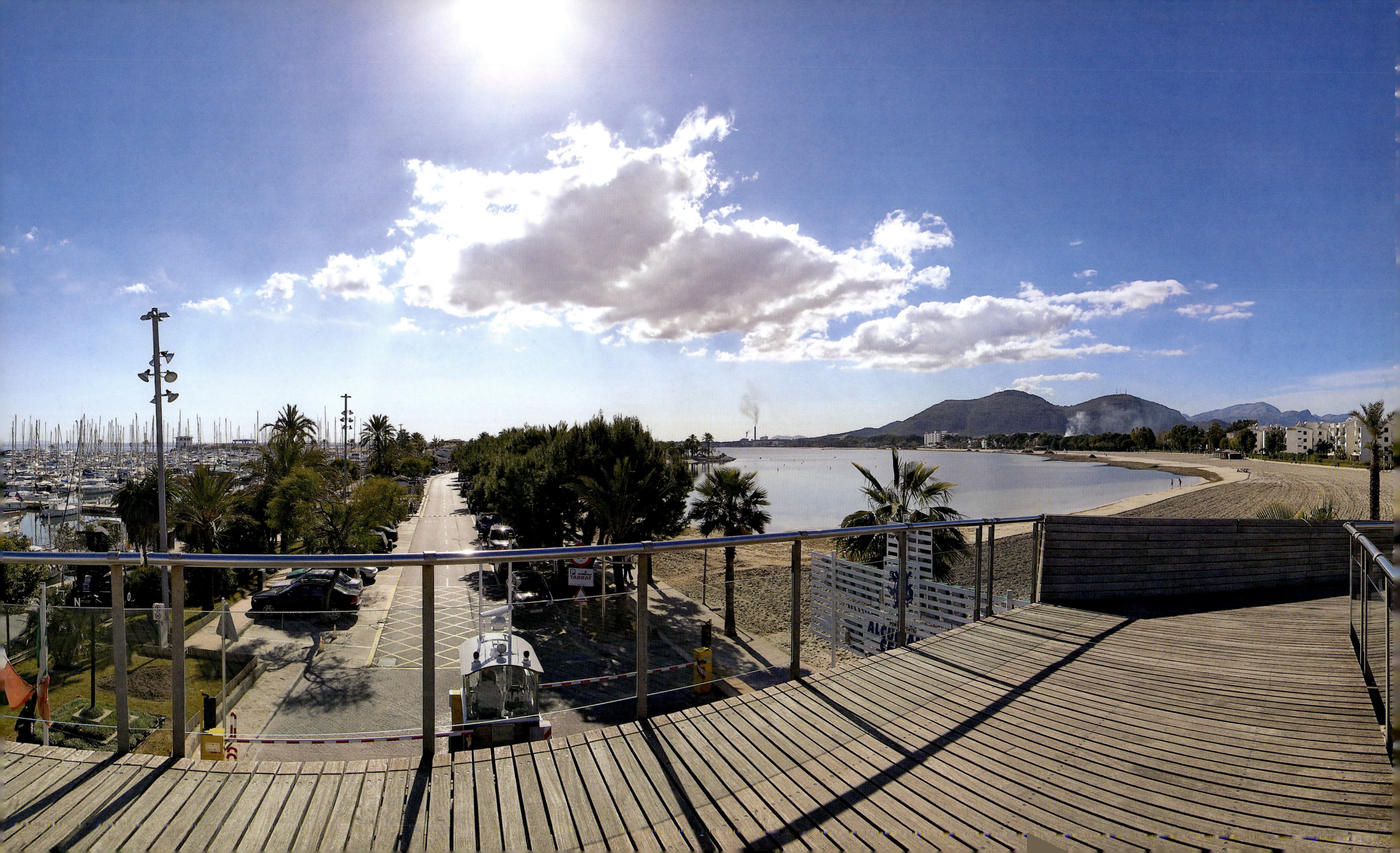

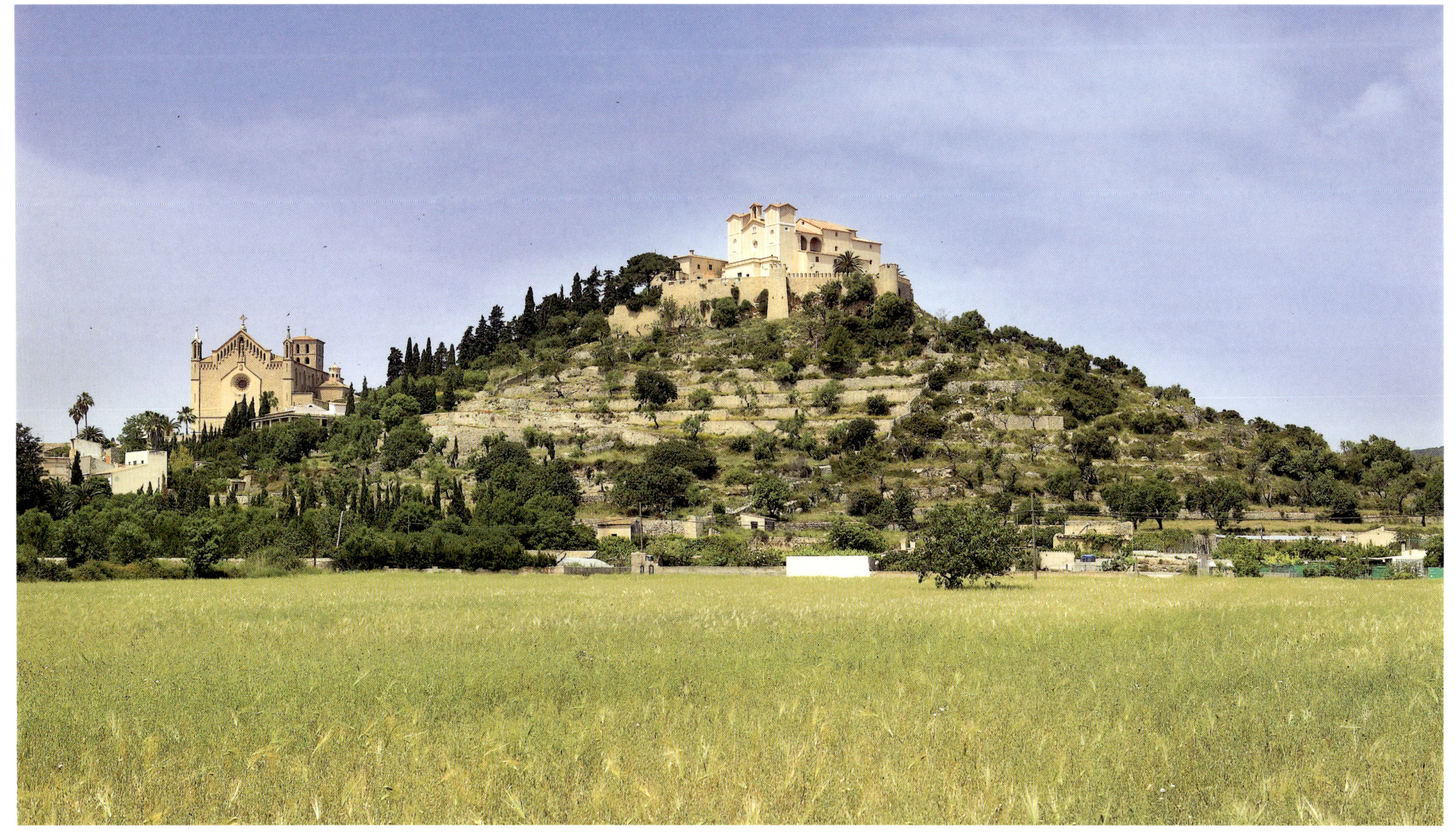

Artà

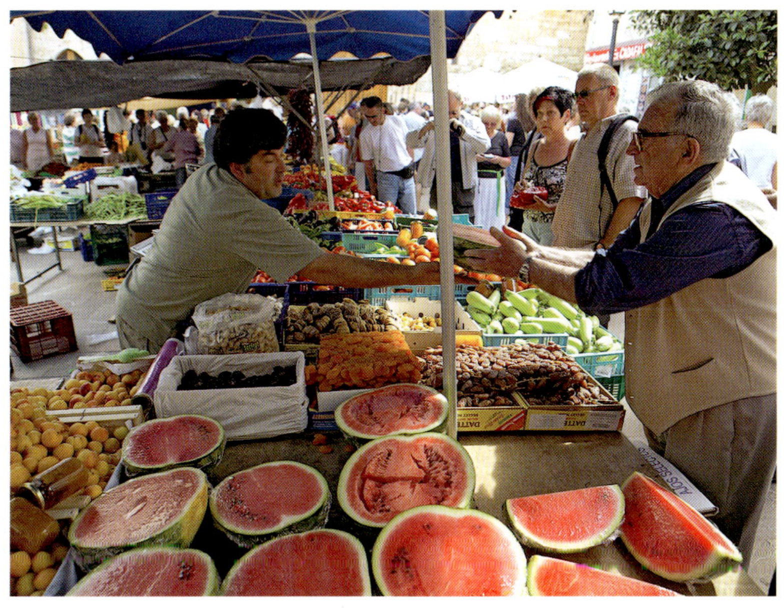

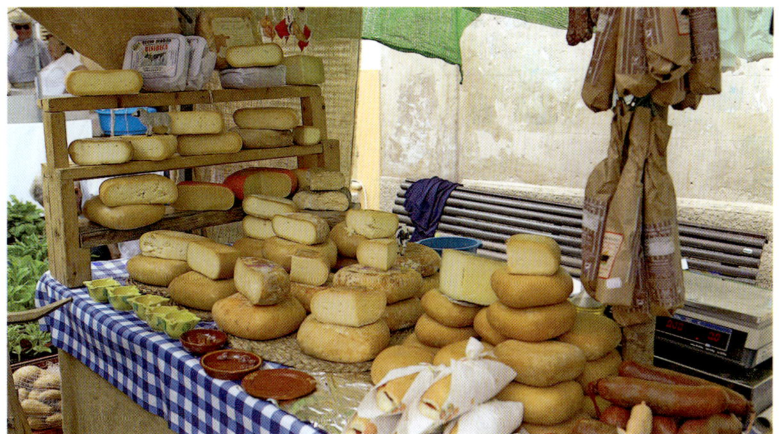

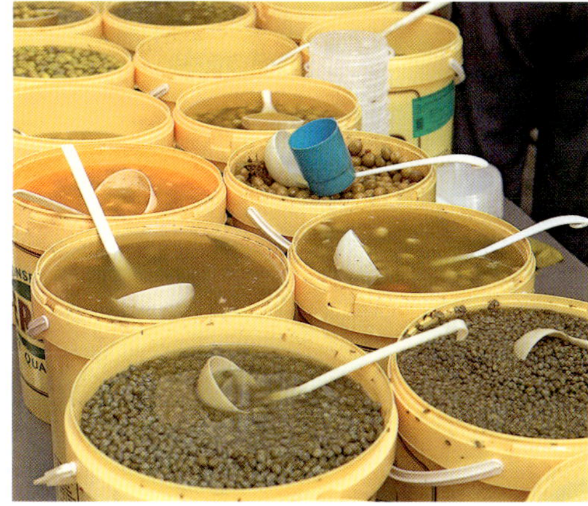

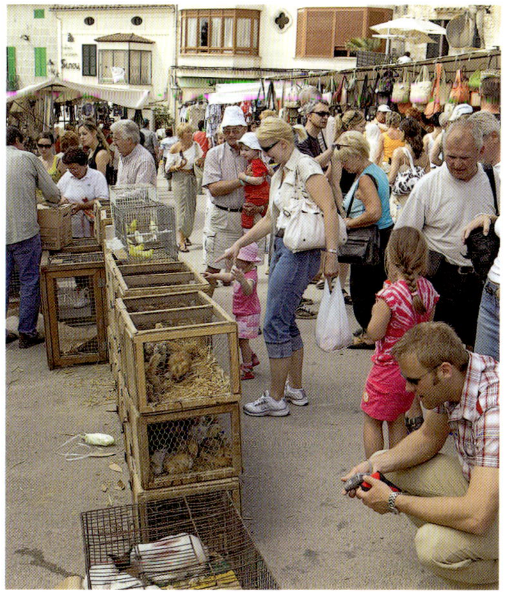

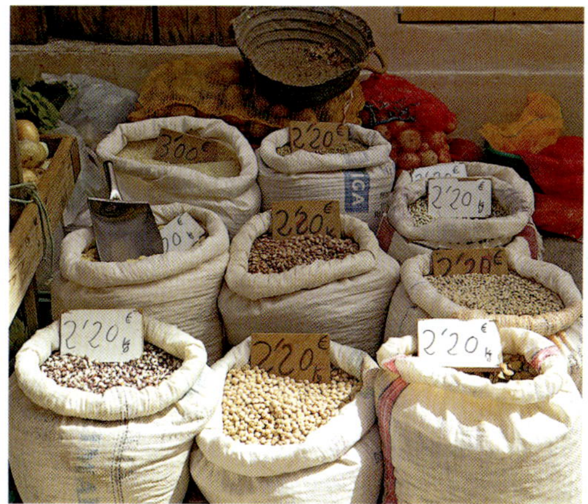

The small village of Artà lies in the area of the Serra Artana in Majorca's east. It is well-known for its dwarf palms (Chamaerops humilis). The fronds are used to make the popular Majorcan baskets.

The coast with the famous dune formation Sa Canova is more than 25 km long and mostly undeveloped.

For more than 700 years, a weekly livestock market has been held every Wednesday in the small rural village of Sineu. The market day begins early with horses, donkeys and cows, after that it is time for small animals and fowl. Other products for sale include fruit, vegetables, crafts and second-hand goods. The surrounding cellar restaurants serve hearty home-made dishes, and the shut-down train station houses the gallery "S'Estació".

Market in Sineu

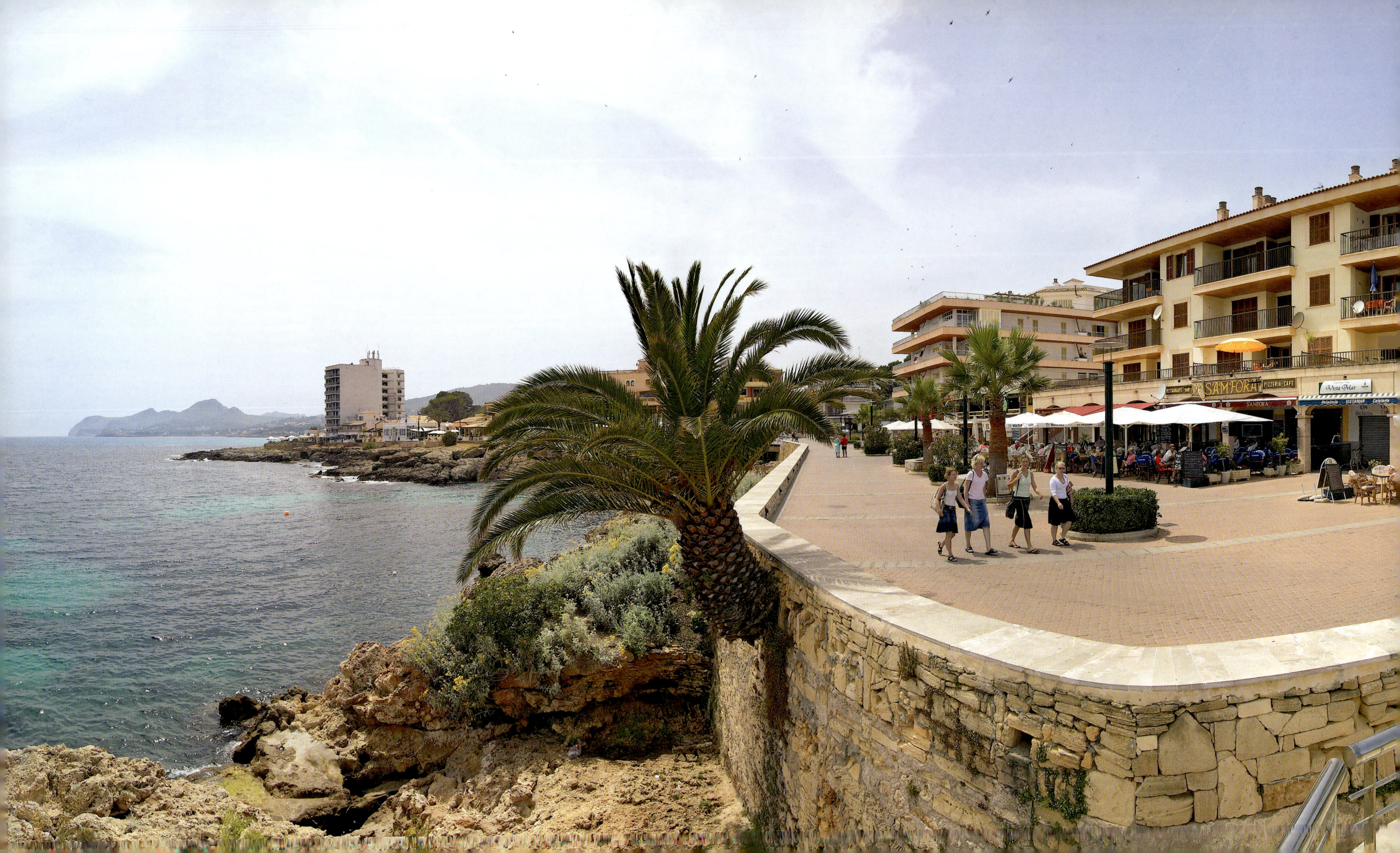

S'AMFORA
PIZZERIA-CAFE
S'AMFORA
Vista Mar
Heladeria VISTAMAR Cafeteria

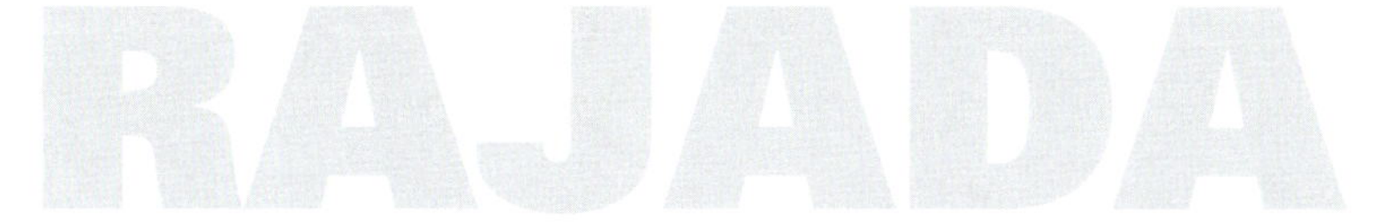

Port de Cala Rajada

The bay of Cala Rajada (bay of rays) is the location of the island's second-most important port, built in the 17th century. Fishermen caught mostly rays and rock lobsters in the area. North of the port, visitors can still see the protected lobster houses.
From here, tour boats go to the neighbouring island of Minorca. To the east, Cala Rajada is bounded by Cap de Capdepera. A footpath leads through jagged rocks to the small cove Punta de Capdepera and the lighthouse "Far de Capdepera".

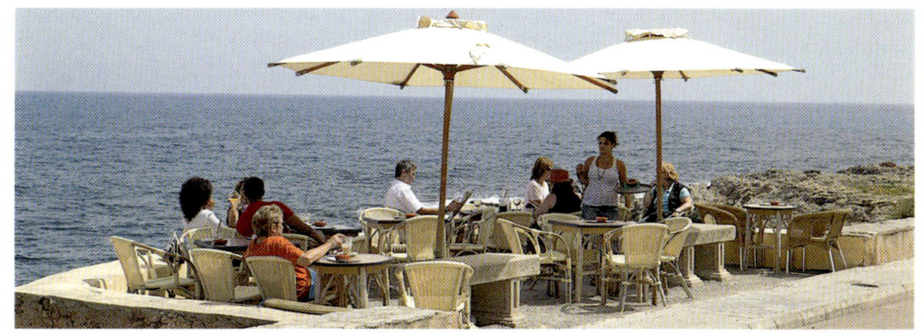

On a hill overlooking the town, banker built a villa in 1911, surrounded by the expansive park "Jardines March", which displays an abundance of Mediterranean plants and about 60 sculptures.

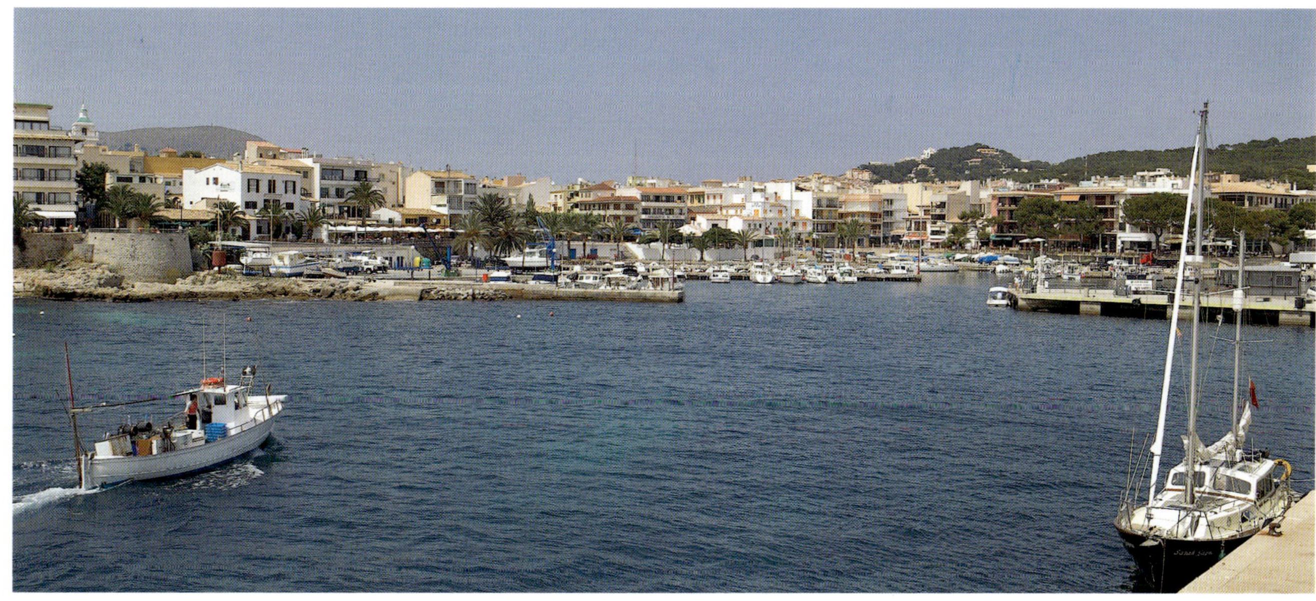

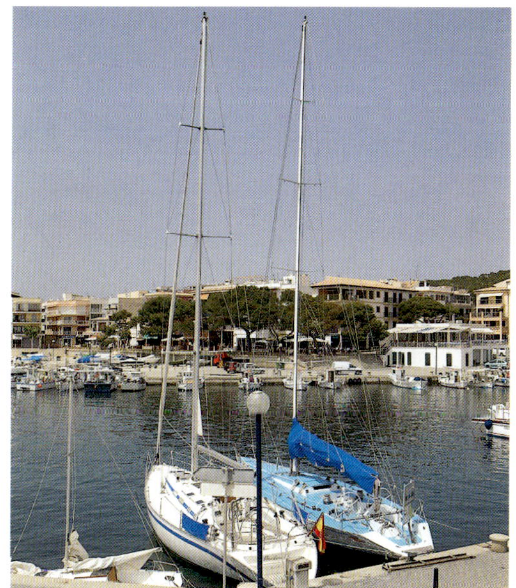

Port de Cala Rajada

360° panoramic photo: Port de Cala Rajada 19

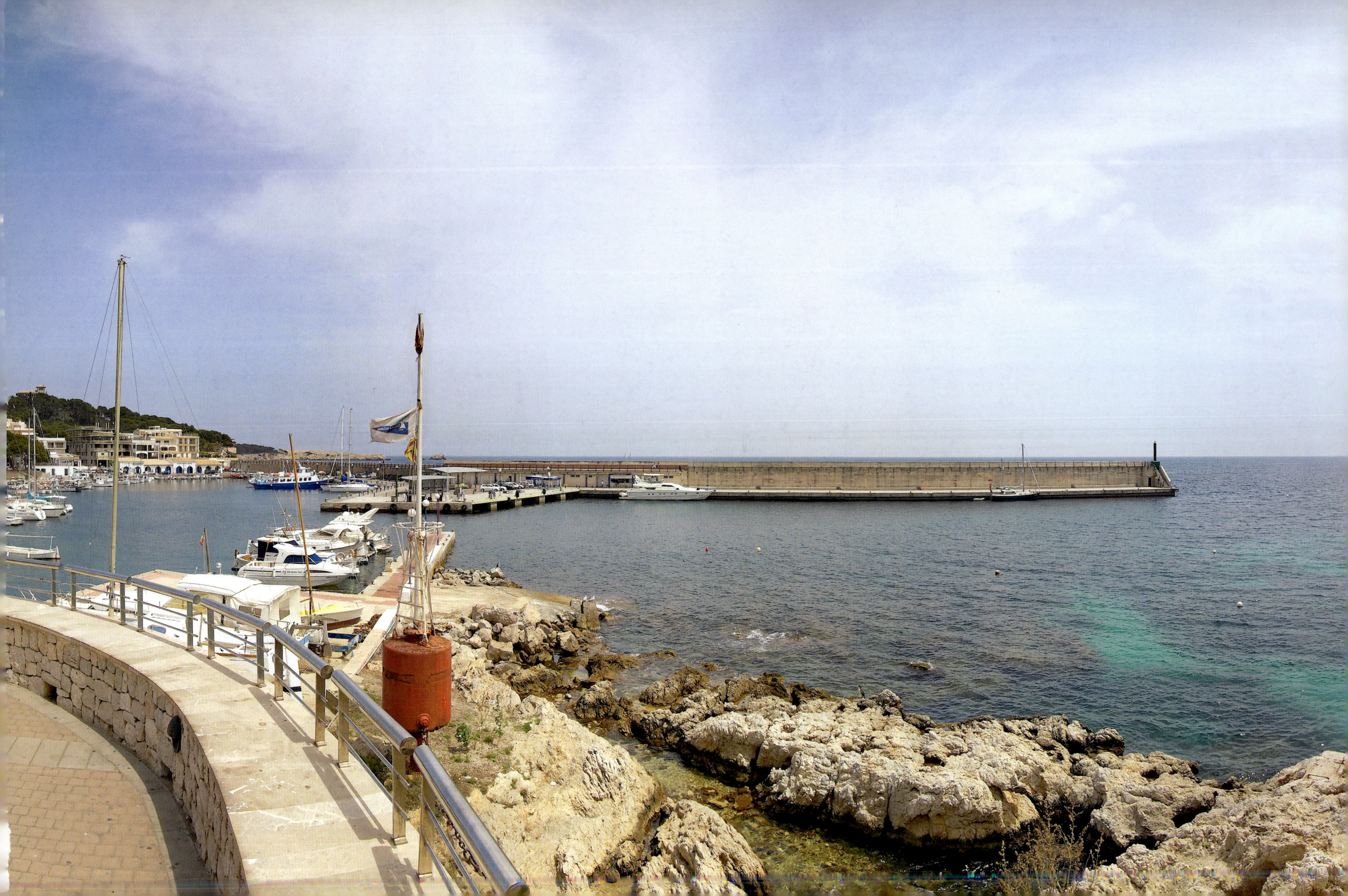

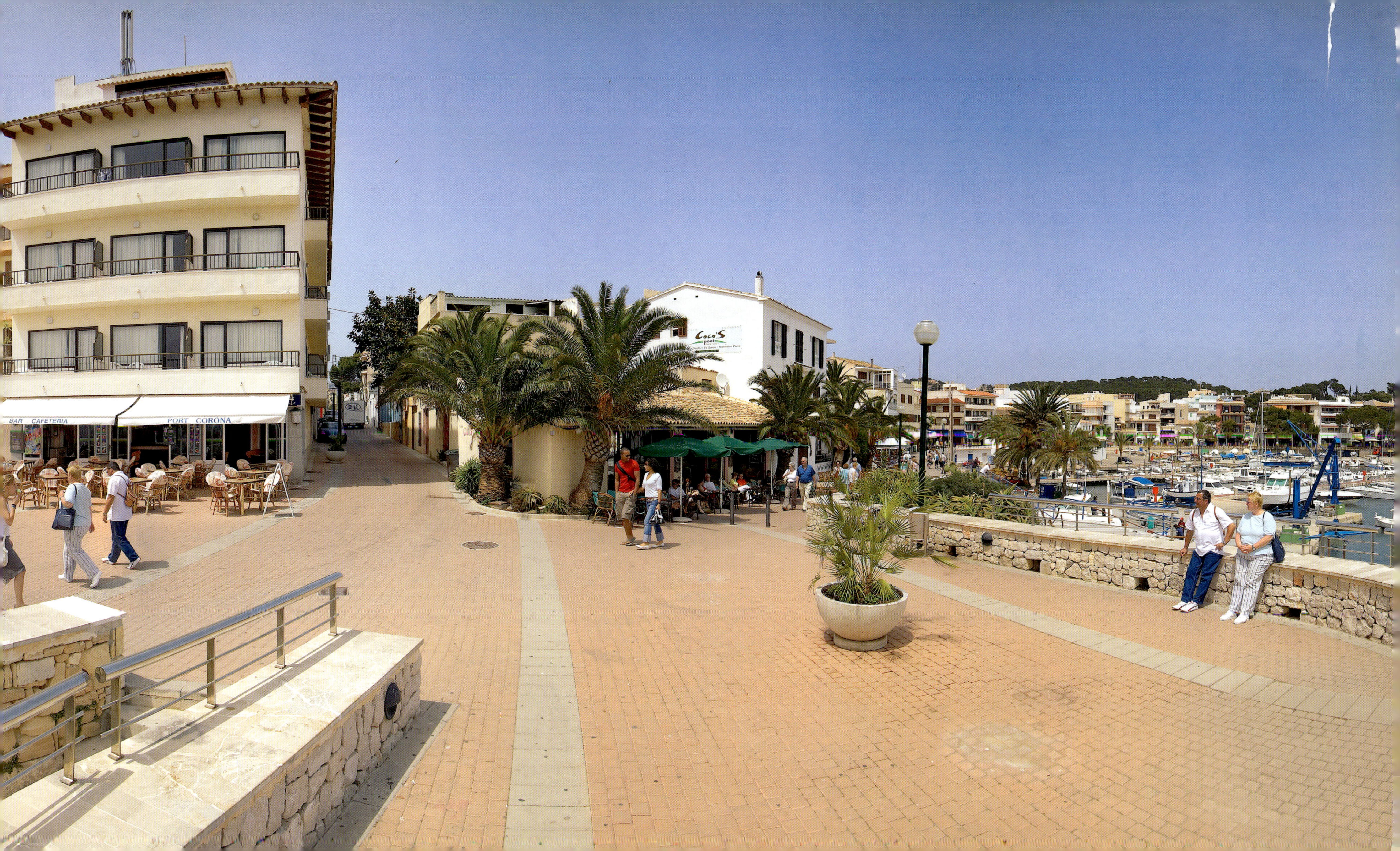
BAR CAFETERIA
PORT CORONA
Coco'S
pool

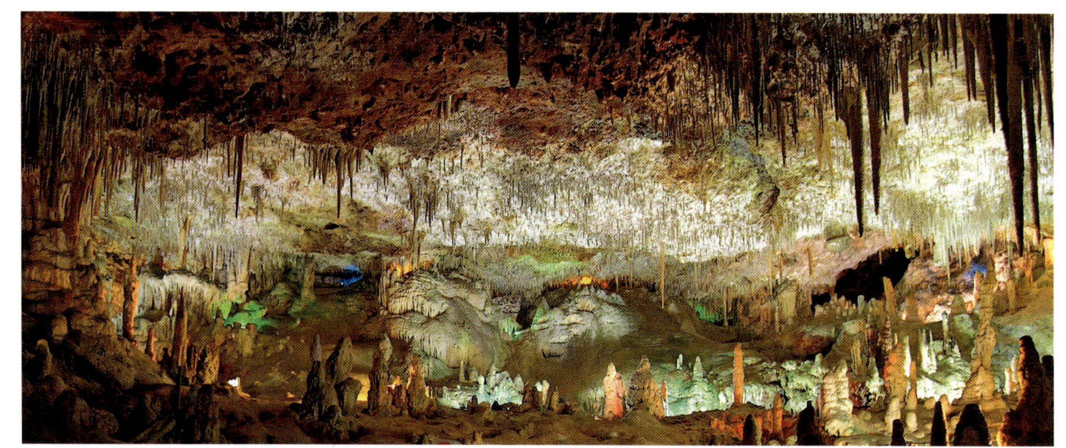

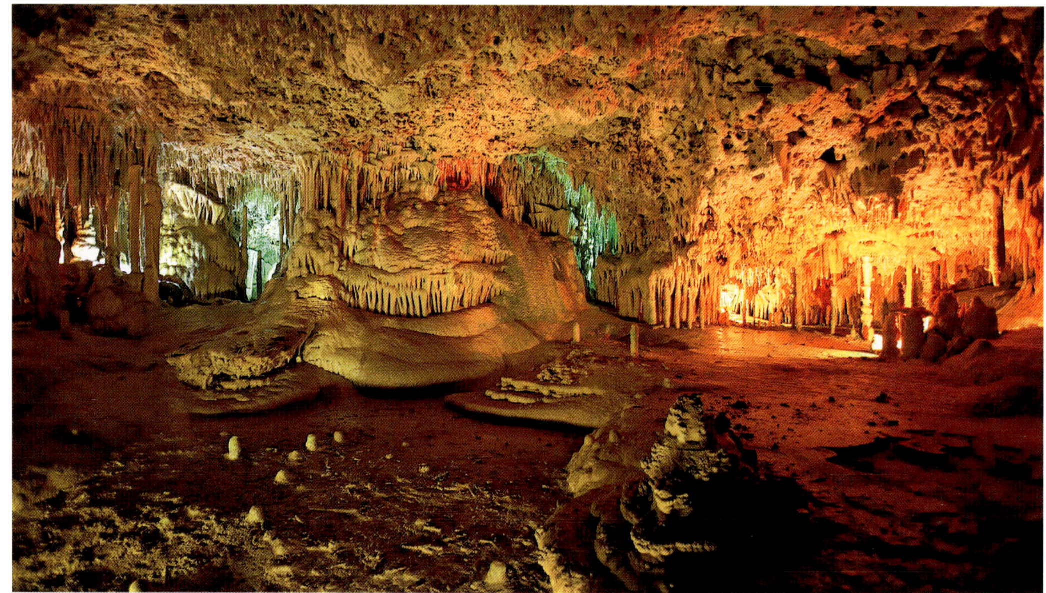

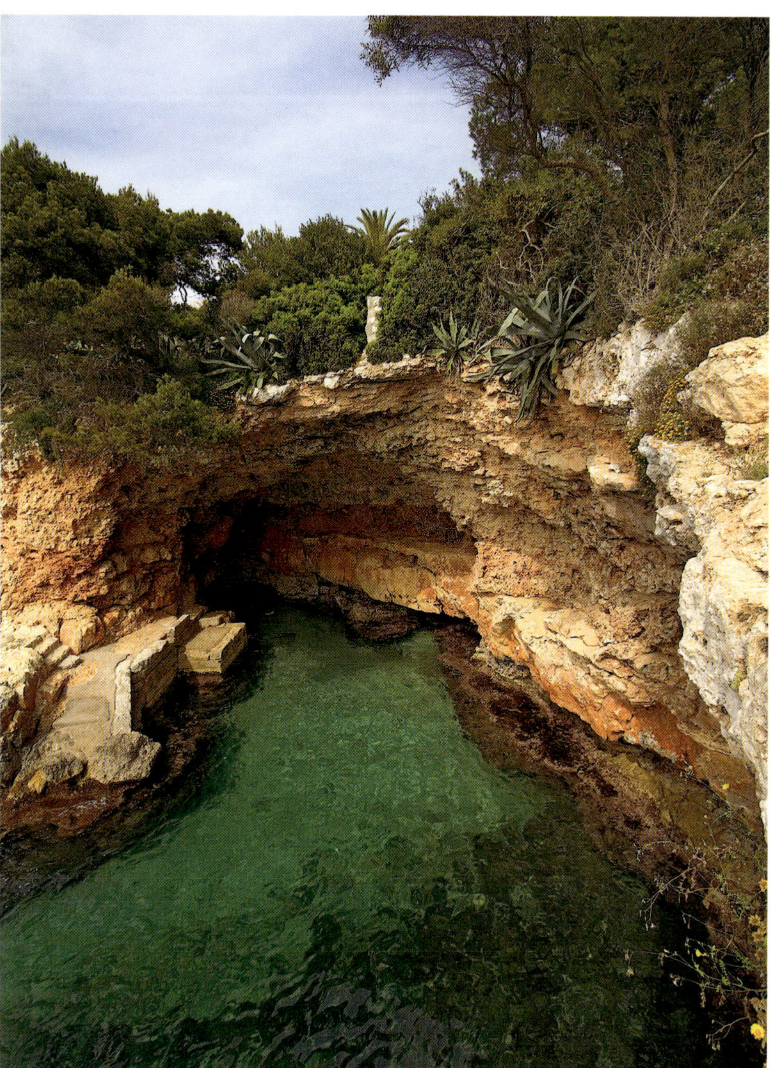

Cuevas dels Hams

The town of Porto Christo (port of Christ), characterized by its marina, whose entrance is protected by rocks, used to be the biggest holiday resort on the east coast.
A 17th-century watchtower overlooks the entrance to the marina bay, with a small cave underneath. A narrow beach, lined by restaurants, is located directly by the thoroughfare. Archaeological discoveries in the marina prove the presence of the Romans, while the uncovered ruins of an early Christian basilica are evidence of settlement in the 5th century. In 1936, Porto Christo was the only Majorcan town involved in the Spanish civil war. With its many historic buildings in the old part of town, Porto Christo still has the charm of an old fishing port.
The system of stalactite caves "Coves del Drac" (dragon lair) outside of the town is the location of Llac Martel, one of the world's largest subterranean lakes. It is the venue of regular concerts, which have become a tourist attraction. "Coves dels Hams" (fishing hook caves) is another cave system with a less expansive subterranean lake.

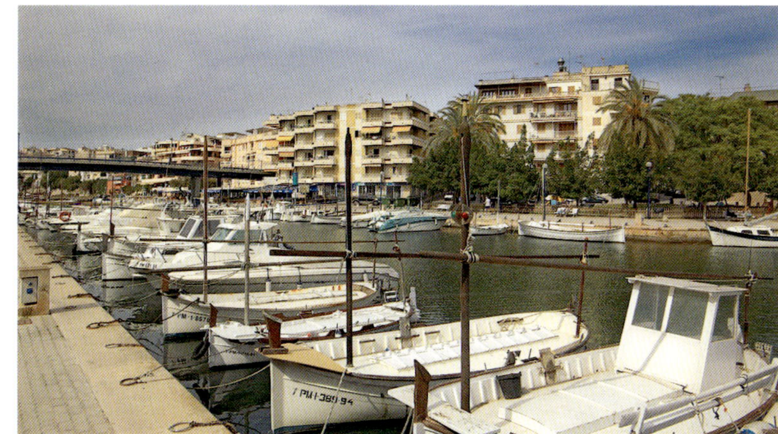

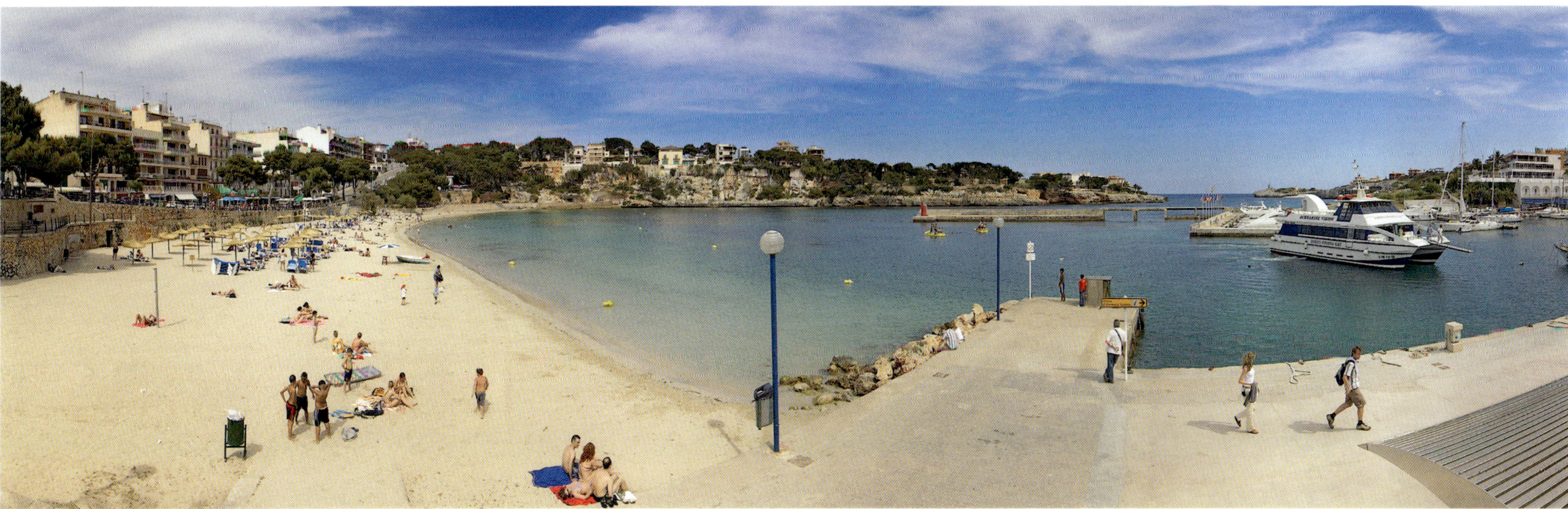

Porto Christo

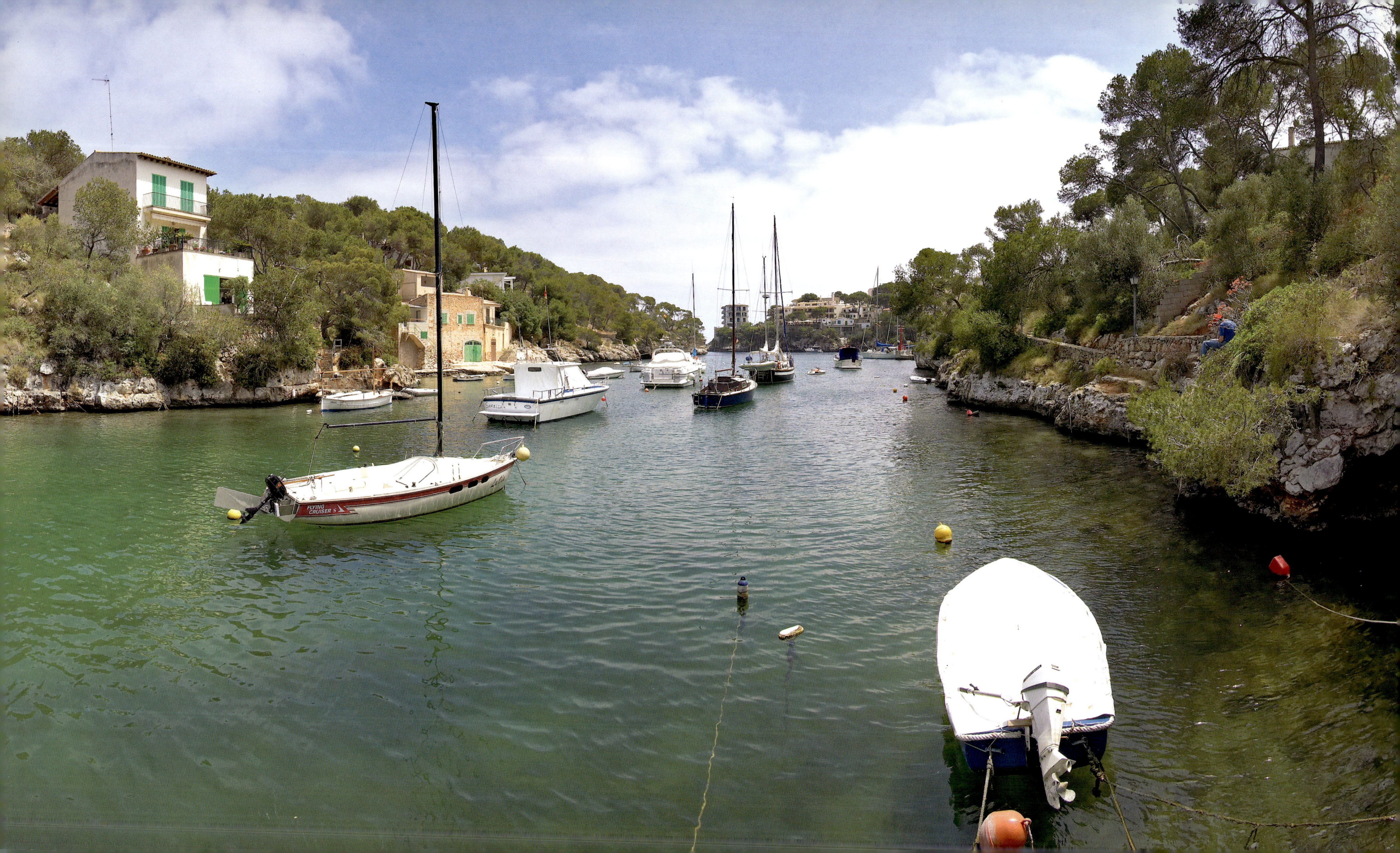
FLYING CRUISER

Torrent des Olms

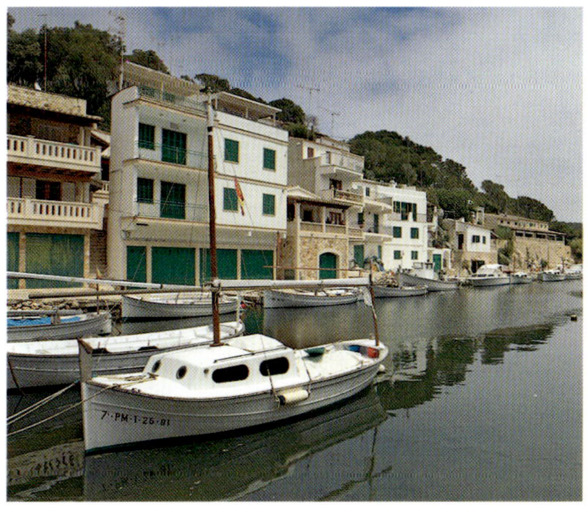

The small village was first documented in 1306, located in a two-part fjord-like bay. The first village church, built in 1938, has been turned into a restaurant. The two river arms Caló d'En Boira and Caló d'En Busques form a Y. Some of the fisherman's huts, built directly into the rock, can only be reached via steep stairs. The old fishing village doesn't have its own beach, but there are swimming pools available. Local fishermen sell their fresh catch in the picturesque harbour. A lovely, if somewhat strenuous hike takes you around the fjords to the lighthouse.

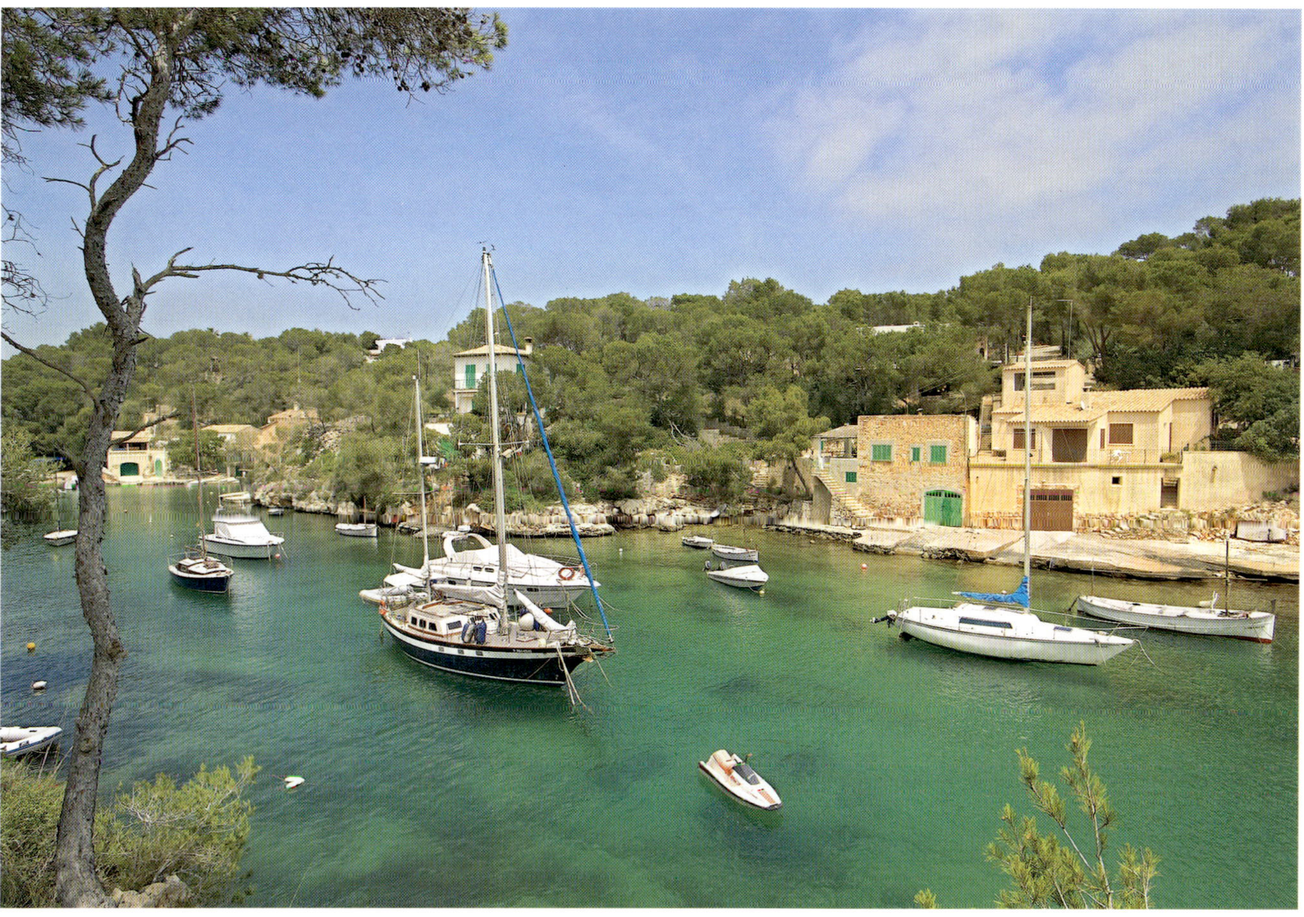

Torrent des Olms

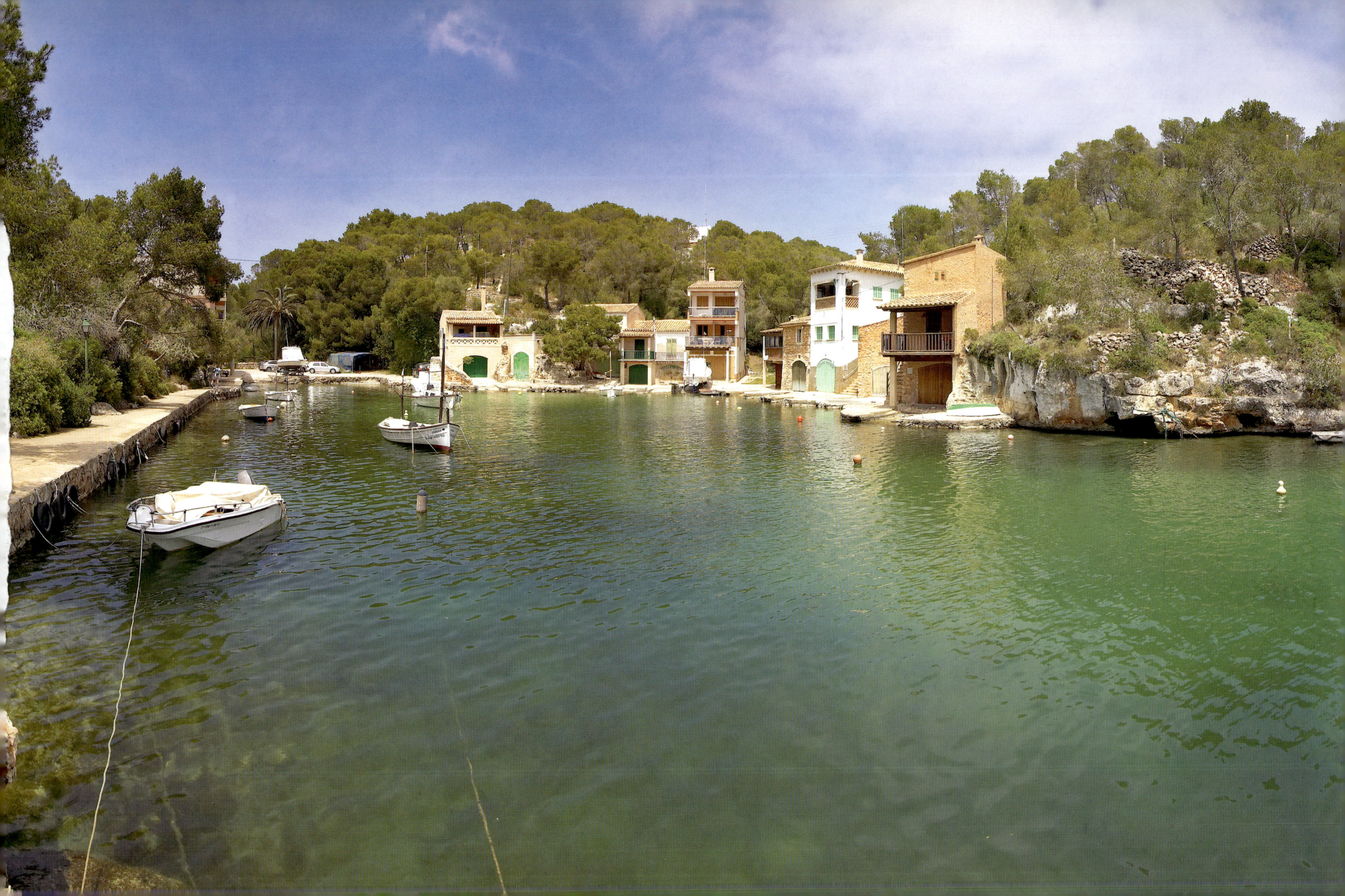

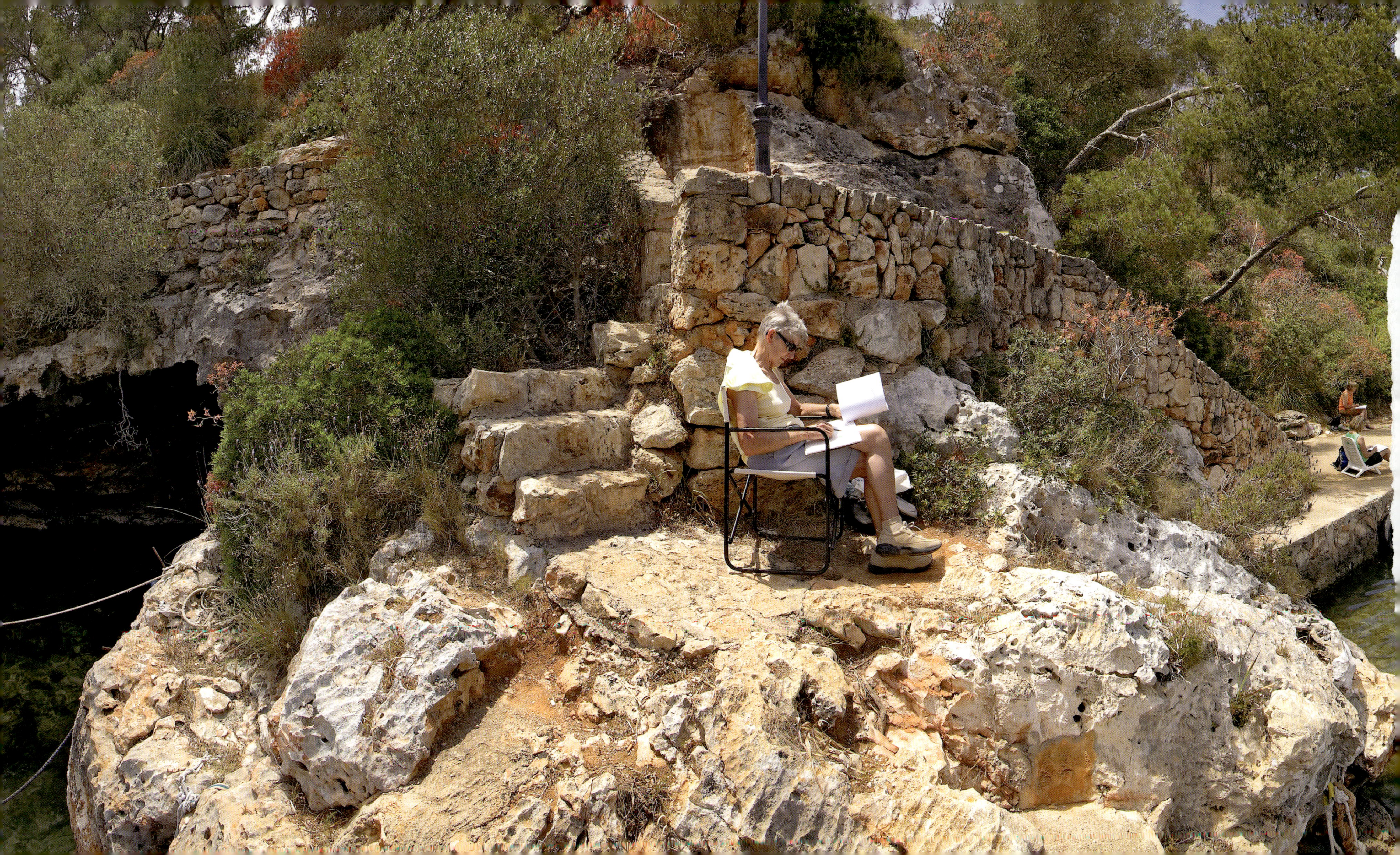

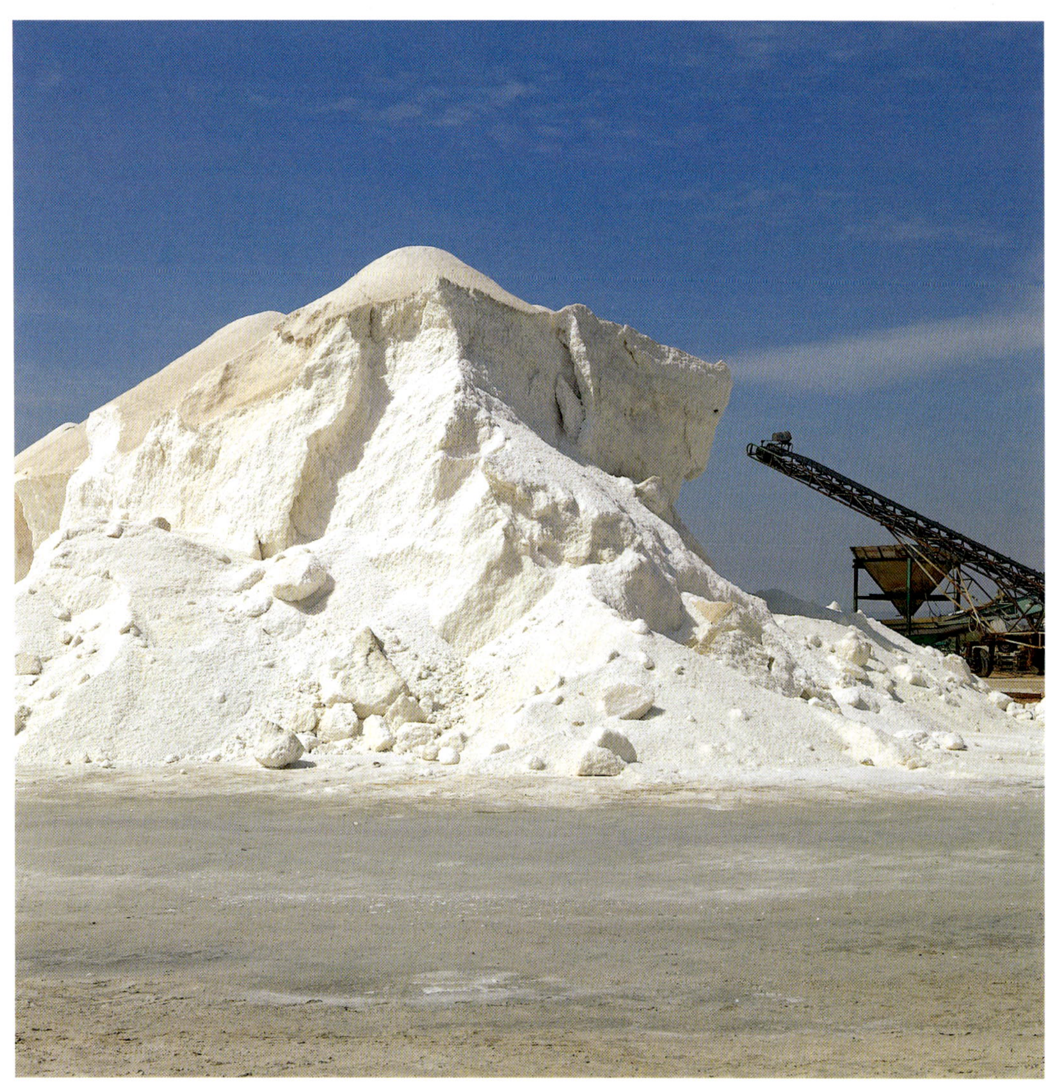

About 50 m wide and 9 km long, the Platja de Es Trenc stretches between Sa Ràpita and Colònia de Sant Jordi. The beach is lined by dunes and pines, and the typical Majorcan beach kiosks (Chiringuitos) provide swimmers with food and beverages.

Behind the dunes lie protected salt fields, the perfect refuge for many birds. Industrial salt production on Majorca began with the foundation of the company "Salines de Llevant". Every year, almost 10,000 t of sea salt are produced, using a 2000-year old technique. In April, sea water is pumped on the salt fields of the area with a total size of 130 ha, where it is left to evaporate over the summer. Starting in September, the remaining salt crystals can be harvested. The salt fields include a shop where you can buy salt in a variety of qualities and flavours.

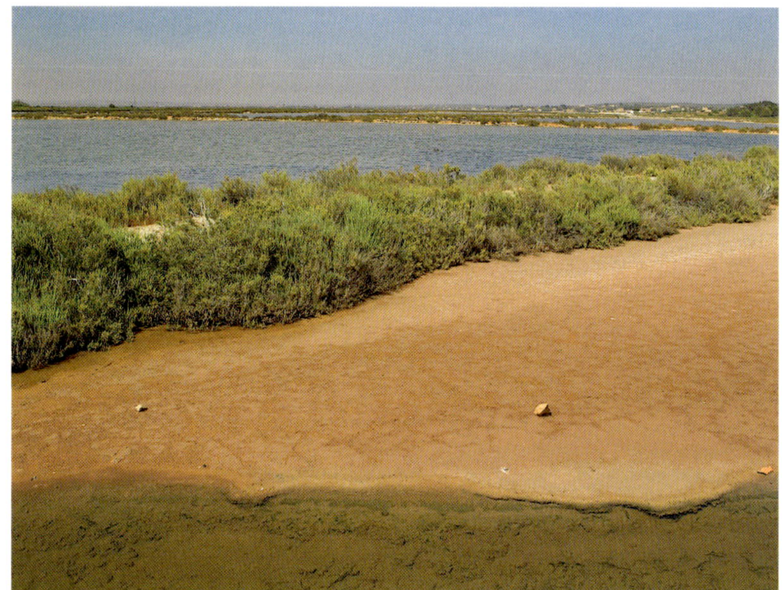

Salt works on Platja de Es Trenc.

Approaching the airport of Palma, you can already see the many windmills on the plains of Pla, whose history predates Christian conquest in 1229. Majorca used to have about 1,000 of these mills, which were in operation in the 17th and 18th century. In earlier times, the windmills were used to process grains, then to pump water for irrigation systems. The oldest of these windmills for water transport was built in 1845 on the plain of Sant Jordi. The windmills have long lost their meaning for Majorcan agriculture, but they are still the island's landmarks and part of the cultural heritage.

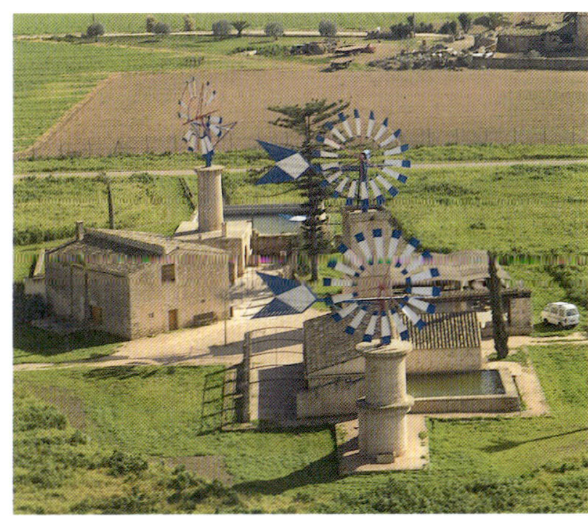

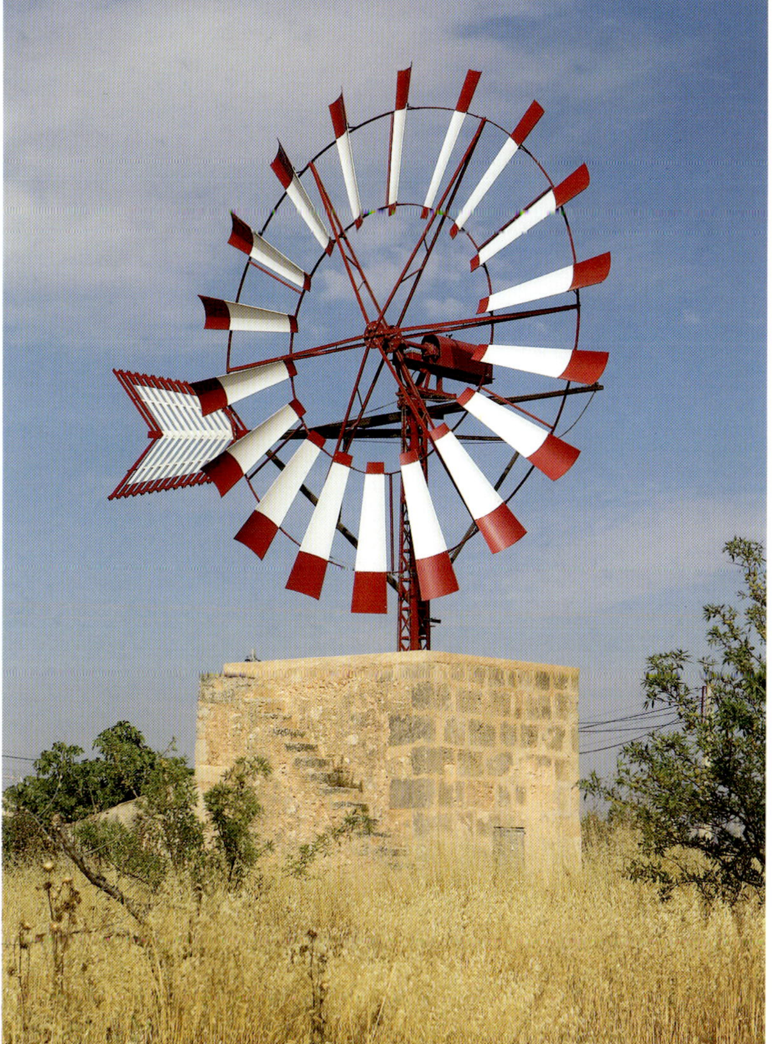

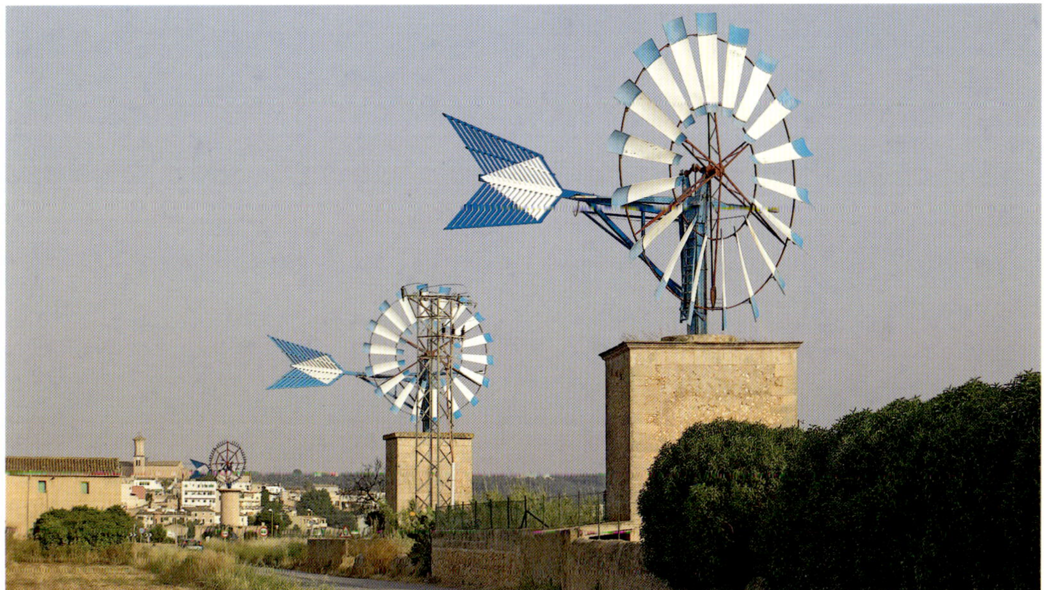

Long time ago the windmills have lost their meaning for Majorcan agriculture, but they are still part of the cultural heritage.

Island Panoramas 360° – Majorca, 1st Edition

ISBN 978-1-877339-48-6

Layout and typesetting	Sabine Weiler
Authors	Helga Neubauer, Wolfgang Vorbeck
Photographs	Werner Weiler
Editorial Officc	NZ Visitor Publications Ltd.
Translation	language networks bv, Amsterdam, Holland
Printed by	Everbest Printing Co Ltd., China

We cannot guarantee that this book has not been struck by erronitis. Should this be the case, we would be greatful if you could point out any errors to us. You can contact us at:

NZ Visitor Publications Ltd.
Level 27, PWC Tower, 188 Quay Street
Auckland, New Zealand
or email us at:
editor@nzpublications.com